PREFACE B

General Editor: JOH

'A description of what the *Preface Books* were intended to be was included in the first volume and has appeared unchanged at the front of every succeeding title: "A series of scholary and critical studies of major writers intended for those needing modern and authoritative guidance through the characteristic difficulties of their work to reach an intelligent understanding and enjoyment of it." This may seem modest enough but a moment's reflection will reveal what a considerable claim it actually is. It is much to the credit of Longman and to their (founding) editor Maurice Hussey and his authors that these words have come to seem no more than a plain statement of fact.'

NATE NEWS

Titles available in the series:

A Preface to Conrad *2nd Edition*	CEDRIC WATTS
A Preface to Ezra Pound	PETER WILSON
A Preface to Greene	CEDRIC WATTS
A Preface to Hardy *2nd Edition*	MERRYN WILLIAMS
A Preface to Hopkins *2nd Edition*	GRAHAM STOREY
A Preface to James Joyce *2nd Edition*	SYDNEY BOLT
A Preface to Jane Austen *Revised Edition*	CHRISTOPHER GILLIE
A Preface to Keats	CEDRIC WATTS
A Preface to Oscar Wilde	ANNE VARTY
A Preface to Samuel Johnson	THOMAS WOODMAN
A Preface to Shakespeare's Comedies	MICHAEL MANGAN
A Preface to Shakespeare's Tragedies	MICHAEL MANGAN
A Preface to Swift	KEITH CROOK
A Preface to Wilfred Owen	JOHN PURKIS
A Preface to Wordsworth *Revised Edition*	JOHN PURKIS
A Preface to Yeats *2nd Edition*	EDWARD MALINS, with JOHN PURKIS
A Preface to the Brontës	FELICIA GORDON
A Preface to Lawrence	GÂMINI SALGÂDO
A Preface to Milton *Revised Edition*	LOIS POTTER
A Preface to T. S. Eliot	RONALD TAMPLIN

Thomas Hardy, 1891

A PREFACE TO

HARDY

MERRYN WILLIAMS

SECOND EDITION

Longman

An imprint of **Pearson Education**

Harlow, England · London · New York · Reading, Massachusetts · San Francisco
Toronto · Don Mills, Ontario · Sydney · Tokyo · Singapore · Hong Kong · Seoul
Taipei · Cape Town · Madrid · Mexico City · Amsterdam · Munich · Paris · Milan

Pearson Education Limited
Edinburgh Gate
Harlow
Essex CM20 2JE
England

and Associated Companies throughout the world

Visit us on the World Wide Web at:
www.pearsoneduc.com

First published 1976
Second edition 1993

ISBN 0 582 43770 9 PPR

British Library Cataloguing-in-Publication Data
A catalogue record for this book can be obtained from the British
Library.

Library of Congress Cataloging-in-Publication Data
A catalog record for this book can be obtained from the Library of
Congress.

10 9 8 7 6 5 4 3 2 1
04 03 02 01

Set in 10/11pt Baskerville MT
Printed in Malaysia, VVP

Contents

Contents

List of illustrations

Acknowledgements

We are grateful to the following for permission to reproduce copyright material:

Bodley Head, part of Random House UK Ltd, for extracts from *Thomas Hardy And His Readers* edited by L. Lerner and J. Holmstrom; George T. Sassoon for the poem 'At Max Gate' by Siegfried Sassoon from *Collected Poems* (pub. Faber and Faber Ltd).

We are grateful to the following for permission to reproduce illustrations and photographs:

The Beinecke Rare Book and Manuscript Library, Yale University, page 73; the Syndics of Cambridge University Library, pages 105 and 187; Trustees of the Thomas Hardy Memorial Collection, Dorset County Museum, pages 17, 20, 38, 102, 133, 159 and frontispiece.

Foreword to the first edition

A century on from their original reception the Wessex Novels of Thomas Hardy have entered into the national store of fictional masterpieces and are still eagerly read. Possibly Dickens alone of the great Victorian writers can equal or surpass Hardy's continuing success, a thought that would have pleased him most deeply. For many of us, though made aware of the unhappy social conditions of life in Hardy's Dorset, persist in finding colour, humanity and nostalgia present to a degree in the novels that almost excludes the darker emotions. There is still to this day a recognizable Hardy country and it stands fairly free from that more modern rural tragedy that goes by the name of development.

In this most readable, and unexpectedly positive study of Hardy's prose and verse, Merryn Williams offers a variety of scholarly approaches to her subject to demonstrate the depths of his power to release tragic emotion and universal humanity within the closely studied visual realism. In Part One she provides a firm historical perspective, reminding us that Hardy, for all his apparent isolation, could not escape the pervasive influence of the scientists and agnostics of Victorian England. We are invited to consider especially Charles Darwin, Thomas Huxley, John Stuart Mill and Matthew Arnold. The last-named writer's key poem, 'Dover Beach', quoted on p. 69, seems now to be part of a range stretching all the way to Beeny Cliff in Cornwall (see p. 160), that Cliff without a Name, the setting of one of the most imaginative of all post-Darwinian fantasies, that to be found in Hardy's *Pair of Blue Eyes*. [. . .]

Incidentally, one wonders why it is that no art historian seems to have offered the genre paintings of the Pre-Raphaelite period or even the popular engravings for the Victorian drawing-room as unsuspected sources of Hardy's imagination. He was, after all, much more than a man devoted to a single art. In his diaries and notebooks we are continually aware of his discussions of paintings, architecture, music and even the problems of modern philosophy as discussed in the distinguished periodical, *Mind*. It seems to me quite possible that these magazine engravings with their almost operatic emotions could to some degree have influenced the drama of some of the stories which he wrote for just such illustration. The one reprinted on p. 105 is one example among the many that have never been reprinted.

Dr Williams continually seeks to dismiss the image of Hardy as a pessimist. There is, of course, no doubt that the tragic novels have their bitterness and bleakness, but we tend to ignore the more optimistic side of his character and writings. Where else can we find better and more delightful images of fields, woods and heaths or a more Franciscan love of the animal creation, devoid of sentimentality, in his period? Because it is the expressed aim of this book to draw attention to the positive aspect of his art I have chosen to quote a brief incident in *The Woodlanders*, said to have been his own favourite, and one of the Novels of Character and Environment. That last word arouses in us images of the conservationist and the environmentalist. Hardy anticipates us in this tree-planting episode of *The Woodlander*:

> What he [Giles Winterborne] had forgotten was that there were a thousand young fir trees to be planted in a neighbouring spot which had been cleared by the wood-cutters, and that he had arranged to plant them with his own hands. He had a marvellous power of making trees grow. Although he would seem to shovel in the earth quite carelessly there was a sort of sympathy between himself and the fir, oak, or beech that he was operating on; so that the roots took hold of the soil in a few days. He put most of these roots towards the south-west; for he said, in forty years' time, when some great gale is blowing from that quarter, the trees will require the strongest holdfast on that side to stand against it and not fall.

MAURICE HUSSEY
General Editor

Maurice Hussey died suddenly in June 1991. The Publishers and author would like to pay tribute to his wisdom, inspiration and friendship as Editor of Preface Books. He will be sadly missed.

Preface to the second edition

Since this book was first published, in 1976, Hardy studies have changed drastically. At that time there was no reliable biography and not very much criticism ('Wanted: Good Hardy Critic' was the name of a famous article by Philip Larkin). Arnold Kettle pointed out in a lecture of 1966 (the same year as Larkin's article) that, as with Dickens some time earlier, everyone thought he was a great writer except the highbrows and academics. Hardy had always been enormously popular with the general reader but little serious work was done on him for thirty or forty years after his death.

Now everything is different. There have been two major biographies, by Robert Gittings and Michael Millgate. New books covering almost every aspect of his work come out every year. Novels like *Tess* which were controversial in their time are set texts in schools and universities, where students have voted him one of their favourites (another literary headline was 'Hardy Rules OK'). In his birthplace, Dorset, he is a major tourist attraction, and he has reached a whole new non-literary audience by way of the screen. The popular film of *Far from the Madding Crowd* (1967) was followed by the BBC TV *Mayor of Casterbridge* (1978, now available on video) and Roman Polanski's film *Tess* (1979). There have been many other TV and radio adaptations.

If we have to sum up his appeal in a few words, we may say that he describes an old-fashioned (and therefore 'quaint' and 'picturesque' world) with a modern sensibility. He is somewhere on the shadow–line between nineteenth– and twentieth–century literature; he was born in the early years of Queen Victoria, in a countryside with no railways or electricity and where many people were illiterate, and he lived to see the first great modern war and the first general strike. The Wessex of the novels has gone, but his attitudes to class divisions and education, to war, to religion, to relations between men and women, to animals and 'green' issues, are all likely to strike a chord with today's readers. He is seen as a man born ahead of his time, 'one of us'.

'Women', 'class' – these are words often used as slogans. Hardy is now very popular with feminists, a fact which would have surprised his first wife. However, despite the failure of his first marriage, he always protested publicly against what he called man's inhumanity to woman. He is less popular with some who think him a snob, on the basis of Gittings' *Young Thomas Hardy* (1975) which accused him of concealing his humble origins to make a better impression on middle-class readers. My own view is that he had little choice. We can hardly imagine the rigidity of class divisions in Victorian England; what distinguishes Hardy from thousands of men who painfully climbed out of the class they were born into is that he understood what was going on and used it to write major novels. Change, progress, conservatism, tradition: these are the raw materials of his work.

Reading over this book, several years after it was first written, I felt I had given too much attention to Hardy's novels (or rather, the Novels of Character and Environment) at the expense of the rest of his work. So I have written a new chapter on the short stories and *The Dynasts* and greatly expanded the one on the poetry. I have also revised Chapter One to take account of what we now know about Hardy the man.

M.W.

To John with love.

'But criticism is so easy, and art so hard: criticism so flimsy, and the life-seer's voice so lasting.'

(Thomas Hardy, writing about William Barnes)

Part One
The Writer and his Setting

Chronological table

1866		Swinburne's *Poems and Ballads*.
1867	Returned to Dorchester. Began *The Poor Man and the Lady*.	
1870	Met Emma Gifford at St Juliot in Cornwall.	Education Act. Dickens died. Franco-Prussian war.
1871	*Desperate Remedies* published.	
1872	Designed schools for London Board. *Under the Greenwood Tree*.	Joseph Arch's Union. George Eliot's *Middlemarch*.
1873	*A Pair of Blue Eyes*. Suicide of Horace Moule.	
1874	*Far from the Madding Crowd* appeared in *Cornhill Magazine*. Married Emma Gifford in London; they moved to Surbiton.	
1875	*The Hand of Ethelberta*.	
1876–8	Lived in Sturminster Newton, Dorset; wrote *The Return of the Native*.	
1878–80	At Upper Tooting; *The Trumpet-Major*.	
1880–1	Wrote *A Laodicean* during a serious illness.	George Eliot died.
1881	Moved to Wimborne, Dorset.	
1882	Went to Darwin's funeral. *Two on a Tower*.	

1883	Moved permanently to Dorchester; wrote *The Dorsetshire Labourer*.	
1885	*The Mayor of Casterbridge*	
1886		William Barnes died.
1887	*The Woodlanders*	D. H. Lawrence born.
1888	*Wessex Tales*	
1891	*Tess of the d'Urbervilles*.	
1892	Father died.	
1894	*Life's Little Ironies*.	
1895	*Jude the Obscure*.	
1898	*Wessex Poems*.	
1899		Boer War began.
1901	*Poems of the Past and the Present*.	Queen Victoria died.
1902		End of Boer War.
1904	First part of *The Dynasts*.	
1905	Honorary degree from Aberdeen University.	
1906	Second part of *The Dynasts*	Liberals won general election; Labour Party got 30 seats.
1908	Third part of *The Dynasts*.	
1909	*Time's Laughingstocks*. President of Society of Authors.	Swinburne died.

1910	Awarded Order of Merit. First revision of Wessex Novels.	
1912	Emma Hardy died on 27 November.	
1913	Honorary degree from Cambridge University.	
1914	Married Florence Dugdale. *Satires of Circumstance.* On war committee of writers.	Great War began.
1915	Sister Mary died.	
1916	Visited German prisoners of war in Dorchester.	
1917	*Moments of Vision.*	Russian Revolution.
1918		End of war.
1920	Honorary degree from Oxford University.	
1922	*Late Lyrics and Earlier.*	
1925	*Human Shows.* Honorary degree from Bristol University.	
1928	Died, 11 January. *Winter Words* published later the same year.	

1 Hardy's life

Childhood and youth

Thomas Hardy was born on 2nd June 1840, in a small thatched cottage in the hamlet of Higher Bockhampton three miles from Dorchester. It was a picturesque place. There were several quaint-looking houses, with 'trees, clipped hedges, orchards, white gate-post-balls' in the avenue of cherry trees which led to the cottage, and behind it stretched the vast expanse of Egdon or Puddletown Heath. The cottage is still standing, and is used as a Hardy museum, but the other houses, the cherry trees and much of the heath have gone.

Fifty years earlier the heath had come up to the door, and bats had flown in and out of the house when the first Thomas Hardy moved in with his wife. This was the novelist's grandfather. He is said to have used the house for smuggling brandy, a tradition that plays its part in Hardy's story 'The Distracted Preacher'. His son, the second Thomas Hardy, was a skilled violinist and a 'master mason', self-employed in 1840 but later to expand his business and employ other men. They became a modestly well-off family, but his brother remained an ordinary labourer, and his wife, Jemima Hand, had had a deprived childhood:

> By reason of her parent's bereavement and consequent poverty under the burden of a young family, Jemima saw during girl-hood and young womanhood some very stressful experiences of which she could never speak in her maturer years without pain, though she appears to have mollified her troubles by reading every book she could lay hands on.
>
> (*The Life of Thomas Hardy*, F.E. Hardy, 1962, p. 8)

Her own mother, a prosperous farmer's daughter, had married a servant, been disinherited and spent the rest of her life in poverty. Class barriers, marriage between classes and the rise and fall of individuals would loom large in the novels of Thomas Hardy.

After moving about Dorset and London working for various families as a cook, Jemima became involved with the young mason and at the end of 1839 found herself pregnant. A marriage was fixed up, and five months later the third Thomas was born. Hardy naturally did not mention these facts, but in 'A Tragedy of Two

Ambitions' he makes the hero discover that 'his father had cajoled his mother in their early acquaintance, and had made somewhat tardy amends. . . . It was the last stroke, and he could not bear it'. As a writer he would show constant sympathy for the illegitimate child.

The mother had a difficult labour, and the baby was thought to be dead at first, but the nurse revived him just in time. There were three more children, Mary, born in 1841 and her brother's special friend, Henry born in 1851 and Katharine in 1856. None of them married, and there were no Hardys in the next generation.

Hardy often seems to have felt that there was something wrong with his family and that it was doomed to die out. At one time the Hardys had been well known in Dorset; one ancestor had founded Hardye's Grammar School in Elizabethan times and another had been the Admiral Hardy who was with Nelson when he died. They had owned a good deal of land, but lost it. Hardy noted in 1888, 'The decline and fall of the Hardys much in evidence hereabout . . . So we go down, down, down', and he would discover that the outside world regarded him and his family as peasants. Possibly that is why he brooded over the decline of ancient families in *The Woodlanders* and *Tess of the D'Urbervilles*, and created a family marked down by fate and unfit for marriage in *Jude the Obscure*.

Little Thomas remained a sickly child; for the first few years his parents did not expect him to live and apparently he heard them say so. He was precocious, 'being able to read almost before he could walk, and to tune the violin when of quite tender years'. The musical talent came from his father, the love of words from his mother. She was, he said, 'essentially a literary woman – nearly blinded herself by reading', and she bought him all the books she could afford, for example Dryden's translation of Virgil, Johnson's *Rasselas* and Bunyan's *Pilgrim's Progress*. He enjoyed dressing up in a tablecloth and reciting services from the prayer book, and everyone thought that as he was no good at anything else he would have to be a parson. The family went regularly to Stinsford church, which Hardy would immortalize under the name of Mellstock, and this church, where many of his ancestors were buried, was 'to him the most hallowed spot on earth':

> In this connection he said once – perhaps oftener – that although invidious critics had cast slurs upon him as Nonconformist, Agnostic, Atheist, Infidel, Immoralist, Heretic, Pessimist, or something else equally opprobrious in their eyes, they had never thought of calling him what they might have called him much more plausibly – churchy; not in an intellectual sense, but in so far as instincts and emotions rule. As a child, to be a parson had

> been his dream; moreover, he had had several clerical relatives who had held livings; while his grandfather, father, uncle, brother, wife, cousin, and two sisters had been musicians in various churches over a period covering altogether more than a hundred years.
>
> *Life.* p. 376)

Unconscious of religious controversy, he soaked in the atmosphere of this small country church and gradually acquired a deep knowledge of the Bible. At eight he was sent to the village school and learned arithmetic and geography. After a year he seemed much stronger, and his mother, who wanted him to 'get on', moved him to Isaac Last's Academy in Dorchester. He walked the three miles there and back through the country lanes every day.

It was a Nonconformist school but took pupils from all kinds of backgrounds. Isaac Last was 'an exceptionally able man, and a good teacher of Latin', and it seems that the boy was lucky to find so good a school in a quiet country town. He became an outstanding pupil, won a Latin prize, and learned advanced mathematics and French. But he shunned the other schoolboys. He 'loved being alone', and he was already showing signs of the extreme sensitivity which would plague him later in life. He has recorded that, like his character Jude, he 'did not wish to grow up . . . to be a man, or to possess things, but to remain as he was, in the same spot, and to know no more people than he already knew (about half a dozen)'. He also saw things, as a boy, which he remembered for the rest of his life: a frozen bird, a shepherd boy who later starved to death, and two public hangings. One was of a woman who had killed her husband, and it is likely that this was in his mind when he wrote *Tess*.

He left school in 1856. His parents had been concerned about what to do with him, for although he was obviously highly intelligent it was not normal for one of their background to progress to public school and then one of the ancient universities. But a family friend, John Hicks, an architect who practised in South Street, Dorchester, offered to take the boy into his office, and this was agreed. Even that offended the local parson. According to Michael Millgate's biography 'he never forgot . . . the humiliation of sitting in Stinsford Church at his mother's side in that early summer of 1856 while the Reverend Mr Shirley preached against the presumption shown by one of Hardy's class in seeking to rise, through architecture, into the ranks of professional men' (p. 55).

Hicks was a genial man who encouraged him to go on studying the classics. Hardy would get up at four or five and read Greek or Latin for a few hours before walking to work; he also discussed theology with another of Hicks's pupils, and he had a remarkably helpful friend who saw that he did not stagnate mentally.

This was Horace Moule, a young man eight years older than himself who had just left Cambridge to become a freelance writer. His father, Henry Moule, the vicar of Fordington, was a devoted clergyman who had saved hundreds of lives when cholera broke out in the Dorchester slums. Horace was a brilliant scholar who had, however, failed to take his degree and suffered from alcoholism and depression. He was very kind to the young Hardy, introduced him to liberal theology and literary criticism, and advised him about his career. He felt compelled to tell the boy to go on with architecture as there was no other obvious way for him to earn a living. Nevertheless, at about the same time, Hardy began to write poetry.

At twenty-one, eager for wider horizons, he 'started alone for London, to pursue the art and science of architecture on more advanced lines'. An early photograph shows a boyish-looking youth with a carefully cultivated moustache. He found a place with Arthur Bloomfield, in Adelphi Terrace, and stayed there for the next five years. The great city overwhelmed him at first, but he soon got used to it,

> knowing every street and alley west of St Paul's like a born Londoner, which he was often supposed to be; an experience quite ignored by the reviewers of his later books, who, if he only touched on London in his pages, promptly reminded him not to write of a place he was unacquainted with, but to get back to his sheepfolds.
>
> (*Life*, p. 62)

These were the years which completed his education. During the day he worked conscientiously at architectural drawings, and in his spare time went round the museums and art galleries and read voraciously. He still dreamed of going to Oxford or Cambridge, but this was obviously unrealistic; a later plan was to go to theological college and qualify at a lower level, but he gave up the idea at the age of twenty-five when he realized that he was no longer a Christian. The history of his early hopes is reflected in *Jude the Obscure* and in a remarkable short story, 'A Tragedy of Two Ambitions'. In the end he never got any high educational qualification, which he always regretted. Later he would collect four honorary degrees.

> His environment cut him off from any tradition of culture that might have instilled into him that critical sense that was not implanted by nature. When he came to maturity, he made a conscientious effort to get over this disability. Hardy was a great

self-educator, and his novels are marked by the fruits of his labours . . . They have the touching pedantry of the self-educated countryman naively pleased with his hardly acquired learning. Indeed, it is the inevitable defect of a spontaneous genius like Hardy's that it is impervious to education. No amount of painstaking study got him within sight of achieving that intuitive good taste, that instinctive grasp of the laws of literature, which is the native heritage of one bred from childhood in the atmosphere of a high culture.

(David Cecil, Hardy the Novelist, pp. 145–6).

What this means, presumably, is that Hardy did not have the public school and Oxbridge education which the English upper class assumes is the only one worth having. Neither did Lawrence, Dickens, the Brontës, Jane Austen or George Eliot. Nor, among poets, did Blake, Keats, Clare, Wilfred Owen or Shakespeare. (Many people think it would have been impossible for someone who went to the grammar school at Stratford-on-Avon to write Shakespeare's plays.) This appalling attitude helps to explain why so many Victorian critics patronized Hardy, telling him to write about sheep and cows and to leave philosophy to his betters.

In fact, Hardy was more fortunate in his education than most people. He went to a very good school and had very good teachers outside it; without this background, it is unlikely that he would have found the will-power to go on educating himself in his spare time. He was interested in a very wide range of subjects. He knew classical literature and mathematics as well as the average undergraduate in those days, and more important, by the end of his time in London he thoroughly knew the classics of our own literature – Shakespeare, the King James Bible and the English poets (especially Wordsworth and Shelley) who, until our own century, were never studied in Oxford or Cambridge.

By the time he reached London he was determined to be a poet, but he did not try to get introductions to famous writers, as a more pushy young man would have done. Although he was living near two of the writers he most admired, Browning and Swinburne, he never met them in those days. He once sat next to Dickens in a coffee-shop and he heard John Stuart Mill give an open-air speech. But he did not presume to think that he himself would ever be famous. He wrote a good many poems in the 1860s and sent them to magazines, which invariably sent them back.

In many ways, he was excited by London. He watched from his office windows as Charing Cross Bridge and the Embankment went up, and helped the Midland Railway to carry a cutting through Old St Pancras churchyard, sweeping away many hundreds of tombs.

He visited the Great Exhibition of 1862 and the Science Museum, and won two architectural prizes. But a good deal of his time in the capital must have been miserable. He was lonely, although he sometimes saw his friend Moule, and he was deeply shocked by the squalor, vice and human misery in the richest city on earth. As his early religious convictions weakened and died, he began to feel 'a passion for reforming the world'. One of his early poems, 'Dream of the City Shopwoman', expresses the frustration he felt at this time:

> O God, that creatures framed to feel
> A yearning nature's strong appeal
> Should writhe on this eternal wheel
>   In rayless grime;
>
> And vainly note, with wan regret,
> Each star of early promise set;
> Till Death relieves, and they forget
>   Their one Life's time!

By 1867 he was beginning to be ill, partly because of the stench of river-mud near his office and partly because he shut himself up every evening to read. His employer told him to go down to the country for a rest, and Hardy thought he might stay there. The business of getting on in the world repelled him, but he left his books and papers in London and went back to Dorchester to spend the summer working for Mr Hicks. His family were shocked by how pale he looked, but after a few weeks in the country he was much better.

Tryphena, Emma and the early novels

It was not until a hundred years later, when a book called *Providence and Mr Hardy*, by Lois Deacon and Terry Coleman, was published that the world knew anything about Hardy's love affair with his cousin Tryphena Sparks. The evidence is fragmentary and mostly comes from alleged statements by Tryphena's daughter, who died a very old woman in 1965. All we know is that when Hardy returned to Dorset he saw a good deal of Tryphena, who had been a child when he left for London and was now sixteen, and that when she died, twenty-three years later, he wrote a poem, 'Thoughts of Phena', which called her 'my lost prize'.

The few surviving photographs of Tryphena show a 'bright-eyed vivacious girl' with a 'pile of dark hair', like Sue in *Jude the Obscure* with whom she has been connected. Again like Sue, she was a brilliant girl, who so impressed the education authorities that she was made a headmistress at twenty-one. In 1867 she was a student-teacher at the village school in Puddletown, where her parents lived. She and Hardy are said to have gone for long walks on the heath together and possibly became engaged.

That is probably the whole story. But Deacon and Coleman, having revealed that a relationship with Tryphena did exist, went on to make some lurid suggestions – that she and Hardy had an illegitimate son, that Horace Moule came between them and that they could not marry because they turned out to be too closely related. This caused a sensation in the literary world and for a time it was widely believed; John Fowles in his famous novel *The French Lieutenant's Woman* (1969) discussed it at some length and concluded that it was true. But the suggestions propounded in *Providence and Mr Hardy* are now discredited.

Over the next few years the ties between the two cousins were weakened. Tryphena went away to training college in London, got her own school in Plymouth and eventually married someone else. Hardy, meanwhile, was unsure what he wanted to do with his life. He did not feel seriously committed to architecture, but poetry seemed to offer him no future, nor could he get married until he was an established professional man. So, while continuing to work occasionally for Hicks, he began his first novel, *The Poor Man and the Lady, by the Poor Man*. His experiences of life in Dorset and London had made him a radical, and there are several signs that he had suffered bitterly from being treated as a social inferior. In 1867 the British labour movement was in its infancy, and there were very few people, even in London, who called themselves Socialists. Yet Hardy had written what he himself called a Socialist novel, and in that respect he was a long way ahead of his time. He even depicted what had never yet happened, large gatherings of working men in Trafalgar Square.

He sent the novel to Macmillan in 1868. In later years they would become his main publishers, but while they admired some of *The Poor Man and the Lady*, they felt it was too uneven to be printed. The publisher told him that 'your description of country life among working men is admirable', but he felt the young author was too prejudiced against the upper class:

> The utter heartlessness of *all* the conversation you give in drawing-rooms and ball-rooms about the working-classes, has some ground of truth, I fear, and might justly be scourged as you aim at doing, but your chastisement would fall harmless from its very excess. . . . Nothing could justify such a wholesale blackening of a class but large and intimate knowledge of it.

He next tried the firm of Chapman and Hall, and was invited to London to meet their reader, the novelist George Meredith. The older man warned him that 'if he printed so pronounced a thing he would be attacked on all sides by the conventional reviewers, and his future injured'. He suggested that Hardy should put the book aside and write one with a more conventional plot.

The Poor Man and the Lady is now lost, but ten years afterwards Hardy turned it into a long short story, 'An Indiscretion in the Life of an Heiress'. This cut out some, but not all, of the radical passages, and gives a good idea of the young Hardy's style. He would write much better things later, but even his first crude attempts at fiction were impressive.

He went back to Dorset (working in Weymouth as an architect) and began to write *Desperate Remedies*. This was a murder and mystery story, strongly influenced by Wilkie Collins, which he believed to be 'quite below the level of *The Poor Man and the Lady*'. There are good bits of writing in it, but it was a bizarre way for Hardy to start his career. He sent it off in March 1870.

In the same month he went down to Cornwall, at his employer's request, to estimate the cost of repairs to St Juliot Church. The parish, on the north coast, was a very lonely one, and the journey of a hundred miles by road and rail took him all day. In the evening he arrived at the rectory, where he was to stay, and where there lived an elderly clergyman, the Reverend Caddell Holder, his much younger wife, and her sister, Emma Gifford, who was Hardy's own age, twenty-nine.

The two girls were the daughters of a Plymouth solicitor and their uncle was a canon of Worcester Cathedral, later an archdeacon. Socially her family was far above Hardy's but their father drank, and had gone bankrupt, so Emma had no wish to live with him. She must have been lonely in this remote place, for she loved meeting people. She received Hardy alone and was interested in him at once:

> I was immediately arrested by his familiar appearance, as if I had seen him in a dream – his slightly different accent, his soft voice; also I noticed a blue paper sticking out of his pocket. . . . I thought him much older than he was. He had a beard, and a rather shabby greatcoat, and had quite a business appearance. Afterwards he seemed younger, and by daylight especially so. . . . The blue paper proved to be the MS of a poem, and not a plan of the church, he informed me, to my surprise.
>
> (*Life*, p. 70)

Hardy stayed at St Juliot for four days and when he had finished work Emma showed him the countryside, including the massive Beeny Cliff a few miles away. In later years Hardy always associated that romantic landscape with his love for Emma:

13

> I found her out there
> On a slope few see,
> That falls westwardly
> To the salt-edged air,
> Where the ocean breaks
> On the purple strand,
> And the hurricane shakes
> The solid land.

When he went down to St Juliot he may still have been engaged to Tryphena, and he did not marry Emma for another four years. But he was attracted by her vivacity, by what he called her *aliveness*, although there were differences between them (most obviously, class differences; she took it for granted that she should ride her pony everywhere while he walked). At the time this did not seem important. He went to Cornwall several more times to see her; they wrote to each other and he told her about his hopes of becoming a novelist.

Desperate Remedies was accepted by the firm of Tinsley, on condition that Hardy paid them seventy-five pounds. It was a bold step for a young man with not much money, but he paid it nevertheless, and got most of it back. The novel, which came out anonymously in 1871, sold quite well. But Hardy was bitterly upset by a review in the *Spectator* which attacked 'the author's daring to suppose it possible that an unmarried lady owning an estate could have an illegitimate child'. Horace Moule, who published a kindlier review, told him not to worry. Hardy would find that he needed the encouragement of his friends if he was to go on writing, for he was and remained hyper-sensitive to hostile criticism.

Still, he wanted his next novel to be quite different, and over the next few months, while continuing to design Gothic churches, he prepared a much shorter book, *Under the Greenwood Tree*. Macmillan were doubtful about taking it, and Hardy very nearly threw the manuscript away. He was so depressed that he wrote to Emma to say he was giving up literature. Some women would have let him do it, for he needed a steady income before they could get married. But Emma believed in his work, and urged him to go on writing.

At first he took no notice and went on working doggedly at architecture. But he was impressed when Moule, too, advised him not to give up. He then bumped into Mr Tinsley, who asked for another novel. Hardy did not respond at first, but finally dug out his manuscript and sent it off without looking at it. *Under the Greenwood Tree* was published in 1872. It 'met with a very kindly and gentle reception', although not many copies were sold. The story was shorter than most Victorian novels and although pleasant

to read it was not exciting. He could not risk becoming a professional writer on the strength of such a mild success.

Tinsley then made a proposal which would alter his whole career
and dominate his life for the next twenty-odd years. He asked him
for another, longer novel which would run for twelve months as a
serial in his magazine and then be published in book form. Soon
afterwards Leslie Stephen, the editor of the *Cornhill Magazine*, who
had been greatly impressed by *Under the Greenwood Tree*, made a
similar request. Hardy, who was living in London again and
drawing designs for the new Board Schools (education had been
made compulsory in 1870), thought it over carefully and agreed. It
seemed he had a real chance to devote himself to literature and still
earn a living.

At this time most established and successful novelists, including
some of the greatest of the age, first published their work as a weekly
or monthly serial in one of the circulating magazines. These
magazines (examples are Dickens's *Household Words* and *All the Year
Round* in which several of his own novels first saw the light) had an
enormous public because more and more people were learning to
read in the second half of the century and they were considerably
cheaper than books. After serialization these novels came out in
hardback (usually in three volumes) and found their way to the
public libraries where they reached another vast group of readers.
Quite often the final version was very different from the serial one;
Hardy himself made several changes before they came out in book
form, as we shall see.

The advantage of this way of publishing novels was that they
reached a much wider public than the work of Scott or Jane Austen
had done. It also made it possible for an author to live entirely on
his work and, if it was popular, to make a fortune. But there were
drawbacks. A writer had to produce the sort of novel that his public
and his editor wanted. He had to work to a deadline and to see that
each instalment was equally interesting and action-packed; if it was
not, readers might stop buying the magazine. Even the length was
not under his control for he was under great pressure to produce a
novel which would fill three volumes. (This led to a good deal of
'padding' and unnecessary sub-plots.) He also had to see that his
work contained nothing which could conceivably offend anyone.
The magazines were designed for family reading, and almost
everybody believed that the young girls into whose hands they
might fall must be carefully shielded from dangerous knowledge;
this led to the famous dictum that an author must never write
anything which 'might bring a blush to a young person's cheek'.
This did not mean working-class girls, like Tess Durbeyfield, who
had always had the facts of life forced on them at an early age and

in an extremely brutal way, but the daughters of middle-class families, 'young ladies', whose education had been satirized by Dickens:

> Nothing disagreeable should ever be looked at. Apart from such a habit standing in the way of that graceful equanimity of surface which is so expressive of good breeding, it hardly seems compatible with refinement of mind. A truly refined mind will seem to be ignorant of the existence of anything that is not perfectly proper, placid, and pleasant.
>
> (*Little Dorrit*, Book 2, Ch. 5)

Later Hardy was to rebel against the 'young person's' tyranny, but in 1872 it never occurred to him that anyone could be offended by his writings, and even if he had known about the possible difficulties he would probably have done the same thing. He was anxious to get married, anxious to give up the architectural work which consumed so much of his time, and although he still valued poetry more highly than any other art he said that his main ambition was to be 'considered a good hand at a serial'.

He asked his employer for a holiday and went into the country, where he wrote most of *A Pair of Blue Eyes*. When it began to appear in print he gave notice that he would not be coming back, and his career as an architect stopped. The novel was well received; it was, indeed, the best that Hardy had yet written. It was a love story, set in Cornwall, and the fair-haired heroine, Elfride, was in many ways very like Emma Gifford. Some critics have gone further, and suggested that the young architect, Stephen Smith, who wants to marry her, is a portrait of Hardy himself. Hardy denied this strongly, but it is a fact that this novel, like *The Poor Man and the Lady*, deals with class and its effect on relationships. Elfride's father rejects Stephen when he is discovered to be the son of a labourer, and Hardy was having trouble with Emma's family at around the same time. When he and Emma went to see her father to ask his consent to get engaged, Mr Gifford made it clear that he was not welcome. He is said to have described Hardy as 'a low-born churl who has presumed to marry into my family'.

Hardy classified *A Pair of Blue Eyes* among a group of his works which he called Romances and Fantasies, 'as if to suggest its visionary nature'. It is not one of his great books. But it does have an interest and poetry of its own, and Hardy was glad to know that it was admired by Tennyson and Coventry Patmore, two of the most popular poets of the day. When it came out in the standard three-volume edition Hardy's name appeared on the cover for the first time. Horace Moule again wrote an encouraging review.

Next month, June 1873, Hardy went up to Cambridge to see him.

Emma Lavinia Gifford
(afterwards Mrs Thomas Hardy)
1870

Emma Hardy

Horace Moule

They sat up talking until late at night, and next morning climbed on the roof of King's College chapel and looked out over the flat country to Ely cathedral. Hardy never forgot that morning, for it would be the last time he saw his friend. In September Moule committed suicide in his rooms at Queens' College by cutting his throat while his brother was in the next room. For Hardy this was one of the most horrifying experiences of his life.

As has been said, Moule had an alcohol problem. There were also rumours about his private life; at forty-one he was unmarried, is said to have had a child by a 'low' woman from Dorset, and had possibly been engaged to a woman of his own class who had broken with him. What is certain is that he was a man of great talent who had failed to fulfil his promise. Hardy, whose own career was just opening out, very possibly felt that he owed it to Moule. It has been suggested that Knight in *A Pair of Blue Eyes* is a portrait of his friend; certainly he was thinking of him twenty years later when he began to write *Jude the Obscure*. At the end of his life, when he was over eighty, he wrote or passed for publication the poem 'Standing by the Mantelpiece', based on their last meeting. The figure of Horace Moule, then, would haunt him for another half a century.

He was living at home (from where he attended Moule's funeral in Fordington churchyard) and writing *Far from the Madding Crowd.* He always found that the quietness of Dorset, and the rhythms of country life, helped him to do good work. The new novel began to appear in the *Cornhill* early in 1874. It was published anonymously, and one reviewer suggested, to Hardy's surprise, that George Eliot might be the author. 'If *Far from the Madding Crowd* is not written by George Eliot', this review continued, 'then there is a new light among novelists'. But not all the criticism was so positive. Leslie Stephen was a distinguished intellectual, but he dared not overlook his readers' prejudices if he wanted them to go on taking his magazine. He warned Hardy that the seduction of Fanny Robin must be treated 'gingerly', and when 'three respectable ladies' wrote in to complain about 'an improper passage' he was quite upset. When Hardy pointed out that *The Times* had praised the same passage Stephen retorted, 'I spoke as an editor, not as a man. You have no more consciousness of these things than a child'.

The story was illustrated by a young professional woman, Helen Paterson, better known by her married name of Helen Allingham. Hardy was surprised to find that she was not a man, but later called her 'the best illustrator I ever had'. Helen went on to paint several beautiful scenes of country cottages and landscapes which fetch high prices today. Hardy met her and speculated, forty years later, that they might have married. It would certainly have been an interesting, and maybe a fruitful union.

Possibly this should have warned him that he ought not to marry Emma, but they had already waited four years, and on 17th September 1874 they had a quiet wedding in London. Hardly any of their relations were there. After a short honeymoon abroad, they went to live in Surbiton.

Architecture and literature

Hardy was struck off the list of the Architectural Association in 1872 for not having paid his subscription; in the same year, as we have seen, he decided to become a full-time writer. He had few regrets. Architecture had been chosen for him by his parents rather than taken up freely, and except for short periods of amateur work he never practised it again.

Yet in some ways it must have seemed the natural career for him; all the Hardys for the last four generations had been master-masons. 'For Hardy craftmanship was innate' (a modern architect has written), 'something inherited from his master-mason father and forebears who could think and work in no other way' (C.J.P. Beatty, Introduction to *The Architectural Notebooks of Thomas Hardy*). He went on with it for long enough to make sure that he could have earned a living, and his one surviving notebook shows that he took his work seriously. He was 'an all-round man' like his hero, Jude Fawley; sketches of Gothic pillars and winged angels alternate, in his notebook, with detailed notes about drains. He worked not only on churches but also on labourers' cottages, railway buildings and schools. Some of these experiences went into his later writing, particularly the weak but interesting novel *A Laodicean*. The heroes of *The Poor Man and the Lady*, *Desperate Remedies* and *A Pair of Blue Eyes* are all young architects and the hero of *Jude the Obscure* a stonemason.

During the years when Hardy was learning his trade English architecture was undergoing great changes. Glass and iron were used much more, in structures like the Crystal Palace and the roof of Paddington Station. With this increased modernity, architecture began, in other ways, to look backwards. A.C. Pugin (1812–52) had made the public more aware of the beauty of medieval buildings, and during the early years of Queen Victoria a great campaign of church restoration began. Most churches and cathedrals were in a bad state. They had been neglected for many hundreds of years, and if they had not been drastically repaired they would probably be in ruins today. But the Victorians were insensitive craftsmen. They tore down a great deal of beautiful medieval work, which was lost for ever, and put in greatly inferior work of their own. An entire building might be pulled down sometimes:

> The original church, hump-backed, wood-turreted, and quaintly hipped, had been taken down, and either cracked up into heaps of road-metal in the lane, or utilised as pig-sty walls, garden seats, guard-stones to fences, and rockeries in the flower-beds of the neighbourhood. In place of it a tall new building of modern Gothic design, unfamiliar to English eyes, had been erected on a new piece of ground by a certain obliterator of historic records who had run down from London and back in a day.
>
> (*Jude the Obscure*, Part 1, Ch. 1)

This is how Hardy describes the destruction of 'Marygreen' village church in *Jude*. We have seen how he called himself 'churchy', in a strictly non-religious sense, and the village church in its role as the 'historic record' of the community seemed to him worth preserving. 'The human interest in an edifice ranks before its architectural interest, however great the latter may be,' he once said. This was in a speech to the Society for the Protection of Ancient Buildings, which had been founded by William Morris to resist the restorers' vandalism. Hardy was an active member of this society in his later years, partly because he felt guilty that as a

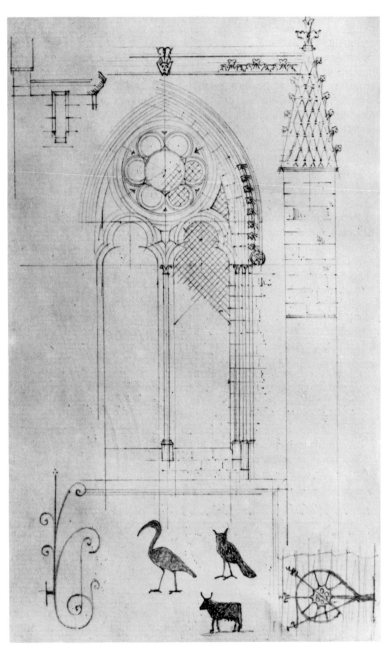

Gothic art and architecture in Hardy's sketchbook

young man he had been forced to destroy a lot of fine Gothic work. In the same speech he had some interesting things to say about the role of an architect who is asked to restore a decaying church:

> The true architect, who is first of all an artist and not an antiquary, is naturally most influenced by the aesthetic sense, his desire being, like nature's, to retain, recover, or recreate the idea which has become damaged, without much concern about the associations of the material that idea may have been displayed in . . . Thus if the architect have also an antiquarian bias he is pulled in two directions – in one by his wish to hand on or modify the abstract form, in the other by his reverence for the antiquity of its embodiment. Architects have been much blamed for their doings in respect of old churches, and no doubt they have much to answer for. Yet one cannot logically blame an architect for being an architect – a chief craftsman, constructor, creator of forms – not their preserver.

By this time he had begun to feel that 'medievalism was as dead as a fern-leaf in a lump of coal; that other developments were shaping in the world . . . in which Gothic architecture and its associations had no place'. This suggestion is made in *Jude*, where the stone-mason-hero arrives in Christminster (Oxford) to find that his work will consist of patching up the ancient colleges. Here Hardy shows a preference for modern over medieval. The carvings in the stone-mason's yard 'were marked by precision, mathematical straightness, smoothness, exactitude: there in the old walls were the broken lines of the original idea; jagged curves, disdain of precision, irregularity, disarray'.

He felt that there was no point in merely copying the great work of the past; the true architect was like an artist, a 'creator of forms'. In a poem, 'The Abbey Mason', about the birth of the Perpendicular style in England, he says of the architect of Gloucester cathedral:

> He did but what all artists do,
> Wait upon Nature for his cue.

The reason he liked Gothic architecture was that it related closely to natural things – leaves, animals, or (as in this poem) a pattern of raindrops. His notebook is full of drawings of plants, animals and birds, either in their natural state or transmuted into stone carvings. Art must remain close to the rhythms of life, and he went on feeling this after he had given up architecture for literature:

> That the author loved the art of concealing art was undiscerned. For instance, as to rhythm. Years earlier he had decided that too regular a beat was bad art. He had fortified himself in his opinion

by thinking of the analogy of architecture, between which art and that of poetry he had discovered, to use his own words, that there existed a close and curious parallel, both arts, unlike some others, having to carry a rational content inside their artistic form. He knew that in architecture cunning irregularity is of enormous worth, and it is obvious that he carried on into his verse, perhaps in part unconsciously, the Gothic-art principle in which he had been trained – the principle of spontaneity, found in mouldings, tracery, and such-like – resulting in the 'unforeseen' (as it has been called) character of his metres and stanzas, that of stress rather than of syllable, poetic texture rather than poetic veneer; the latter kind of thing, under the name of 'constructed ornament', being what he, in common with every Gothic student, had been taught to avoid as the plague. He shaped his poetry accordingly, introducing metrical pauses, and reversed beats; and found for his trouble that some particular line of a poem exemplifying this principle was greeted with a would-be jocular remark that such a line 'did not make for immortality'. The same critic might have gone to one of our cathedrals (to follow up the analogy of architecture) and on discovering that the carved leafage of some capital or spandrel in the best period of Gothic art strayed freakishly out of its bounds over the moulding, where by rule it had no business to be, or that the enrichments of a string-course were not accurately spaced; or that there was a sudden blank in a wall where a window was to be expected from formal measurement, have declared with equally merry conviction, 'This does not make for immortality'.

(*Life*, pp. 300–1)

This tells us a good deal about the theory behind Hardy's poetry. If the works of Pope and Dryden, written almost uniformly in heroic couplets, may be compared with the classical churches and mansions which were being built at the same time by Wren and others, it is helpful to see Hardy's verse as the product of an age when Gothic architecture was coming back into fashion. It is built on the principle which Ruskin saw behind the medieval cathedrals – there are no rules, the artist-builder may try out as many different styles as he wants. Almost all Hardy's poems are constructed with care, but they often took his readers by surprise, for he experimented with several unfamiliar metres, many of which he had invented himself. His guiding principle was that an architect must not copy Gothic art, any more than a poet should copy other poets, for in the long run a copy was dead. What he could do was learn from this free and flexible architecture how to develop his own skills, and create an art-form which would speak to the needs of his own age.

Hardy's early training was never forgotten, and when he was quite an old man people noticed how he could immediately grasp all the details of a building. Apart from the many references in his work to churches and architects, there are several slight touches which remind the reader of his special knowledge, as in this description of Sherborne from *The Woodlanders* (Ch. 5):

The churches, the abbey, and other medieval buildings on this clear bright morning having the linear distinctness of architectural drawings, as if the original dream and vision of the conceiving master-mason were for a brief hour flashing down through the centuries to an unappreciative age.

Another passage, from *The Mayor of Casterbridge* (Ch. 4), shows that he was accustomed to looking at towns with an architect's eye:

To birds of the more soaring kind Casterbridge must have appeared on this fine evening as a mosaic-work of subdued reds, browns, greys, and crystals, held together by a rectangular frame of deep green. To the level eye of humanity it stood as an indistinct mass behind a dense stockade of limes and chestnuts, set in the midst of miles of rotund down and concave field. The mass became gradually dissected by the vision into towers, gables, chimneys, and casements, the highest glazings shining bleared and bloodshot with the coppery fire they caught from the belt of sunlit cloud in the west.

It was his architectural training that enabled him to say that Casterbridge met the countryside in a *mathematical* line, and that *Jude the Obscure* was 'almost *geometrically* constructed'. There are many other examples in his work of how he had been affected by his training. But in 1874 he had virtually given up architecture, and was being recognized as a good novelist for the first time.

The middle years

When *Far from the Madding Crowd* came out in book form in 1874, Hardy found to his surprise that he had made a breakthrough. Whenever he and his wife went into London they saw people carrying copies, and on both sides of the Atlantic the novel got good reviews. One of the most interesting was by the young Henry James:

Mr Hardy describes nature with a great deal of felicity, and is evidently very much at home among rural phenomena. The most genuine thing in his book, to our sense, is a certain aroma of the meadows and lanes – a natural relish for harvesting and sheep-washings. He has laid his scene in an agricultural county, and his characters are children of the soil – unsophisticated country-folk. . . . Everything human in the book strikes us as factitious and insubstantial; the only things we believe in are the sheep and the dogs. But, as we say, Mr Hardy has gone astray very cleverly, and his superficial novel is a really curious imitation of something better.

This was to be the tone of most reviewers towards Hardy for the next twenty years. Again and again they would tell him that simple rural scenes were his proper subject-matter, and that his best novel was *Far from the Madding Crowd*. Perhaps this was why he made his next book, *The Hand of Ethelberta* (1875), as different as possible. This was a comedy about a butler's daughter who gate-crashes high society (as, indeed, Hardy was beginning to do, for he could not tell his London friends that some members of his family, like Ethelberta's, were servants), and eventually marries a wicked old peer. It was badly received by the public, who wanted him to go on writing about country life, and Hardy noted unhappily, 'It was, in fact, thirty years too soon for a Comedy of Society of that kind – just as *The Poor Man and the Lady* had been too soon for a Socialist story, and as other of his writings – in prose and verse – were too soon for their date'. As a general observation this had a lot of truth in it, but on this occasion the critics were right. *Ethelberta* is a weak novel; the society scenes are unconvincing, and the whole is distinctly inferior to anything that Hardy wrote about his own people. After finishing it, he wrote nothing for a while. He was moving restlessly about, looking for somewhere to settle, and was not at all sure which direction to take next:

One reflection about himself at this date sometimes made Hardy uneasy. He perceived that he was 'up against' the position of having to carry on his life not as an emotion, but as a scientific game; that he was committed by circumstances to novel-writing as a regular trade, as much as he had formerly been to architecture; and that hence he would, he deemed, have to look for material in manners – in ordinary social and fashionable life as other novelists did. Yet he took no interest in manners, but in the substance of life only. So far what he had written had not been novels at all, as usually understood – that is pictures of modern customs and observances – and might not long sustain the interest of the circulating library subscriber who cared mainly for those things. On the other hand, to go about to dinners and clubs and crushes as a business was not much to his mind. Yet that was necessary meat and drink to the popular author.

(*Life*, p. 104)

This uncertainty about his talents, his real strength as one who wrote about 'the substance of life', went very deep. It is now that we find him reading Addison, Macaulay, Newman, Gibbon and *The Times* leaders in an attempt to polish his style. It led to the many disastrous attempts at sophisticated prose which disfigure his novels, and it would shape the pattern of his life for many years to come. Even after he had made the decision to live close to his roots in Dorset, he went to London every year to study 'modern customs and observances' for as long as Emma was alive. She enjoyed it more than he did, but all his life Hardy seems to have felt that he needed the approval of 'the world', and seems to have been unhappy if he did not get it. He also made notes for some novels about 'fashionable life', to be written if the public would accept nothing else. Fortunately it never happened, and almost the only way these experiences touched his work was in some short stories about titled ladies, published as *A Group of Noble Dames* in 1891.

After a short rest from writing he got his nerve back. He and Emma rented a cottage in Sturminster Newton, in the Vale of Blackmoor, and he settled down to write *The Return of the Native*. The two years they spent in the country were described by him as 'our happiest time'.

It is hard to say when their relationship began to fail. They had not been able to spend long periods of time together before they got married, and afterwards deep differences began to appear. There was an intellectual gulf; Emma, like most women, had had a scrappy education and was not outstandingly gifted like (for instance) Helen Allingham or Tryphena Sparks. And there was a class gulf; Hardy's family, who had lived very near the poverty line and spoke with broad Dorset accents, always said he had 'married a lady'. Jemima had not wanted him to get married at all and disliked Emma from the start.

Less than a year after their wedding, Hardy wrote a poem, 'We Sat at the Window', which concluded that the marriage had been a mistake:

> Wasted were two souls in their prime,
> And great was the waste, that July time
> When the rain came down.

Almost certainly, he did not feel like this all the time. Emma was an exciting companion; she was very involved in his work (which she copied out) and they seem to have got on better when they were away from his family. But after three years he sadly noted that their young maid was about to have an (illegitimate) baby, 'Yet never a sign of one is there for us'.

In every other way the years at Sturminster Newton were good ones. The new novel was set on Puddletown Heath, which had played so great a part in his life, and his childhood memories of the mummers, the reddleman and stories about Napoleon were interwoven with the theme of a hero born ahead of his time. This was a Hardy-like hero, who is deeply attached to his birthplace, who has been given the chance to 'get on' but is not happy with it, and who has married a woman of whom his mother disapproves. It is significant that it took him noticeably longer to complete (some two years) than his previous novels, suggesting that it was a much more personal and ambitious work. It was certainly his finest book yet and represented the beginnings of his most distinctive and uncompromising work. But his publishers made him alter the ending of the sub-plot, and, although the ending he actually wrote is a good one, this depressed him. He must have been still more depressed when the novel was published in 1878 and reviewers said it was worse than his earlier work. Indeed, they would go on saying for several years that each new novel was less good than *Far from the Madding Crowd*. That book had been planned before Horace Moule died and, ever since, he had been intensely conscious of waste and tragedy. Victorian readers, who expected a happy ending with the good and bad suitably rewarded and punished, found this hard to take.

The Return of the Native did not even sell out. Hardy moved back to London, and relapsed to a lower level of work. Around this time he got his first request for a short story (there was always room for them in magazines) and went on writing them for the next fifteen years. In 1878, living in lodgings at Upper Tooting, he began to do research on the Napoleonic wars, which had always fascinated him. By the end of 1879 he had finished *The Trumpet-Major* and it was published the following year. This novel is pleasant and entertaining but rather slight compared to the one which had gone before. While it was still running as a serial Hardy had promised to begin work on another novel, but before he had written more than one instalment he realised he was ill. The doctor found he had an internal haemorrhage and told him to stay in bed for six months.

Lying with his feet above his head, and in a good deal of pain, he dictated the rest of *A Laodicean* to Emma; it was published in 1881. He did not feel particularly creative in the circumstances, but he was determined to do it, for the publishers would have been in an awkward position if he had let them down and there was very little money for his wife if he died. The result of all this was a long and poor novel. Some parts of it are memorable for his discussions of Gothic architecture, and it also shows his interest in the discoveries of modern science, such as railway engineering and a device for faking photographs (unheard of at the time). But on the whole it was a book which Hardy preferred to forget. It is usual to lay the whole blame on the fact that he was a sick man when he wrote it, but the first few chapters, written before he became ill, are little better than the rest. It seems more likely that the move to London had had a bad effect on him, 'residence in or near a city tended to force mechanical and ordinary productions from his pen'. As soon as he was better he and Emma decided to move back to the country.

They found a little house in the picturesque town of Wimborne Minster, and almost as soon as they had settled there Hardy began to feel more cheerful:

> Our garden . . . has all sorts of old-fashioned flowers, in full bloom: Canterbury Bells, blue and white, and Sweet Williams of every variety, strawberries and cherries that are ripe, currants and gooseberries that are almost ripe, peaches that are green, and apples that are decidedly immature.
>
> (*Life*, pp. 149–50)

A comet gave him the idea for a new story, about a young man in a remote village who wants to be an astronomer. In the Preface to *Two on a Tower* he said that 'this slightly-built romance' had been inspired by the wish 'to set the emotional history of two infinitesimal lives against the stupendous background of the stellar universe, and to impart to readers the sentiment that of these contrasting magnitudes the smaller might be the greater to them as men'. He wrote it quickly, in about six months, and it was published in 1882. It was not one of his greatest novels, but it was intended to be a serious story about man's place in the universe, about achievement, and about self-sacrifice. He was therefore taken aback when the book was criticized for being 'immoral' and a satire on religion. It was not the first or last time that his novels would be attacked on these grounds.

Soon afterwards, in April 1883, an article on Hardy by Havelock Ellis appeared in the *Westminster Review*. It showed a warm appreciation for him:

> The English agricultural labourer is a figure which few novelists have succeeded in describing. Few, indeed, have had an opportunity of knowing him. George Eliot, who has represented so much of the lower strata of English rural life, has not reached him. At best he is only visible in the dim background. . . . It is difficult to find anywhere fit company for the quaint and worthy fellowship, so racy of the earth, who greet us from the pages of *Far from the Madding Crowd* and *The Return of the Native*.

Most people still tended to think of Hardy as the author of *Far from the Madding Crowd*, though he had written five novels since that one, and to assume that the one thing he could do supremely well was paint pictures of English rural life. But it was less usual for critics to perceive that Hardy was the *only* considerable novelist to write about agricultural workers, a class which was generally treated as rather comic and described, by educated people, by the nickname of 'Hodge'. In July of the same year Hardy published in *Longman's Magazine* an article, 'The Dorsetshire Labourer', which ridiculed this crude conception:

> This supposedly real but highly conventional Hodge is a degraded being of uncouth manner and aspect, stolid under-standing, and snail-like movement. His speech is such a chaotic corruption of regular language that few persons of progressive aims consider it worth while to enquire what views, if any, of life, of nature, or of society, are conveyed in these utterances. . . . But suppose that, by some accident, the visitor were obliged to go home with this man . . . he would, for one thing, find that the language, instead of being a vile corruption of cultivated speech, was a tongue with grammatical inflection . . . the unwritten, dying Wessex English. . . .
>
> Six months pass, and our gentleman leaves the cottage, bidding his friends goodbye with genuine regret. The great change in his perception is that Hodge, the dull, unvarying, joyless one, has ceased to exist for him. He has become disinte-grated into a number of dissimilar fellow-creatures, men of many minds, infinite in difference; some happy, many serene, a few depressed; some clever, even to genius, some stupid, some wanton, some austere; some mutely Miltonic, some Cromwellian; into men who have private views of each other, as he has of his friends; who applaud or condemn each other; amuse or sadden themselves by the contemplation of each other's foibles or vices; and each of whom walks in his own way the road to dusty death. Dick the carter, Bob the shepherd, and Sam the ploughman, are, it is true, alike in the narrowness of their means and their general open-air life; but they cannot be rolled together again into such a Hodge as he has dreamed of, by any possible enchantment.

This article, with its clear message that people who worked on the land must be treated as fully human, in some ways marked a turning-point in Hardy's career. From now on he would commit himself to writing novels about Dorset and its people, and would produce his greatest work. This turning-point had been prefigured in his efforts with *The Return of the Native*. What was new was not just a return to novels about Dorset but a sense of vindication from Havelock Ellis and a decision not to bend to the whims of London critics and audiences. This new sense of purpose and identity was also symbolized in his decision to settle permanently in Dorchester. Over the last ten years he and his wife had been moving restlessly from town to country and back again, never staying for long in one place. Perhaps they lacked the stability which a family would have given them, and they must have realized by now that they were never going to have children. But in the summer of 1883 they took lodgings in Dorchester, and Hardy (perhaps against Emma's wishes) began to design a house about a mile out of town. It was finished in another two years, and named Max Gate. He would write all the rest of his novels and later poetry there.

Meanwhile he was working on *The Mayor of Casterbridge*. Almost certainly it turned out well because he refused to be rushed (although it did have to be trimmed for serial publication, like all his later novels) and, more fundamentally, because he had now fully discerned and accepted his particular identity and strength as a novelist. A good deal of the real Dorchester went into Hardy's portrait of Casterbridge, and the hero, Michael Henchard, is one of his most vital characters. But he had some trouble getting it published, and not all the copies were sold; reviewers complaining that it was gloomy. Fortunately Hardy was becoming more and more indifferent to public opinion. Moving back to home base seems to have given him confidence, and from then on his novels would become steadily more unorthodox and more individual.

He finished *The Mayor* just before moving into Max Gate, and his next novel, *The Woodlanders*, was written entirely in the study there. Published in 1887, it was his favourite work, although not many people agreed at the time. Some called it disagreeable, or even immoral. But it was enough of a success, both with readers and in his own judgement, to make him happy to continue on the road he had chosen.

He was now contemplating a more ambitious work than any he had yet written. In September 1888 he went to look at some of the houses and lands which his family were said to have owned, generations ago, and wrote:

> The Vale of Blackmoor is almost entirely green, every hedge being studded with trees. On the left you see to an immense distance, including Shaftesbury. The decline and fall of the Hardys much in evidence hereabout. . . . 'All Woolcombe and Froom Quintin belonged to them at one time'.

Out of this grew the idea for a story, set in the Vale of Blackmoor, which would deal with the decline and fall of ancient families. This mingled with memories of the woman he had seen hanged for a crime of passion, and with his own knowledge about the exploitation of village girls. He began to write *Tess of the D'Urbervilles*, although it was not known by that name at first; in the manuscript the heroine was called Rose Mary Troublefield. This is a corruption of Turberville, the real name of an aristocratic Norman family which had died out and is commemorated in the Dorset church of Bere Regis.

He offered the first few chapters to a magazine editor without, apparently, seeing anything controversial about them. They were sent back, 'virtually on the score of its improper explicitness'. He could not yet afford to do without serial publication, so he spent the year 1890 cutting up the novel, leaving out some parts and drastically altering others, to make it fit for the 'young person'. He claimed to do this in a spirit of cynical amusement, but in an essay which he wrote that year, 'Candour in English Fiction', it can be seen that he bitterly resented what he was being forced to do. 'The great bulk of English fiction of the present day is characterized by its lack of sincerity', he stated, and the reason for this was that writers were forced to rely for their livelihood on the magazines from which any frank treatment of sex or religion was carefully excluded:

> It may be urged that abundance of great and profound novels might be written which should require no compromising, contain not an episode deemed questionable by prudes. This I venture to doubt. In a ramification of the profounder passions the treatment of which makes the great style, something unsuitable is sure to arise; and then comes the struggle with the literary conscience. The opening scenes of the would-be great story may, in a rash moment, have been printed in some popular magazine before the remainder is written; as it advances month by month the situations develop, and the writer asks himself, what will his characters do next? . . . On his life and conscience, though he had not foreseen the thing, only one event could possibly happen, and that therefore he should narrate, as he calls himself a faithful artist. But, though pointing a fine moral, it is just one of those issues which are not to be mentioned in respectable magazines and select libraries. The dilemma then confronts him, he must either whip and scourge those characters into doing something contrary to their natures . . . or, by leaving them alone to act as they will, he must bring down the thunders of respectability upon his head, not to say ruin his editor, his publisher, and himself. . . .
>
> If the true artist ever weeps it probably is then, when he first discovers the fearful price that he has to pay for writing in the English language – no less a price than the complete extinction, in the mind of every mature and penetrating reader, of sympathetic belief in his personages.

Although his argument may be less than totally honest – it is difficult to believe that he had 'not foreseen' how *Tess* would end – it is still a powerful plea for freedom of expression. When the novel was published, unexpurgated, at the end of 1891, it was a sensation. There were some hostile reviews (which, as usual, upset Hardy out of proportion), but most critics were enthusiastic. On censorship, George Gissing noted privately that 'after Hardy's *Tess*, one can scarcely see the limits of artistic freedom'. Sales were enormous, as with all controversial novels; Hardy had become one of the most widely read English authors at home and abroad.

A glimpse of him in the early 1890s is provided by a journalist, Raymond Blathwayt, who wrote after an extended interview:

> Mr Hardy is in himself a gentle and a singularly pleasing personality. Of middle height, with a very thoughtful face and rather melancholy eyes, he is nevertheless an interesting and an amusing companion. . . . His wife . . . is so particularly bright . . . so evidently a citizen of the wide world, that the, at first, unmistakable reminiscence that there is in her of Anglican ecclesiasticism is curiously puzzling and inexplicable to the stranger.

Hardy showed him round Max Gate and talked about his latest novel. On the character of Tess he said:

> 'She had done exactly what I think one of her nature under similar circumstances would have done in real life. It is led up to right through the story. One looks for the climax. One is not to be cheated out of it by the exigencies of inartistic conventionality. And so there come the tears of faithful tragedy in place of the ghastly and affected smile of the conventionally optimistic writer.'

He said that the public's growing willingness to accept tragic endings was a hopeful sign for the future. Blathwayt went on to say:

> 'And the ultimate result of your book, Mr Hardy, will be, I hope, that a greater freedom will exist for the decent, grave consider-ation of certain deep problems of human life.'
>
> 'Well,' replied Mr Hardy with a smile, 'that would be a very ambitious hope on my part. Remember I am only a learner in the art of novel writing. Still I do feel very strongly that the position of man and woman in nature, things which everyone is thinking and nobody is saying, may be taken up and treated frankly. Until lately, novelists have been obliged to arrange situations and *dénouements* which they knew to be indescribably unreal, but dear to the heart of the amiable library subscriber.

See how this ties the hands of a writer who is forced to make his characters act unnaturally, in order that he may produce the spurious effect of their being in harmony with social forms and ordinances.

Everything Hardy said and wrote at this time suggests he was moving in the direction of greater realism, and this tendency can be seen, still more clearly, in his next (and last) novel, *Jude the Obscure*, published in 1895. For some time he had been thinking of a story about a young man who failed to go to Oxford and committed suicide (like Horace Moule). Later he dropped the idea of a suicide, and something which happened in 1890 again made him alter his plans. While he was in a train on the way to London he found himself thinking about Tryphena, and composed the first few lines of a poem, 'Thoughts of Phena'. (He had been drafting or making notes for poems, though not publishing them, all through his novel-writing career.) It was, he said, 'a curious instance of sympathetic telepathy', for Tryphena was dying. They had had no contact with each other for some twenty years. In the preface to *Jude* he said that parts of the novel had been suggested by 'the death of a woman' in the year Tryphena died.

Opinion has always been divided about this novel, which is the story of two cousins who fall in love but each marry the wrong person, as well as the story of a young working man who is excluded from Oxford. Some people, notably Swinburne, thought it one of the greatest things Hardy ever wrote. Others found it depressing and a failure, and this included the majority of those who reviewed it. Typical headlines for such reviews were 'Jude the Obscene', 'Hardy the Degenerate', and 'The Anti-Marriage League'. This last was written by Mrs Margaret Oliphant, herself a fine and under-appreciated novelist. But she and Hardy were incompatible, and, as a woman, she was suspicious of any philosophy which seemed to reduce women to sex objects and to devalue the importance of children. She wrote:

Nothing so coarsely indecent as the whole history of Jude in his relations with his wife Arabella has ever been put in English print – that is to say, from the hands of a Master. There may be books more disgusting, more impious as regards human nature, more foul in detail, in those dark corners where the amateurs of filth found garbage to their taste; but not, we repeat, from any Master's hand.

The novel was banned from public libraries, and a bishop announced that he had burned it. Although many other voices defended it, Hardy felt almost ill at finding himself in the middle of the biggest literary scandal for years. He did not believe the book was immoral; his only aim had been to write honestly, but at the time he made no public attempt to defend himself and retreated into his shell. The 1912 preface to *Jude*, and poems like 'Wessex Heights' and 'In Tenebris', give some idea of his suffering. And there were other problems which the public knew nothing about.

Mrs Oliphant was not the only woman to find Hardy's views on marriage offensive. Emma felt betrayed; her nephew wrote that 'my aunt, who was a very ardent Churchwoman and believer in the virtues and qualities of women in general, strongly objected to this book'. As she grew older she had become more devout; Hardy writes of Jude 'that Sue and himself had mentally travelled in opposite directions . . . events which had enlarged his own views of life, laws, customs, and dogmas, had not operated in the same manner on Sue's'. We do not know exactly when he and Emma began to be miserable, though, as we have seen, Hardy already had doubts about their marriage, but Blathwayt in 1892 was the last outsider to describe them as a united couple, and also the last to say anything good about Hardy's wife.

Emma's striking looks had faded; the girlish manner which had seemed enchanting in her twenties seemed absurd in her fifties. One observer called her 'an excessively plain, dowdy, high-stomached woman with . . . a severe cast of countenance', and reported the comment, 'Mrs Hardy. Now you may understand the pessimistic nature of the poor devil's work'. Other cruel remarks from those who met them in the later years of their marriage (for they continued to appear in public together) are on record.

Emma has been typecast as a commonplace woman who dragged her husband up to London for parties (although in fact there were times when he went there without her). It would be more true to say that she was a woman of strong views and strong character who could not adapt to her expected social role. 'It is so silly of her though isn't it', wrote one visitor, 'not to rejoice in the privilege of being wife to so great a man?' In happier times Emma had helped her husband by copying out and discussing his novels; now she felt he had no more use for her. 'If he belongs to the public in any way, years of devotion count for nothing', she wrote, claiming also that he kept her at a distance 'lest the dimmest ray should alight upon me of his supreme glory'. In the 1890s there were many society women eager to take him up and for a time he fell in love with one of them, Mrs Florence Henniker. Emma retreated into writing religious pamphlets and bad poetry, which she tried, sometimes successfully, to get published.

She embarrassed him; he caused her pain. There were no children or shared structure of beliefs to sustain the marriage. Yet they went on living under one roof, taking long bicycle rides together and making a fuss of their pets (one thing they did agree about was animal welfare). Hardy doubtless believed, as he often said, that marriage to the wrong person was agonizing, but he did not realize that his feelings for Emma had never quite died.

Meanwhile, he tried to rebuild his life as far as possible. He prepared his novels for a new general edition, which came out in 1895. But he was determined not to write any more fiction, partly because of the hostility to *Jude* but even more because he had secretly thought of himself as a poet all his adult life. He had now made enough money from his novels to do as he wanted. In 1898 he brought out his first collection, *Wessex Poems*, some of which had been written more than thirty years earlier. This, incidentally, caused more unhappiness to Emma, as several had been inspired by other women. He would go on writing poetry exclusively for the rest of his life. The public, which had never thought of him as anything but a novelist, took some time to get used to the change-over, but gradually, as younger readers grew up, he became recognized as a great poet.

In the early years of the twentieth century he began work on *The Dynasts*, 'an epic-drama of the war with Napoleon', which he had been planning for years. It was born out of the deep interest in Napoleon which he shared with many writers of his own and the previous generation, and aimed to give a broad picture of what happened to Europe (and Dorset) at this time of upheaval. The whole work is imbued with a sense of the horrors of war (the recent South African war had inspired several shorter poems). It took him some six years to write, and was published in three parts in 1904, 1906 and 1908.

The Dynasts is little read today. But it was a heroic attempt to write a modern epic, and as such was widely praised. Indeed, Hardy must have been surprised at how respectable he was becoming. He was getting to be a grand old man of letters; Aberdeen University gave him a doctorate in 1905. He refused a knighthood, but accepted a greater honour, the Order of Merit, in 1910.

Emma, Florence and the later years

On the last pages of *Wessex Poems* Hardy had placed 'I Look into my Glass', one of his most famous lyrics, perfect in its stark simplicity:

> I look into my glass,
> And view my wasting skin,

And say, 'Would God it came to pass
My heart had shrunk as thin!'

For then, I, undistrest
By hearts grown cold to me,
Could lonely wait my endless rest
With equanimity.

But Time, to make me grieve,
Part steals, lets part abide;
And shakes this fragile frame at eve
With throbbings of noontide.

Believing that his marriage to Emma was dead, he found himself increasingly attracted to other women, although he seldom did anything about it other than write poetry. In 1906 he was in his mid-sixties, looked frail and probably thought he had not many more years to live. It was around this time that he met a young woman, Florence Dugdale, who probably introduced herself as an admirer of his work. Florence, the daughter of an Enfield schoolmaster, had been born in 1879 and so was almost forty years younger. She had trained as a teacher, and published articles and children's stories, but her poverty and bad health stood in the way of her becoming a writer. Hardy sympathized intensely, found her small literary jobs and recommended her to editors. As the relationship (one doubts if it was a full-blooded affair) deepened, he invited her to Max Gate where she got on friendly terms with Emma. In the lovely poem 'After the Visit' he speaks of her 'mute ministrations to one and to all/Beyond a man's saying sweet'. Florence must have seemed everything that Emma was not – youthful, quiet, intelligent, sympathetic. But the poem ends 'that which mattered most could not be'; he saw no hope that they could ever marry.

Possibly he had not noticed that Emma was unwell; certainly they had been on distant terms for some time when she died suddenly in his presence on 27th November 1912. It was an unspeakable shock. Looking back over the years, he could only remember the long-ago time when they had fallen in love, and much of what had happened since seemed to him to be more his fault than hers. He found a manuscript among her papers, headed 'What I Think of my Husband', which deepened his feelings of guilt. Over the next few months he wrote poem after poem about her and these became a cycle, called 'Poems of 1912–13', which are among the greatest elegies in English. 'The Voice' is a winter poem set in Dorset, and dated (December 1912) only a few weeks after Emma's death:

Woman much missed, how you call to me, call to me,
Saying that now you are not as you were
When you had changed from the one who was all to me,
But as at first, when our day was fair.

Can it be you that I hear? Let me view you, then,
Standing as when I drew near to the town
Where you would wait for me: yes, as I knew you then,
Even to the original air-blue gown!

Or is it only the breeze, in its listlessness
Travelling across the wet mead to me here,
You being ever dissolved to wan wistlessness,
Heard no more again far or near?

Thus I; faltering forward,
  Leaves around me falling,
Wind oozing thin through the thorn from norward,
  And the woman calling.

The picture of the elderly man, groping after what he knows to
be a ghost, is heart-rending. In the spring of 1913 he revisited
Cornwall, to explore Emma's home territory on the anniversary of
their meeting, and produced further magnificent poems. Florence
was not impressed.

By this time she had moved into Max Gate to work as his
secretary, and they were quietly married in February 1914. The
Great War which broke out six months later appalled Hardy. He
had been fascinated by the European wars of the previous century,
but had believed (in spite of his 'pessimism') that men were slowly
growing more rational. Privately he wrote that 'the world, having
like a spider climbed to a certain height, seems slipping back to
what it was long ago.'

However, he accepted the official version that England was
fighting for its life and offered to help in any way he could. He
joined the Writers' War Committee and wrote several mildly
patriotic poems which had a wide circulation. But he never hated
Germans or took part in the really vicious propaganda which was
so common during those years. He visited wounded prisoners of
war in Dorchester and tried to persuade them that the war was not
against Germany as such. There was a personal sadness too; a
distant cousin, Frank George, whom he had planned to make his
heir, was killed. Two years after it finally ended he wrote 'And there
was a Great Calm', which asked if there had been any real reason
for the war:

Calm fell. From Heaven distilled a clemency;
There was peace on earth, and silence in the sky;
Some could, some could not, shake off misery:
The Sinister Spirit sneered: 'It had to be!'
And again the Spirit of Pity whispered, 'Why?'

Afterwards his life settled down into a quiet routine. He was nearly eighty now, and too old to go far from home, but he continued to write poetry prolifically. Florence, at some cost to her health and nerves, provided him with a peaceful working environment and was a pleasant hostess to the many admirers who called at Max Gate. His novels were accepted as having permanent value (after the war, no one was likely to call them too pessimistic) and a new generation of poets had grown up to revere him. One was Siegfried Sassoon, who became a good friend and organized a birthday tribute from forty-three younger poets. Hardy was very touched. 'It was almost his first awakening to the consciousness that an opinion had silently grown up as it were in the night, that he was no mean power in the contemporary world of poetry.'

In 1920 the University of Oxford (having finally forgiven him for *Jude*) awarded Hardy an honorary doctorate, seven years later than Cambridge. An undergraduate, Charles Morgan, showed him around the city and reflected, 'It seemed very strange to be driving solemnly up the High and down the Broad with the author of *Jude*.' Another observer noted that Hardy had changed in thirty years from 'a rather rough-looking man, dressed very unlike his fellows, with a very keen alert face and a decided accent of some kind', to 'a refined, fragile, gentle little old gentleman, with . . . a gentle and smooth voice and polished manners'.

Morgan thought, though, that some of the passion of the younger man was still there below the surface:

> He was not simple; he had the formal subtlety peculiar to his own generation; there was something deliberately 'ordinary' in his demeanour which was a concealment of extraordinary fires. . . . There was in him something timid as well as fierce, as if the world had hurt him and he expected it to hurt him again. But what fascinated me above all was the contrast between the plainness, the quiet rigidity of his behaviour, and the passionate boldness of his mind.

This contrast was explored by Siegfried Sassoon in a poem, 'At Max Gate':

Old Mr Hardy, upright in his chair,
Courteous to visiting acquaintance chatted
With unaloof alertness while he patted

Hardy and Florence Dugdale on the beach at Aldeburgh, circa 1909

The sheep dog whose society he preferred.
He wore an air of never having heard
That there was much that needed putting right.
Hardy, the Wessex wizard, wasn't there.
Good care was taken to keep him out of sight.

Head propped on hand, he sat with me alone,
Silent, the log fire flickering on his face.
Here was the seer whose words the world had known.
Someone had taken Mr Hardy's place.

He went on living quietly in the country, writing poetry almost
on his highest level and working with Florence on the authorized
biography which would eventually be published under her name.
He used to walk regularly to Stinsford and see that the family graves
were in good order. He was still interested in everything that went
on around him, literature, religion and politics, never showing the
faintest trace of senility. In November 1927 Florence noted, 'Speaking about ambition T. said today that he had done all that he meant
to do, but he did not know whether it had been worth doing. His
only ambition, so far as he could remember, was to have some poem
or poems in a good anthology like the Golden Treasury'.

He had prepared a collection of poems, *Winter Words* (his eighth)
for publication on his ninetieth birthday, but was never to see it in
print. According to Florence he had a great burst of creativity in
the last months of 1927, but when he went to his study on December
11th he found for the first time that he could not work. Although
his mind never weakened, he was finally wearing out, having
survived most of his generation, and he died aged eighty-seven on
11th January 1928.

He had wished to be buried in Stinsford churchyard, but
Florence, against her better judgement, was persuaded to let his
body be divided so that there could be a great national funeral in
Westminster Abbey. So his heart lies in Stinsford and his ashes in
Poets' Corner next to Dickens. It was a final irony, for he had been
a divided person, and a few years earlier had written a mocking
poem about the Abbey's refusal to have a memorial to Byron in the
same place.

2 Hardy the countryman

To understand Hardy's life and work we need to know something about nineteenth-century Dorset, the region which lay at the heart of what he called Wessex, and where most of his novels are set. When Hardy was growing up it was very different from the rest of England. It had its own culture, its own traditions, even its own language, in a sense.

It was a very remote and old-fashioned county. When Hardy wrote about it in his novels, he was often asked, 'even by educated people', where exactly it lay. Traditions lingered on for a long time in this neighbourhood. Hardy's grandmother remembered hearing the news of the French Revolution, and many men still living had joined the militia to fight Napoleon, when it looked as if Dorset would be invaded from the sea. These memories were very real to him; he knew a great deal more about his ancestors, who had lived, died and been buried in Dorset, than most of us do about ours. Some of his earliest memories were of 'men in the stocks, corn-law agitations, mail-coaches, road-waggons, tinder-boxes, and candle-snuffing'. He had also seen or heard of such customs as the skimmity ride, the maypole, the mummers who gave the play of St George and the Dragon at Christmas, the old-fashioned hiring fairs for farm labourers, and the sale by husbands of wives. But things were changing. When he was seven the railway came to Dorchester, and Hardy noted with regret that this killed off the countryside's traditional ballads – 'the orally transmitted ditties of centuries being slain at a stroke by the London comic songs that were introduced' (*Life*, p. 21). This is a complaint which we often hear in our own century, from Scotland to Eastern Europe, wherever the culture of a country or province is superseded by a new 'pop culture' without roots there. The ballads were not the only thing Hardy regretted. His family had a long connection with the cultural life of the parish which had ended when he was only one year old. For forty years before that, his grandfather, and then his father and uncle, had been the nucleus of a little group of musicians who accompanied the services at Stinsford church. In those days it was normal for such groups, rather than an organ, to provide the church music, and there was a small gallery for the players which has long since been pulled down. They were excellent performers: 'the Hardy instrumentalists, though no more than four, maintained an easy superiority over the large groups in parishes near'. Hardy drew a detailed and loving picture of this little group in an early novel, *Under the Greenwood Tree*, although he

> invented the personages, incidents, manners, etc., never having seen or heard the choir as such, they ending their office when he was about a year old. He was accustomed to say that on this account he had rather burlesqued them, the story not so adequately reflecting as he could have wished in later years the poetry and romance that coloured their time-honoured observances.
>
> > (*Life*, p. 12)

Hardy felt a deep respect for these people, and a deep regret that choirs like this should have been abolished all over the West Country when he was a boy. He noted that the musicians were 'mainly poor men and hungry', but very good at and devoted to their work, which included playing at weddings and parties as well as in church. Not surprisingly, when the village choirs were killed the attendance at the village church (which also had the disadvantage of being associated with the landlords) began to decline.

Later Hardy came to think that one of the most important events of his childhood had been the Great Exhibition which was held in London in 1851:

> For South Wessex, the year formed in many ways an extraordinary chronological frontier or transit-line, at which there occurred what one might call a precipice in Time. As in a geological 'fault' we had presented to us a sudden bringing of ancient and modern into absolute contact, such as probably in no other single year since the Conquest was ever witnessed in this part of the country.
>
> > ('The Fiddler of the Reels')

Special 'exhibition trains' were laid on, and literally thousands of people, who had never left their village or got on a train before, were whirled up to London to see the wonders of modern science and industry. Hardy did not go, but already as a boy he had begun to feel the contrast between old and new. Dorchester was an old-fashioned place, just as he was to describe it later in *The Mayor of Casterbridge*, but, compared with Higher Bockhampton, it seemed very modern:

> Owing to the accident of his being an architect's pupil in a county town of assizes and aldermen, which had advanced to railways and telegraphs and daily London papers; yet not living there, but walking in every day from a world of shepherds and ploughmen in a hamlet three miles off, where modern improve-

ments were still regarded as wonders, he saw rustic and borough doings in a juxtaposition peculiarly close. To these externals may be added the peculiarities of his inner life, which might almost have been called academic – a triple existence unusual for a young man – what he used to call, in looking back, a life twisted of three strands – the professional life, the scholar's life, and the rustic life, combined in the twenty-four hours of one day.

(*Life*, pp. 31–2)

This 'triple existence' was in fact to continue all the rest of his life, for as well as being a scholar and a professional man Hardy would always remain deeply committed to the Dorsetshire countryside, its people and its culture. Instinctively, he felt that he belonged here, although at a very early stage he began to be conscious of something beyond.

William Barnes and 'provincialism'

When Hardy was working at John Hicks's office in South Street, he would often look in next door, where the Reverend William Barnes kept a school. Hardy used to ask his advice about knotty problems in Greek and Latin grammar; he was an expert on all kinds of linguistic problems and later they became friends in spite of forty years' difference in age. Barnes was one of Hardy's greatest teachers at this formative time in his life.

This extraordinary man, probably the best-known person in Dorchester, was born a farmer's son in the Vale of Blackmore in 1801. He took an external degree at Oxford and eventually became a clergyman, during which time he taught himself an amazing number of languages. 'He was almost always ready', Hardy wrote, 'with definite and often exclusive information on whatever slightly known form of human speech might occur to the mind of his questioner, from Persian to Welsh, from the contemporary vernaculars of India to the tongues of the ancient British tribes' (*Thomas Hardy's Personal Writings*, ed. Harold Orel, p. 102). But his particular love was the Dorsetshire dialect, and he is remembered today as our only significant dialect poet outside Scotland. Not that he is remembered widely, because many readers are naturally reluctant to tackle poems which they assume will be very difficult. Hardy was conscious of this obstacle when he wrote, in the Preface to a new edition of his friend's work:

I chance to be (I believe) one of the few living persons having a practical acquaintance with letters who knew familiarly the Dorset dialect as it is spoken now. Since his death, education in the West of England, as elsewhere, has gone on with its silent and inevitable effacements, reducing the speech of this country to uniformity, and obliterating every year many a fine old local word. The process is always the same: the word is ridiculed by the newly taught; it gets into disgrace; it is heard in holes and corners only; it dies.

(PW, p. 76)

This was all the more sad, from Hardy's point of view, because he felt that Barnes, at his best, had been a very great poet. He was essentially a writer of simple lyrics; he did not often go deeply into social conditions, but his descriptions of nature were often lovely – Hardy cited his phrase 'the blue-hilled worold' to describe the landscape of Blackmore Vale. He was also deeply impressed with Barnes's poetry about the people of Dorset, particularly one called 'The Wife-a-Lost'. This sad little poem is not difficult to translate into ordinary English:

> Since I noo mwore do zee your feäce,
> Up-steäirs or down below,
> I'll zit me in the lonesome pleäce,
> Where flat-bough'd beech do grow.
> Below the beeches' bough, my love,
> Where you did never come,
> An' I don't look to meet ye now,
> As I do look at hwome.

> Since you noo mwore be at my side,
> In walks in zummer het,
> I'll goo alwone where mist do ride
> Drough trees a-drippèn wet:
> Below the rain-wet bough, my love,
> Where you did never come,
> An' I don't grieve to miss ye now,
> As I do grieve at hwome.

> Since now bezide my dinner bwoard
> Your vaïce do never sound,
> I'll eat the bit I can avword,
> Ä-vield upon the ground;
> Below the darksome bough, my love,
> Where you did never dine,
> An' I don't grieve to miss ye now
> As I at hwome do pine.

What Hardy admired about poems like these was that they used the regional dialect *seriously*. Most writers only put it into the mouths of their 'comic rustics', a vulgarization of the real country people which never failed to make him angry. As he said in 1908, in the Preface to Barnes's poems:

> For some reason or none, many persons suppose that when anything is penned in the tongue of the countryside, the primary intent is burlesque or ridicule, and this especially if the speech be one in which the sibilant has the rough sound, and is expressed by Z. Indeed, scores of thriving story-tellers and dramatists seem to believe that by transmuting the flattest conversation into a dialect that never existed, and making the talkers say 'be' where they would really say 'is', a Falstaffian richness is at once imparted to its qualities.
>
> <div align="right">(<i>PW</i>, p. 78)</div>

Hardy's own use of dialect was considerably more subtle and varied than the older poet's. As a young man he tried writing a few poems in broad Dorset, but they were not a success. In his novels, the less well-educated characters do normally speak in the language of the province, but Hardy was careful not to reproduce their speech phonetically, as Barnes had done:

> The rule of scrupulously preserving the local idiom, together with the words which have no synonym among those in general use, while printing in the ordinary way most of those local expressions which are but a modified articulation of words in use elsewhere is the rule I usually follow.
>
> <div align="right">(<i>PW</i>, p. 92)</div>

He was more reluctant than Barnes to use words which would not have been easily understood by his readers. Occasionally he showed how the older people, like Grammer Oliver in *The Woodlanders*, used expressions like 'ch woll' or 'Ich woll' for 'I will'.* Even an educated girl like Tess Durbeyfield speaks dialect sometimes: 'Had it anything to do with father's making such a mommet of himself in thik carriage this afternoon? Why did 'er? I felt inclined to sink into the ground with shame!' (*Tess*, Ch. 3). But, normally, Hardy found that he could give his readers a good idea of the rhythm and quality of west country speech without actually using dialect words:

> 'My brother-in-law told me, and I have no reason to doubt it,' said Creedle, 'that she'll sit down to her dinner with a gown hardly higher than her elbows. "O, you wicked woman!" he said to himself when he first see her, "you go to the Table o' Sundays,

---

* The Dorset dialect was in some ways very like German, and Hardy commented on this in a poem, 'The Pity of It', which he wrote in 1915. It seemed to him to make the war all the more tragic.

and kneel, as if your knee-joints were greased with very saint's anointment, and tell off your hear-us-good-Lords as pat as a business-man counting money; and yet you can eat your victuals a-strip to such a wanton figure as that!" Whether she's a reformed character by this time I can't say; but I don't care who the man is, that's how she went on when my brother-in-law lived there.'

(*Woodlanders*, Ch. 4)

And at other times in the Wessex novels he showed how the dialect could be transformed into great literature, as in the labourer Whittle's description of the last days of Michael Henchard:

'He was kind-like to mother when she were here below, sending her the best ship-coal, and hardly any ashes from it at all; and taties, and such-like that were very needful to her. I seed en go down street on the night of your worshipful's wedding to the lady at yer side, and I thought he looked low and faltering. And I followed en over Grey's Bridge, and he turned and zeed me, and said, "You go back!" But I followed, and he turned again, and said, "Do you hear, sir? Go back!" But I zeed that he was low, and I followed on still. Then 'a said, "Whittle, what do ye follow me for when I've told ye to go back all these times?" And I said, 'Because sir, I see things be bad with 'ee, and ye were kind-like to mother if ye were rough to me, and I would fain be kind-like to you." Then he walked on, and I followed: and he never complained at me no more. We walked on like that all night: and in the blue o' the morning, when 'twas hardly day, I looked ahead o' me, and I zeed that he wambled, and could hardly drag along. By that time we had got past here, but I had seen that this house was empty as I went by, and I got him to come back; and I took down the boards from the windows, and helped him inside.'

(*Mayor of Casterbridge*, Ch. 45)

In the hands of a great master like Hardy, or indeed a less great one like Barnes, dialect could become a means of showing how Dorset people felt and thought. But, as Hardy was well aware, it was dying out. The coming of universal education helped to kill it: Tess Durbeyfield speaks 'two languages, the dialect at home, more or less; ordinary English abroad and to persons of quality'. It was also a fact that many of these people thought it was vulgar to speak anything except 'ordinary English'; Hardy shows Henchard becoming furious with his daughter because of her 'occasional pretty and picturesque use of dialect words – those terrible marks of the beast to the truly genteel':

The sharp reprimand was not lost upon her; and in time it came to pass that for 'fay' she said 'succeed'; that she no longer spoke of 'dumbledores' but of 'humble bees'; no longer said of young men and women that they 'walked together', but that they were 'engaged' that she grew to talk of 'greggles' as 'wild hyacinths'; that when she had not slept she did not quaintly tell the servants next morning that she had been 'hag-rid', but that she had 'suffered from indigestion'.

(Mayor of Casterbridge, Ch. 20)

Hardy's own feelings about the substitution of correct, but colourless English phrases for the 'pretty and picturesque' words come over very clearly. Although he could only use them sparingly in his novels, he wrote:

It must, of course, always be a matter for regret that, in order to be understood, writers should be obliged thus slightingly to treat varieties of English which are intrinsically as genuine, grammatical, and worthy of the royal title [the King's English] as is the all-prevailing competitor which bears it; whose only fault was that they happened not to be central, and therefore were worsted in the struggle for existence, when a uniform tongue became a necessity among the advanced classes of the population.

(PW, pp. 92–3)

What he was protesting against was the assumption that the dialect of one particular region (London and the south-east) was somehow superior to the dialects of all other regions, and that people must all speak with identical accents and use identical forms of speech if they wished to be 'truly genteel'. Indeed his whole work can be seen as a vindication of the dignity, the essential value of the culture and the people of his own region. After reading Matthew Arnold, he wrote:

Arnold is wrong about provincialism, if he means anything more than a provincialism of style and manner in exposition. A certain provincialism of feeling is invaluable. It is of the essence of individuality, and is largely made up of that crude enthusiasm without which no great thoughts are thought, no great deeds done.

(Life, pp. 146–7)

It was at that time, and still is, customary to run Hardy down because he was a 'provincial' writer. But so were the Brontës and George Eliot and D.H. Lawrence: indeed *Middlemarch*, which is often called the greatest of English novels, is subtitled 'A Study of Provincial Life'. Hardy's attempts to write about the smart London scene which he discovered in later life were almost invariably flat and boring. His best novels were written not only *about* but actually *in* Dorset; he found that he could not work well when he was living anywhere else. And although we may sometimes find a difficult word or phrase in the Wessex novels, Hardy certainly solved the problem of making a dialect readable. Emily Brontë and George Eliot did what Barnes had done and copied dialect straight on to the page, and as a result these parts of their novels are difficult to read. Hardy was more flexible, and he immortalized Dorset forms of speech.

Social conditions in Dorset

'There were few counties in England' (claims a twentieth-century account) 'where more went on beneath the surface of everyday life than in Dorset'.* We have seen that smuggling was normal, and the Hardy family was involved in it. Cranborne Chase (scene of the rape in *Tess*) is said to have been 'the last tract in England to lie entirely outside the confines of law and order'. In 1830 there were riots when half-starved labourers set fire to ricks. In 'The Withered Arm', Hardy describes the hanging of a young man, 'only just turned eighteen, and only present by chance when the rick was fired'. It seems that his father had witnessed just such an execution.

Six years before Hardy was born, a group of labourers in the little village of Tolpuddle, a few miles away across Puddletown Heath, banded together to form a trade union branch. Five of them were Methodists, a fact which automatically made them suspicious characters to parsons and squires. Strictly speaking, trade unions were not illegal, but Lord Melbourne's government meant to stamp them out by any means it could. The men were found guilty of taking an illegal oath (they had sworn to keep faith with each other) and transported to Australia. They became known to history as the Tolpuddle Martyrs. There was a good deal of agitation after the sentence, but it took four years to get all the men back from Australia, and by this time many of them were so disgusted with conditions in England that they emigrated to Canada and never came back. The only one who remained, James Hammett, died in the workhouse and is buried in Tolpuddle churchyard. Hardy must have known this story well. He never spoke of it, but it happened in a county where memories endured for generations and it cannot have failed to impress him.

It is pleasant to know that there are six cottages in Tolpuddle today, each named after one of the Martyrs, for the use of retired

* Firth and Hopkinson, *The Tolpuddle Martyrs* (1934).

agricultural labourers. But at the time the incident did a great deal of harm, and not only to the six men. It killed agricultural trade unionism for the best part of forty years, and during this time the labourers went on suffering, as they had done for as long as anybody could remember. Dorset was one of the very poorest counties in England, and in the absence of railways or big towns it was practically impossible to get away from the land. Years later, in 1902, Hardy wrote to the novelist Rider Haggard:

> As to your first question, my opinion on the past of the agricultural labourers in this county: I think, indeed know, that down to 1850 or 1855 their condition was in general one of great hardship . . . As a child I knew a sheep-keeping boy who to my horror shortly afterwards died of want – the contents of his stomach at the autopsy being raw turnip only.
>
> *(Life,* p. 312)

A popular nineteenth-century song, 'The Fine Old English Labourer', tells us a little about how these people used to live, and why some of them died:

He used to take whatever wage the farmer chose to pay,
And work as hard as any horse for eighteenpence a day;
Or if he grumbled at the nine, and dared to ask for ten,
The angry farmer cursed and swore, and sacked him there and
    then.

He used to tramp off to his work while town folk were a-bed,
With nothing in his belly but a slice or two of bread;
He dined upon potatoes, and he never dreamed of meat,
Except a lump of bacon fat sometimes by way of treat.

He used to find it hard enough to give his children food,
But sent them to the village school as often as he could;
But though he knew that school was good, they must have bread
    and clothes,
So he had to send them to the fields to scare away the crows.

When Hardy was a boy, women and children worked on the land, diseases like cholera still lingered, and the old and sick usually ended up on Dorchester workhouse. This is the place described in *Far from the Madding Crowd,* where Fanny Robin dies with her baby. It was 'a picturesque building':

> The view from the front, over the Casterbridge chimneys, was one of the most magnificent in the country. A neighbouring earl once said that he would give up a year's rental to have at his own door the view enjoyed by the inmates from theirs – and very

probably the inmates would have given up the view for his year's
rental.

(Far from the Madding Crowd, Ch. 40)

Many of Hardy's greatest novels reflect the social realities of
Dorset in the nineteenth century. In *Far from the Madding Crowd* and
The Mayor of Casterbridge he shows us the old-fashioned hiring fairs,
held every year, where labourers stood up to be picked over by
farmers. In *Jude* he shows child labour; in *The Woodlanders* and *Tess*
the system whereby, after living in the same house for three
generations, a family could be turned out of doors. (This only
applied to the better-off villagers; most labourers could be turned
out anyway, whenever the farmer wished.) But in his later novels,
which have a more modern setting than the early ones, we can see
how the system was changing. *Tess* and *Jude* show exactly how
horrible work on the land could be, but the characters are free to
leave the land if they wish. There is a great difference between them
and an earlier generation of people who remained in their villages
for the whole of their lives.

During the 1840s two things happened which would profoundly
alter life in Dorset. One was the extension of the railway to
Dorchester; the other was the abolition of the Corn Laws. The
coming of railways made labourers much more mobile; able to look
for work where they liked if they could not find it at home, and now
free to move to the towns and cities as urbanization grew apace.
The repeal of the Corn Laws by Sir Robert Peel's government (Peel
is the 'Corn Law convert' mentioned in Book 2 of *Jude*) meant that
the country could import cheap grain from abroad when the home
crop failed. This was necessary because people in England and
Ireland were starving, but the farmers claimed that it would ruin
them, and in a sense they were right. Although the full effects were
not felt for another quarter of a century, it meant that the British
corn trade lost most of its old importance. There were two 'great
depressions', in the periods 1875–84 and 1891–99, when the harvest
failed and the country had to buy vast quantities of Russian and
American corn. The farmers lost heavily, and those who had not
already done so began to change over from arable to pasture
farming; as *Tess* indicates, they also began to mechanize. It was
very profitable for them to do so. They only needed about half as
many labourers, and there was a growing demand for more animal
food. People were beginning to eat bacon and eggs for breakfast
instead of bread and potatoes, and the living standards of those
labourers who stayed on the land rose.

By this time there had been several other changes. Education was
making the labourers dissatisfied with their conditions; the growth

of industry was offering them better-paid jobs; and a new Agricultural Labourers' Union was founded in 1872. Its leader, Joseph Arch, was worried at first about its chances:

> I remembered the Labourers' Union in Dorsetshire, started in the thirties – what had become of that? Poor Hammett had had to pay a heavy price for standing up with his fellow-labourers against the oppression. . . . For daring to be Unionists they had been sent to the hulks in Australia. . . . What if the Union we meant to start in this corner of Warwickshire tonight should fall to bits like a badly made box?
>
> (Life of Joseph Arch, Ch. 4)

But it was no longer possible to treat agricultural labourers as the Martyrs had been treated, and although the Union broke up after only twelve years it did what it was intended to do. In many places including parts of Dorset it pushed up wages, and where this could not be done it helped the labourers to move to the towns or abroad. Once started, this process was irresistible. Thousands of labourers left the villages forever, and those who did not give up work on the land altogether tended to move about from place to place, changing jobs every year. This happened often in Dorset, and Hardy shows something of its effects on ordinary people in *Tess*.

What were Hardy's feelings about these great changes? He respected Arch, whom he once heard addressing a public meeting, and he felt that the labourers had been 'greatly wronged' in the days when the farmers had it all their own way. He was glad that their standards of living had gone up so much during his lifetime:

> But changes at which we must all rejoice have brought other changes which are not so attractive. The labourers have become more and more migratory – the younger families in especial, who enjoy nothing so much as fresh scenery and new acquaintance. The consequences are curious and unexpected. For one thing, village tradition – a vast mass of unwritten folklore, local chronicle, local topography, and nomenclature – is absolutely sinking, has nearly sunk, into eternal oblivion. I cannot recall a single instance of a labourer who still lives on the farm where he was born, and I can only recall a few who have been five years on their present farms. Thus you see, there being no continuity of environment in their lives, there is no continuity of information, the names, stories, and relics of one place being speedily forgotten under the incoming facts of the next. For example, if you ask one of the workfolk (they always used to be called 'workfolk' hereabouts – 'labourers' is an imported word) the

names of surrounding hills; streams; the character and circumstances of people buried in particular graves; at what spots parish
personages lie interred; questions on local fairies, ghosts, herbs,
etc., they can give no answer; yet I can recollect the time when
the places of burial even of the poor and tombless were all
remembered, and the history of the parish and squire's family for
150 years back known. Such and such ballads appertained to
such and such a locality, ghost tales were attached to particular
sites, and nooks wherein wild herbs grew for the cure of divers
maladies were pointed out readily.

(Life, pp. 312–13)

Still, he realized that these quaint and charming traditions probably
had to go if the labourers were ever to be freed from their shackles.

It is only the old story that progress and picturesqueness do not
harmonise. They are losing their individuality, but they are
widening the range of their ideas, and gaining in freedom. It is
too much to expect them to remain stagnant and old-fashioned
for the pleasure of romantic spectators.

(PW, p. 181)

What he did regret bitterly, and felt to be quite unnecessary, was
the destruction of the class to which he and his parents had
belonged. Almost every village had at one time had 'an interesting
and better-informed class', consisting of skilled craftsmen, shop-
keepers, and a few other people not directly employed on the land.
They had provided most of the local leadership of Arch's Union,
and were the people who kept the village traditions (such as church
choirs) alive. But towards the end of the century they were gradually
squeezed out by the farmers and landowners who disliked their
independence (Hardy describes the kind of thing which happened
in *Tess*), and by broader economic change. They usually held
cottages on a long lease, and when these leases ended, they generally
had to leave their homes, like the Durbeyfields, or Giles. In the end
there was nobody left in the villages except farmers and labourers,
and village life became poorer as a result.

Hardy summed up, rather sadly, that the modern labourer had
'a less intimate and kindly relationship with the land' than had
been the case in earlier times. In many novels he shows people who
do have this kind of relationship with the land: Gabriel Oak, Marty,
Giles Winterborne, Tess. But his later novels reveal these people in
a tragic light; Marty, Giles and Tess are all destroyed or defeated,
and the hero of his last novel, *Jude the Obscure*, knows nothing about
the dead traditions of his village and dislikes the very thought of
working on the land.

Conclusion: Hardy and nature

In our own age, which has at last begun to think seriously about
our alienation from nature and its consequences, Hardy comes over
as one who wanted to protect and preserve it. He believed strongly
that man was a guardian of nature and had a responsibility to look
after the animal kingdom (like Gabriel Oak) and to pass it on
undamaged to future generations. A good symbol of a living thing
which outlasts individual human lives is a tree. In his first surviving
poem, 'Domicilium', written when he was sixteen, Hardy describes
an oak, 'springing from a seed/Dropped by some bird a hundred
years ago', and this awareness of nature within history never left
him. In *The Woodlanders*, Giles 'put most of these roots towards the
south-west; for, he said, in forty years' time, when some great gale
is blowing from that quarter, the trees will require the strongest
holdfast on that side to stand against it and not fall'.

He knew his own bit of England thoroughly – the countryside,
the buildings and the local traditions; he spent long hours bicycling
through narrow lanes and obscure villages, and he found that he
did his best work when he distanced himself from the madding
crowd. In this sense he undoubtedly was what is called a provincial
novelist, and this comes over very strongly in passages like his
description of the vale of Blakemore or Blackmoor:

> This fertile and sheltered tract of country, in which the fields are
> never brown and the springs never dry, is bounded on the south
> by the bold chalk ridge that embraces the prominences of
> Hambledon Hill, Bulbarrow, Nettlecombe-Tout, Dogbury, High
> Stoy, and Bubb Down. The traveller from the coast ... is
> surprised and delighted to behold, extended like a map beneath
> him, a country differing absolutely from that which he has passed
> through ... Here, in the valley, the world seems to be con-
> structed upon a smaller and more delicate scale; the fields are
> mere paddocks, so reduced that from this height their hedgerows
> appear a network of dark green threads over-spreading the paler
> green of the grass. The atmosphere beneath is languorous, and is
> so tinged with azure that what artists call the middle distance
> partakes also of that hue, while the horizon beyond is of the
> deepest ultramarine. Arable lands are few and limited; with but
> slight exception the prospect is a broad rich mass of grass and
> trees.
>
> (*Tess*, Ch. 2)

Again, if we look at his biography we find the same feeling for
nature in the Dorset region:

So Hardy went on writing *Far from the Madding Crowd* – sometimes indoors, sometimes out, when he would occasionally find himself without a scrap of paper at the very moment that he felt volumes. In such circumstances he would use large dead leaves, white chips left by the wood-cutters, or pieces of stone or slate that came to hand. He used to say that when he carried a pocket-book his mind was barren as the Sahara.

This autumn Hardy assisted at his father's cider-making – a proceeding he had always enjoyed from childhood – the apples being from huge old trees that have now long perished. It was the last time he ever took part in a work whose sweet smells and oozings in the crisp autumn air can never be forgotten by those who have had a hand in it.

(*Life*, p. 96)

Or again, in a passage from his diary for 1884, just before he started writing *The Mayor of Casterbridge*:

When trees and underwood are cut down, and the ground bared, three crops of flowers follow. First a sheet of yellow: they are primroses. Then a sheet of blue: they are wild hyacinths, or as we call them, graegles. Then a sheet of red: they are ragged robins, or as they are called here, robin-hoods. What have these plants been doing through the scores of years before the trees were felled, and how did they come there?

(*Life*, p. 164)

3 Hardy the Victorian

We call Hardy a Victorian because he spent the first sixty years of his life in the nineteenth century and it was that century which formed many of his beliefs. But he was not a *typical* Victorian; to many of us he now seems to exemplify the more modern, adventurous, questioning spirit which came into literature about the turn of the century and led on directly to the work of D.H. Lawrence. Many of the most cherished Victorian beliefs – in Providence, for example – were just those which Hardy found he could not accept. Another way in which he seems atypical is in his preoccupation with the life of the countryside, which we looked at in the last chapter. He was interested in the railways and the ideas they brought, but he did not, like many contemporary novelists, write about industrialization or life in big towns. The consciousness of most educated Victorians, writers or not, was decidedly *urban*; Hardy was very different in this way.

But in other ways he could not help being influenced by the contemporary intellectual climate. This chapter will look briefly at his relationship with various thinkers and currents of thought in his time. The first section tries to show how Hardy fitted into the Victorian literary tradition, and suggests that other novelists did not influence him, except in a negative way. Other poets did, and this section will look at the admiration of Romanticism which he shared with his age, and at the influence of the great Victorian rebel, Swinburne.

The second section is about Hardy's agnosticism, and here he did belong to a very definite tradition. Few ages have been more religious-minded than the Victorian, and Hardy himself, like most other agnostics, had been brought up in a strongly Christian home. One result of this was a strong and naïve belief in what was called Providence, which led to a popular demand that art should be 'uplifting', and illustrate the principles of poetic justice. This accounts for the unnaturally happy endings which are foisted on to so many Victorian novels, and which Hardy, in the end, thoroughly disliked. His pessimism, as the Victorians called it, and his interest in Darwin had a powerful effect on his work.

Perhaps the most distinguished agnostic thinker of the century was John Stuart Mill, who also influenced Hardy in other ways. His teaching on freedom was particularly important, and can be traced in Hardy's novel, *Jude the Obscure*.

Hardy emerges from any study of his ideas as a man of the Left, extremely suspicious of all conventional ideas about politics and religion. But he was a lonely figure all his life and joined no political movement. He took no part in the great debate about the nature of Victorian society and its destiny associated with the names of Carlyle, Ruskin, Morris, Pugin, Kingsley and Disraeli. This had something to do with his comparative isolation from the big towns where most Victorians lived, and also with his own diffidence. He often said that any opinions which he might seem to express in his novels and poems were offered as impressions rather than convictions. Nevertheless, he did have views about society, and particularly strong views about war.

Hardy, the Romantics and Swinburne

If Hardy's style has often been criticized, it is partly because he himself was often very unsure of what was the 'best' technique. At times, remembering the sophisticated public which was only too ready to sneer he became self-conscious and tried to smarten up his writing – usually by sprinkling it with fragments of poetry and long Latin words. Of course this did no good; when Hardy was writing at his best the style came naturally.

It is hard to say whether he was much influenced by other novelists. He admired Fielding, who had lived in the same part of England, and thought that he was not appreciated enough 'as a local novelist'. Dickens was still alive when he first went to London, and the young man often went to hear him reading from his own novels, but they wrote about very different subjects and in still more different ways. At this time, Thackeray was generally thought to be the best living novelist, and in 1863 Hardy wrote home to his sister:

> He is considered to be the greatest novelist of the day – looking at novel-writing of the highest kind as a perfect and truthful representation of actual life – which is no doubt the proper view to take. Hence, because his novels stand so high as works of Art or Truth, they often have anything but an elevating tendency, and on that account are particularly unfitted for young people – from their very truthfulness. People say that it is beyond Mr Thackeray to paint a perfect man or woman – a great fault if novels are intended to instruct, but just the opposite if they are to be considered merely as Pictures.
>
> (*Life*, p. 40)

It is clear from this that Hardy at twenty-three was already aware of the tension between writing with one eye on the public, which largely consisted of 'young people', and writing what he felt to be true. But Thackeray died in the year this was written, and by then a new novelist was appearing on the horizon – George Eliot. Hardy had, as we have seen, the strange experience of being mistaken for her when *Far from the Madding Crowd* was first published in the *Cornhill Magazine*. Like him, she wrote mainly about the countryside, and her ideas on many subjects were not very different from his. He thought that she was a 'great thinker – one of the greatest living', but 'not a born storyteller by any means', and that her novels were not representative of real country life.

The other great novelist of the late nineteenth century was Henry James, but although he and Hardy met several times they were incompatible. James wrote privately that *Tess of the D'Urbervilles* was 'vile', while Hardy accused him of 'saying nothing in infinite sentences'. Later he wrote: 'The great novels of the future will certainly not concern themselves with the minutiae of manners. . . . James's subjects are those one could be interested in at moments when there is nothing larger to think of.'

But during his growing period in London he was reading hardly any novels, and a great deal of poetry. We know that in later life he said that he had always wanted to be a poet, and had only written the novels for money, and, while we need not take this too seriously, it is true that he was influenced by poets much more than by novelists. He had a thorough knowledge of Milton and Shakespeare, yet his real roots were in the English Romantic tradition, the tradition which, in one way or another, helped to form almost all English poets until it was killed by the First World War. It began about the time of the French Revolution, when a group of young poets, of whom Wordsworth was the spokesman, became tired of the artificial and conventional nature of eighteenth-century verse. With the rise of this group strong emotions came back into poetry; new ideas and original verse forms were tried out freely, and a new conception of the poet came into circulation. Instead of stringing platitudes together (like Pope and Johnson) he must 'look in his heart and write'. Naturally, the Romantics were very different from one another. The essence of the Romantic outlook was that each writer should develop his individuality to the full. One other point may be noted: that Romanticism was above all a *democratic* movement. It stressed that literature belonged not just to the civilized few but to the whole people; and the Romantic poets, at least while they were young, were strongly sympathetic to the French Revolution and to progressive ideas.

Wordsworth had insisted in his Preface to *Lyrical Ballads* that poetry must be written in 'the real language of men'. Hardy must have felt very much the same, as he incorporated a good deal of ordinary language, including dialect, in his poems and novels. Perhaps he had more in common with Wordsworth than with any other Romantic writer. He is not a rich and colourful poet like Keats; his language is more often careful, restrained, deliberately sober and plain. And, again like Wordsworth, he is deeply interested in man's relationship to his natural environment – in his case Dorset, in Wordsworth's the Cumberland hills. Like Wordsworth, he writes about men and women who live in constant communion with nature, shepherds, for example, tramps, or rural workers, and he feels that nature provides these people with a permanent source of strength.

As a boy Hardy wrote at least one quite good imitation of Wordsworth, a poem about his father's cottage, 'Domicilium'. At twenty-eight, when he had come back from London and was writing *The Poor Man and the Lady*, he noted in his diary:

> Cures for despair:
> To read Wordsworth's 'Resolution and Independence'
>   "   " Stuart Mill's 'Individuality' (in *Liberty*)
>
> (Life, p. 58)

We must look more closely at Wordsworth's 'Resolution and Independence' to see what he meant. This poem, also known as 'The Old Leech-Gatherer', begins with Wordsworth walking out on to the moors on a beautiful spring day. At first he is happy and cheerful, but then, without warning, he becomes very depressed:

> I heard the skylark warbling in the sky;
> And I bethought me of the playful hare;
> Even such a happy child of earth am I;
> Even as these blissful creatures do I fare;
> Far from the world I walk, and from all care;
> But there may come another day to me –
> Solitude, pain of heart, distress and poverty.

While he is still in this mood he comes across an old man, who makes his living by gathering leeches from the pools on the moor. He is one of those odd characters, like the reddleman in *The Return of the Native*, whose mode of life is so strange and old-fashioned that they seem to belong to another world. But the old man is not held up to us as a curiosity. He is courteous and dignified, and seems perfectly cheerful although the leeches which provide his income are gradually disappearing:

> Once I could meet with them on every side;
> But they have dwindled long by slow decay;
> Yet still I persevere, and find them where I may.

After leaving him the poet finds that he is haunted by the thought of the old man. It makes his own troubles appear petty:

> I could have laughed myself to scorn, to find
> In that decrepit man so firm a mind.
> 'God,' said I, 'be my help and stay secure;
> I'll think of the leech-gatherer on the lonely moor'.

There is something here of the courage of ordinary people which Hardy shows us in books like *The Woodlanders* and *Tess*. It may also have helped to suggest his well-known description of Egdon Heath: 'a place perfectly accordant with man's nature – neither ghastly, hateful, nor ugly: neither commonplace, unmeaning, nor tame: but, like man, slighted and enduring' (*Return of the Native*, Book 3, Ch. 1).

In the same novel Hardy spoke of 'the view of life as a thing to be put up with, replacing that zest for existence which was so intense in early civilization' (Book 3, Ch. 1), and here he seems to be thinking along the same lines as Wordsworth. The instinctive, joyful response to the world which we find in children is not enough, because pain and death are realities which cannot be overlooked. But what is heroic in man is his ability to put up with 'solitude, pain of heart, distress and poverty' and still carry on. This is an essential part of Hardy's philosophy, which the Victorians called pessimism, and which he himself thought was the only realistic and possible creed. That was why Wordsworth's poetry seemed to him so good as a 'cure for despair'.

Surprisingly it seems that Hardy's favourite Romantic poets were Keats and, above all, Shelley. He called him 'our most marvellous lyrist', and was always deeply moved when he 'impinged on the penumbra of the poet he loved'. While in Italy he wrote a poem, speculating about what had happened to 'the dust of the lark that Shelley heard'. Indeed Shelley's 'To a Skylark', and Keats' 'Ode to a Nightingale', were to inspire one of his own most famous poems, 'The Darkling Thrush'. He felt a strong sympathy for both of them as people: Shelley because he had been persecuted for unorthodox ideas, and Keats because he had been abused by the critics (like Hardy himself) and died in obscurity.

This does not mean that Hardy wrote the same kind of poetry as Keats or Shelley. This would hardly have been possible, nearly a hundred years later, and in any case his temperament was very different. But he did find himself in sympathy with many of Shelley's ideas – Shelley who had been sent down from Oxford for writing *The Necessity of Atheism* and whose poem 'Queen Mab' had caused a scandal because of its left-wing and anti-religious ideas. Hardy's own attitude to religion was very much the same as Shelley's. He believed in what he called 'the *spirit* of the Sermon on the Mount', but, except as a very young man, he had no belief in a personal God. Another way in which he was very close to Shelley was in his shrinking from other people's pain. He was much the same kind of man as his hero, Jude Fawley:

> Though Farmer Troutham had just hurt him, he was a boy who could not himself bear to hurt anything. He had never brought home a nest of young birds without lying awake in misery half the night after, and often reinstating them and the nest in their original place the next morning. He could scarcely bear to see trees cut down or lopped, from a fancy that it hurt them; and late pruning, when the sap was up and the tree bled profusely, had been a positive grief to him in his infancy. This weakness of character, as it may be called, suggested that he was the sort of man who was born to ache a good deal before the fall of the curtain upon his unnecessary life should signify that all was well with him again. He carefully picked his way on tiptoe among the earthworms, without killing a single one.
>
> *(Jude, Part 1, Ch. 2)*

Hardy continued throughout his life to be haunted by the suffering of the innocent, particularly of animals. When he was over eighty he expressed the hope that 'whether the human and kindred animal races survive till the exhaustion or destruction of the globe . . . pain to all upon it, tongued or dumb, shall be kept down to a minimum by loving-kindness' (*PW*, p. 53). This has a great deal in common with the beliefs of Shelley, who was a vegetarian, a pacifist, and a believer that tyranny could be defeated by moral force. 'I wish no living thing to suffer pain', Shelley makes the hero say in 'Prometheus Unbound'. Both hated war, unnecessary suffering and any kind of cruelty. The Spirit of the Pities in *The Dynasts*, who looks on in horror as Europe plunges into war, is a very Shelleyan conception.

Another important influence on Hardy's work was Shelley's concept of love. Both writers had unorthodox ideas about marriage, and some of them are discussed at length in the fourth book of *Jude the Obscure* when Sue's husband, after an agonizing private struggle, decides that she would be happier with her lover. He explains his decision to a friend, who is naturally surprised:

> 'I found from their manner that an extraordinary affinity, or sympathy, entered into their attachment, which somehow took away all flavour of grossness. Their supreme desire is to be together – to share each other's emotions, and fancies, and dreams'.
>
> 'Platonic!'
>
> 'Well, no. Shelleyan would be nearer to it. They remind me of – what are their names – Laon and Cythna.'
>
> *(Part 4, Ch. 4)*

Laon and Cythna are the two lovers in Shelley's long narrative poem 'The Revolt of Islam'. There is something ethereal about their love, too:

She moved upon this earth a shape of brightness,
A power, that from its objects scarcely drew
One impulse of her being – in her lightness
Most like some radiant cloud of morning dew
Which wanders thro' the waste air's pathless blue,
To nourish some far desert; she did seem
Beside me, gathering beauty as she grew,
Like the bright shade of some immortal dream
Which walks, when tempest sleeps, the wave of life's dark stream.

The theme of a relationship from which 'all flavour of grossness' has been removed is taken up again when Sue makes Jude 'say those pretty lines ... from Shelley's "Epipsychidion" as if they meant me'. The lines are:

There was a Being whom my spirit oft
Met in its visioned wanderings far aloft ...
A seraph of heaven, too gentle to be human.
Veiling beneath that radiant form of woman.

But Shelley and Hardy believed that love is an affinity of the mind and spirit, a great deal more important than sex. In Shelley the loved object is seen as something radiant, divine, scarcely human, and this is how Jude sees the woman he loves, Sue. It comes as a slight shock, after all this, to realize that 'Epipsychidion' is a poem about the impossibility of faithfulness, which suggests that 'to divide is not to take away' from the person one loves:

I never was attached to that great sect,
Whose doctrine is, that each one should select
Out of the crowd a mistress or a friend,
And all the rest, though fair and wise, commend
To cold oblivion, though it is in the code
Of modern morals, and the beaten road
Which those poor slaves with weary footsteps tread,
Who travel to their home among the dead
By the broad highway of the world, and so,
With one chained friend, perhaps a jealous foe,
The dreariest and the longest journey go.

Shelley's ideas on sexual relationships were unconventional. After he had left his wife for Mary Godwin he suggested that she should live with them as a friend, and in the same way Sue optimistically hopes that she can go on being friends with her husband after she has left him. It would be a mistake, though, to think that Hardy necessarily agreed with Shelley's theories. He did reject the Victorian concept of marriage, and in *Jude the Obscure* he examined several arguments about divorce and free love. But his final conclusion was that 'Shelleyan' characters like Angel Clare and Sue Bridehead did more harm than good. Shelley's theory of love left out too many things – the 'fret and fever, derision and disaster', the human need for deep emotional commitments and the earthly, as opposed to the heavenly, aspects of love.

Jude the Obscure often refers to Shelley, whom Hardy describes as 'the last of the optimists'. Shelley did, indeed, have an idealistic faith in goodness:

> It is a modest thought, and yet
> Pleasant if one considers it,
> To own that death itself must be
> Like all the rest, a mockery.
>
> That garden sweet, that lady fair,
> And all sweet shapes and odours there,
> In truth have never passed away:
> 'Tis we, 'tis ours, are changed: not they.
>
> For love, and beauty, and delight,
> There is no death nor change; their might
> Exceeds our organs, which endure
> No light, being themselves obscure.
>
> ('The Sensitive Plant')

It was far more difficult for Hardy to believe this at the end of the century, when he acquired a reputation for being a 'pessimist'. It looks on balance as if, despite his reverence for Shelley, he finally came to see some of his ideas as naïve.

The Victorian reading public admired Keats and Shelley without really knowing much about them. Controversial facts about these two men, particularly their radicalism, were hushed up, and they gained the reputation of being sweet, sentimental poets who died young because they were too good for the world. The Victorians' favourite writer was Tennyson, the Poet Laureate, while the more difficult and original Robert Browning was largely unread (and the most interesting of them all, Gerard Manley Hopkins, remained virtually unknown until 1918). The genius of the age made fiction the central literary form. Much English poetry had grown dull and stagnant when Algernon Charles Swinburne published his first book in 1866.

Swinburne is today only half-remembered, and we can see now that he was not one of our greatest poets, but his work had an electric effect at the time on young men looking for inspiration. Hardy described this effect, many years later, in his elegy for Swinburne, 'A Singer Asleep':

> It was as though a garland of red roses
> Had fallen about the hood of some smug nun
> When irresponsibly dropped as from the sun,
> In fulth of numbers freaked with musical closes,
> Upon Victoria's formal middle time
> His leaves of rhythm and rhyme.

He went on to describe his own reactions when Swinburne's poem first came out:

> O that far morning of a summer day
> When, down a terraced street whose pavements lay
> Glassing the sunshine into my bent eyes,
> I walked and read with a quick glad surprise
> New words, in classic guise, –
>
> The passionate pages of his earlier years,
> Fraught with hot sighs, sad laughters, kisses, tears;
> Fresh-fluted notes, yet from a minstrel who
> Blew them not naïvely, but as one who knew
> Full well why thus he blew.

This gives us a good idea of the reasons for Swinburne's great appeal for Hardy's generation. He was not in the least a naïve writer; on the contrary he was one of the most 'musical' (Hardy's word) of all English poets. His verse is easy, fluent, and intoxicating. We can get some impression of its quality from the lines from the 'Hymn to Proserpine' which are quoted by Hardy in *Jude the Obscure*:

Thou hast conquered, O pale Galilean; the world has grown grey from thy breath;
We have drunken of things Lethean, and fed on the fullness of death;
Laurel is green for a season, and love is sweet for a day;
But love grows bitter with treason, and laurel outlives not May.
Sleep, shall we sleep after all? for the world is not sweet in the end;
For the old faiths loosen and fall, the new years ruin and rend.
Fate is a sea without shore, and the soul is a rock that abides;
But her ears are vexed with the roar and her face with the foam of the tides.

But Swinburne had more to offer his readers than a beautiful style. Hardy, and his other admirers, felt that his great merit was to have brought passion back into English poetry – 'hot sighs, sad laughters, kisses, tears' – at a time when it had become stodgy and respectable. Swinburne never made any secret of his convictions. Like Shelley, he was a passionate republican and atheist; the poem just quoted makes it clear that he thought Christianity was life-denying. Instead he worshipped the idea of liberty, natural beauty, and passionate physical love. In a notorious poem, 'Dolores', he contrasted 'the lilies and languors of virtue' with 'the raptures and roses of vice', leaving no doubt as to which he preferred.

It need hardly be said that the Victorians were deeply shocked by *Poems and Ballads* and although Swinburne became a hero to many of the younger generation his poetry was abused in the press. Hardy recalled this time, in a letter to a friend, after Swinburne died:

> No doubt the press will say some good words about him now he is dead and does not care whether it says them or no. Well, I remember what it said in 1866, when he did care, though you do not remember it, and how it made the blood of some of us young men boil.
>
> Was there ever such a country – looking back at the life, work, and death of Swinburne – is there any other country in Europe whose attitude towards a deceased poet of his rank would have been so ignoring and almost contemptuous? . . . To use his own words again, 'it makes one sick in a corner' – or as we say down here in Wessex, 'it is enough to make every little dog run to mixen'.
>
> (*Life*, p. 344)

This came after Hardy himself had been savaged for writing *Jude* (a novel which Swinburne praised enthusiastically). 'We laughed and condoled with each other', he noted, 'on having been the two most abused of living writers; he for *Poems and Ballads*, and I for *Jude the Obscure*' (*Life*, p. 325).

Why did Hardy admire Swinburne so greatly? He himself was a very different kind of poet – less showy and more genuine, we may feel now – and his own work is quite free from the 'decadent' quality which made Swinburne's so exciting to the youth of his day. Part of his admiration had to do with the literary tradition in which he had been raised. The Victorians like poetry to be 'musical' and to deal with beautiful and romantic subjects; Tennyson was a great master of this kind of poetry and so was Swinburne, in his own way. But perhaps even more of Hardy's enthusiasm was for Swinburne as a bold and independent thinker. Like him, Swinburne was what we would now call a humanist, one who believed that man, not God, was the most important being in the universe. He asserted this, deliberately provocatively, in his 'Hymn of Man', which announced that God was dead:

By the name that in hell-fire was written, and burned at the point
  of thy sword,
Thou art smitten, thou God, thou art smitten; thy death is upon
  thee, O Lord.
And the love-song of earth as thou diest resounds through the wind
  of her wings –
Glory to Man in the highest! for Man is the master of things.

With his atheism went the belief that there was no such thing as Providence, and that man is necessarily alone and must work out his own destiny:

> Save his own soul's light overhead,
> None leads him, and none ever led,
> Across birth's hidden harbour-bar,
> Past youth where shoreward shallows are,
> Through age that drives on towards the red
> Vast void of sunset hailed from far,
> To the equal waters of the dead;
> Save his own soul he hath no star,
> And sinks, except his own soul guide,
> Helmless in middle turn of tide.
>
> (Prelude to *Songs Before Sunrise*)

These were some of Hardy's favourite lines (he often quoted 'Save his own soul hath no star', which is the motto for Book 2 of *Jude the Obscure*). As we shall see in the next section, he believed that the universe was, by its nature, indifferent to man and his feelings and hopes. Both writers tended to see man as a lonely and heroic figure, 'slighted and enduring'. They were both 'pessimists' in the sense of believing that man must solve his own problems, without any help from a superhuman power.

During his later years Swinburne wrote hardly anything of importance. The promise of his early work (he had started publishing poetry many years before Hardy) was never fulfilled. Today, although his collected works fill several volumes, he is remembered only for a few lyrics, but even in his decline he still had useful things to say about the nature and purpose of literature, for instance when he discussed the doctrine (very fashionable at the turn of the century) of 'art for art's sake':

The well-known formula of art for art's sake . . . has like other doctrines a true side to it and an untrue. Taken as an affirmation, it is a precious and everlasting truth. No work of art has any worth or life in it that is not done on the absolute terms of art. . . . On the other hand, we refuse to admit that art of the highest kind may not ally itself with moral or religious passion, with the ethics or the politics of a nation or an age. . . . In a word, the doctrine of art for art's sake is true in the positive sense, false in the negative; sound as an affirmative, unsound as a prohibition.

(Quoted in Harold Nicolson, *Swinburne*, p. 183.)

If he read this, Hardy must have agreed with every word. Towards the end of his career as a novelist he complained bitterly about the people who denied him the right to speak freely, and one of his reasons for turning to poetry was that this made it easier for him to express his ideas. It was natural that both he and Swinburne should find themselves unpopular in an age which feared originality. For this reason Hardy had a fellow-feeling for Swinburne more than for any other living writer, one akin to his affection for Shelley, and he records rather touchingly in the *Life* that after he had written 'A Singer Asleep' he 'gathered a spray of ivy and laid it on the grave of that brother-poet of whom he never spoke save in words of admiration and affection' (*Life*, p. 349). Figures such as Wordsworth, Shelley and Swinburne struck a chord with, and helped to articulate, Hardy's own feelings as an outsider who had formed his own unconventional views on subjects as varied as religion, literature and romantic love. It is not surprising, therefore, that he was drawn also to radical voices in other fields.

Hardy, the Agnostics and 'Pessimism'

In 1859 two books came out which would have a profound effect on the young Hardy; John Stuart Mill's *On Liberty*, and *The Origin of Species* by Charles Darwin. Twenty-three years later, when he went to Darwin's funeral in Westminster Abbey, Hardy said that he had been 'among the earliest acclaimers' of his work. At that time, he was in the minority. Conventional people tended to make fun of *The Origin of Species*, an unpretentious book which turned out, in the end, to be as revolutionary as the theories of Copernicus and Galileo.

Darwin had observed during his researches in South America that certain animals showed slight but quite definite differences from the animals on islands only a few miles away. Such observations suggested a whole new theory about the origins of life. Had differences between species been created when God made the world, as was taught in the Book of Genesis? Or was it not more likely that they all belonged to the same species, and had evolved their own differences to suit their special conditions of life? Darwin came to the conclusion that vast numbers of species had existed at one time, but several had died out; those which survived being the ones which had best adapted to their environment. This became popularly known as the doctrine of the *survival of the fittest*.

Darwin's discoveries could be applied to human beings as well as animals. He did not, as many people thought, say that man was descended from the monkeys, but he did think that men and monkeys were collateral descendants of one ancestor. It was a theory that shook Victorian Christianity to its foundations. For if life evolved under its own laws, if it was not true that Adam and Eve and the animals had been created just as they were in the Garden of Eden, then there was no need for God. Just as fundamentally, Darwin posited a world the evolution of which was determined not by rationality, goodness or the intervention of a divine will but by the struggle for survival in which victory went to the strong. Even if God did exist, he now seemed impossibly remote and the universe a darker, more threatening and meaningless place.

As a matter of fact scientists had suspected for some time that parts of the Bible were inaccurate. Geologists like Charles Lyell (1795–1875) had become convinced, from their study of fossils, that the earth was much older than the six-thousand-odd years which the theologians claimed. But this was not the sort of thing that could be said aloud in Victorian England, where a highly bigoted form of Christianity was taught in the churches and schools. Darwin literally could not face publishing his discoveries for years because he knew how unpopular they would make him. When his book finally did come out, and the storm broke, he took no further part in the controversy. Most of the propaganda work for his theories was done by T.H. Huxley.

A distinguished biologist in his own right, Huxley is mainly remembered as the champion of Darwin and as the man who invented the word 'agnostic'. An agnostic means 'one who does not know', and Huxley maintained that human beings *cannot* know whether or not God exists:

> It is wrong for a man to say that he is certain of the objective truth of any proposition unless he can produce evidence which logically justifies that certainty. This is what Agnosticism asserts; and, in my opinion, it is all that is essential to Agnosticism. That which Agnostics deny and repudiate, as immoral, is the contrary doctrine, that there are propositions which men ought to believe, without logically satisfactory evidence, and that reprobation ought to attach to the profession of disbelief in such inadequately supported propositions.
>
> (*Agnosticism and Christianity*)

This is presumably the kind of argument which Hardy was thinking of when he showed Tess discussing religion with Alec d'Urberville, using arguments which he does not repeat but which 'might possibly have been paralleled in . . . Huxley's *Essays*'. She has picked them up from her husband, Angel Clare, who is typical of the educated young men who were beginning to turn to agnosticism in the latter half of the century. Hardy met Huxley in London a few times and thought very highly of him, 'speaking of him as a man who united a fearless mind with the warmest of hearts and the most modest of manners' (*Life*, p. 122).

While he was still very young Hardy became absorbed in the problem which worried almost all educated Victorians, of whether the Christian faith which he had been brought up to believe in was true. For many people, it was agony to believe that it might not be. Tennyson's great poem 'In Memoriam' (1850), written about his beloved friend Arthur Hallam who died suddenly at the age of twenty-two, put into words what many thousands were thinking and feeling. How could God be all-powerful and all-loving, in face of the overwhelming fact of human suffering? Pain and death were more real to the Victorians than to us, at a time when tuberculosis was a killer disease and about half of all children never grew up. And when one turned from the human to the animal world, it seemed even more frightening. Tennyson wrote about the dilemma of one:

> Who trusted God was love indeed
> And love creation's final law –
> Tho' Nature, red in tooth and claw
> With ravine, shrieked against his creed.

This was written earlier than *The Origin of Species*, but Darwin's book did still more to weaken the idea that love was the final law of the universe. Tennyson himself resolved his doubts in the end, but other distinguished poets, like Matthew Arnold and A. H. Clough, could not; nor could many other intellectuals. Even some churchmen began to feel that Christianity would have to be brought up to date. In 1860 a group of them published a controversial book, *Essays and Reviews*, which made a deep impression on the young Hardy when it was lent to him by Horace Moule. But it seems that at quite an early age he began to move away from the liberal Christianity which Moule believed in and towards an acceptance of Darwinism, and all its implications. One of his finest poems, 'In a Wood', begun in 1887, shows how he saw even trees as 'red in tooth and claw':

> Pale beech and pine so blue,
>   Set in one clay,
> Bough to bough cannot you

    Live out your day?
When the rains skim and skip,
Why mar sweet comradeship,
Blighting with poison-drip
    Neighbourly spray?

Heart-halt and spirit-lame,
    City-opprest,
Unto this wood I came
    As to a nest;
Dreaming that sylvan peace
Offered the harrowed ease –
Nature a soft release
    From men's unrest.

But, having entered in,
    Great growths and small
Show them to men akin –
    Combatants all!
Sycamore shoulders oak,
Bines the slim sapling yoke,
Ivy-spun halters choke
    Elms stout and tall.

Touches from ash, O wych,
    Sting you like scorn!
You, too, brave hollies, twitch
    Sidelong from thorn.
Even the rank poplars bear
Lothly a rival's air,
Cankering in black despair
    If overborne.

Since, then, no grace I find
    Taught me of trees,
Turn I back to my kind,
    Worthy as these.
There at least smiles abound,
There discourse trills around,
There, now and then, are found
    Life-loyalties.

This is a fine satirical retort to the complacent Victorian assumption that nature represented peace and innocence – 'every prospect pleases, and only man is vile'. On the contrary, Hardy is arguing, *all* life is pervaded by the struggle for existence, and it can only be made bearable by human solidarity. He wrote this poem at about the same time as *The Woodlanders* and if we turn to the novel we find many similar images. There is a well-known passage, often quoted to show Hardy's morbid frame of mind, which describes what actually happens in woods, 'The leaf was deformed, the curve was crippled, the taper was interrupted; the lichen ate the vigour of the stalk, and the ivy slowly strangled to death the promising sapling'. The trees are 'wrestling for existence, their branches disfigured with wounds resulting from their mutual rubbings and blows'. The animal world shows the same pattern – 'owls that had been catching mice in the outhouses, rabbits that had been eating the winter-greens in the gardens, and stoats that had been sucking the blood of the rabbits'. Even human beings, at their worst, are no less ruthless; we see in this novel how men and women struggle for the possession of houses, lands and people, and how some of them fail to survive. A philosophy called 'social Darwinism', which was quite fashionable at this time although Darwin did not sanction it, taught that human society illustrated the scientific principle of 'the survival of the fittest'; in other words the weak and incompetent were unsuccessful in life while the strong and clever naturally got to the top. Hardy had something to say about this in *The Mayor of Casterbridge*, and in *Jude the Obscure* he rejected it completely. He argued here that the greatest of mankind are usually failures, and that a successful man is 'as cold-blooded as a fish and as selfish as a pig' – in other words, something less than human.

This meant that there was no room for optimistic assertions like Browning's 'God's in his heaven: all's right with the world', which was a commonplace for many for Hardy's contemporaries. 'God's *not* in his heaven: all's *wrong* with the world', Angel Clare says in anguish in *Tess*. Hardy himself noted wryly that most philosophers 'cannot get away from a prepossession that the world must somehow have been made to be a comfortable place for man' (*Life*, p. 179). But increasingly, Hardy's generation was coming to feel that the world was frightening, planless, and dangerous. Matthew Arnold wrote in his poem 'Dover Beach':

> The world which seems
> To lie before us like a land of dreams,
> So various, so beautiful, so new,
> Hath really neither joy, nor life, nor light,
> Nor peace, nor certitude, nor help from pain;
> And we are here as on a darkling plain,
> Swept with confused alarms of struggle and flight,
> Where ignorant armies clash by night.

This famous and beautiful image seems very appropriate to the world which Hardy created in his poems and novels, so appropriate, in fact, that one of the best books on Hardy, by Harvey C. Webster, is actually called *On a Darkling Plain*. Man must create his own values, for, living in a universe of cruelty and chaos, he will find no guidance from anything outside himself.

A great many of the more thoughtful and intelligent Victorians turned to agnosticism, among them John Stuart Mill, Herbert Spencer and George Eliot. Like Hardy, this great novelist had been brought up to be a devout Christian, and even her agnosticism had a religious tinge. She expressed her feelings in a nutshell:

> She, stirred somewhat beyond her wont, and taking as her text the three words which have been used so often as the inspiring trumpet-calls of man – the words *God, Immortality, Duty* – pronounced, with terrible earnestness, how inconceivable was the *first*, how unbelievable the *second*, and yet how peremptory and absolute the *third*.
>
> (G.S. Haight, *George Eliot*, p. 464)

The agnostics were well aware of the difficulties involved in keeping hold of the idea of duty while abandoning the idea of God. Then as now, many people believed that if religion lost its hold men would become completely immoral. Hardy dramatizes this issue in the argument between Alec and Tess:

> 'Why, you can have the religion of loving-kindness and purity at least, if you can't have – what do you call it – dogma.'
>
> 'O no! I'm a different sort of fellow from that! If there's nobody to say, "Do this, and it will be a good thing for you after you are dead; do that, and it will be a bad thing for you," I can't warm up. Hang it, I am not going to feel responsible for my deeds and passions if there's nobody to be responsible to; and if I were you, my dear, I wouldn't either!'
>
> She tried to argue, and tell him that he had mixed in his dull brain two matters, theology and morals, which in the primitive days of mankind had been quite distinct. But . . . she could not get on.
>
> (*Tess*, Ch. 47)

Long before he wrote this, Hardy had accepted the basic agnostic principle that 'theology' and 'morals' were two different things. Few people could have been more concerned with 'morals' than he was, but by the time he was twenty-five he had lost most of his youthful beliefs. As we have seen, he had some idea of studying to be a clergyman, but he decided in the end 'that he could hardly take the step with honour while holding the views which on examination he found himself to hold' (*Life*, p. 50). At about the same time he was reading Cardinal Newman, the leader of the Oxford Movement and perhaps the most brilliant orthodox thinker of the nineteenth century. But he was not convinced:

> July 2 1865, Worked at J. H. Newman's *Apologia*, which we have all been talking about lately. A great desire to be convinced by him. . . . Only – and here comes the fatal catastrophe – there is no first link to his excellent chain of reasoning, and down you come headlong.
>
> (*Life*, p. 48)

Later he said that Newman had 'a feminine nature, which first decides and then finds reasons for having decided'. He himself would not indulge in wishful thinking. However much he might want to believe in Christianity (and poems like 'The Impercipient' and 'The Oxen' suggest that he did want to sometimes) he refused to let himself be persuaded against his judgement. He went on being an agnostic all his life.

The triumph of Agnosticism can be seen in another later influence, Leslie Stephen, whom Hardy described as 'the man whose philosophy was to influence his own for many years, indeed, more than that of any other contemporary'. He wrote several essays on religion and morals, of which the most famous is 'An Agnostic's Apology':

> Overpowered, as every honest and serious thinker is at times overpowered, by the sight of pain, folly, and helplessness, by the jarring discords which run through the vast harmony of the universe, we are yet enabled to hear at times a whisper that all is well, to trust to it as coming from the most authentic source, and to know that only the temporary bars of sense prevent us from recognizing with certainty that the harmony beneath the discords is a reality and not a dream. This knowledge is embodied in the central dogma of theology. God is the name of the harmony; and God is knowable. Who would not be happy in accepting this belief, if he could accept it honestly? Who would not be glad if he could say with confidence: 'The evil is transitory, the good eternal; our doubts are due to limitations destined to be abolished, and the world is really an embodiment of love and wisdom, however dark it may appear to our faculties'. And yet, if the so-called knowledge be illusory, are we not bound by the most sacred obligations to recognize the facts? Our brief path is dark enough on any hypothesis. We cannot afford to turn aside after every *ignis fatuus* without asking whether it leads to sounder footing or to hopeless quagmires. Dreams may be pleasanter for the moment than realities; but happiness must be won by adapting our lives to the realities.

Hardy was in the central agnostic tradition when he denied that there was any such thing as Providence – a force which made everything in the world work towards good. This was one of the Victorians' favourite beliefs. Wordsworth wrote about 'Nature's holy plan'; Browning 'never dreamed, though right were worsted, wrong would triumph'. To Hardy these assertions seemed intolerably smug. In his later novels, which became steadily more unconventional, he drove home the message that there is no supernatural force which looks after the innocent:

It grew darker, the fire-light shining over the room. The two biggest of the younger children had gone out with their mother; the four smallest, their ages ranging from three-and-a-half years to eleven, all in black frocks, were gathered round the hearth babbling their own little subjects. Tess at length joined them, without lighting a candle.

'This is the last night that we shall sleep here, dears, in the house where we were born,' she said quickly. 'We ought to think of it, oughtn't we?'

They all became silent; with the impressibility of their age they were ready to burst into tears at the picture of finality she had conjured up, though all the day hitherto they had been rejoicing in the idea of a new place. Tess changed the subject.

'Sing to me, dears,' she said.

'What shall we sing?'

'Anything you know; I don't mind.'

There was a momentary pause; it was broken, first, by one little tentative note; then a second voice strengthened it, and a third and a fourth chimed in unison, with words they had learnt at the Sunday-school –

> Here we suffer grief and pain,
> Here we meet to part again;
> In Heaven we part no more;

The four sang on with the phlegmatic passivity of persons who had long ago settled the question, and there being no mistake about it, felt that further thought was not required. With features strained hard to enunciate the syllables they continued to regard the centre of the flickering fire, the notes of the youngest straying over into the pauses of the rest.

Tess turned from them, and went to the window again. Darkness had now fallen without, but she put her face to the pane as though to peer into the gloom. It was really to hide her tears. If she could only believe what the children were singing; if she were only sure, how different all would now be; how

'But Mr Hardy, Mr Hardy, if you only knew all the circumstances': *cartoon by Will Dyson (1880–1938)*

confidently she would leave them to Providence and their future kingdom! But, in default of that, it behoved her to do something: to be their Providence: for to Tess, as to some few millions of others, there was ghastly satire in the poet's lines.

(*Tess*, Ch. 51)

If Tess is to play Providence, and save the children from the workhouse, she will have to live with a man she hates. We may think now that it is greatly to Hardy's credit that he doesn't shrink from showing us how and why this girl is destroyed. But in his own time most people criticized his novels for their 'morbidity' and 'pessimism', and many readers today still have the impression that Hardy is a gloomy and depressing writer. It is worth looking at what he himself had to say:

As to pessimism. My motto is, first correctly diagnose the complaint – in this case human ills – and ascertain the cause: then set about finding a remedy if one exists. The motto or practice of the optimists is: Blind the eyes to the real malady, and use empirical panaceas to suppress the symptoms.

(*Life*, p. 383)

It saddened him that critics approached his work with an ignorant prejudice against his 'pessimism' which they allowed to stand in the way of fair reading and fair judgement' (*Life*, p. 402). He preferred to describe himself as a 'meliorist', that is, one who believes that the world can be made better, if people try. But he insisted, in a poem, 'In Tenebris', from which he often quoted, that 'if way to the Better there be, it exacts a full look at the Worst'. It was no good pretending that pain did not exist or did not matter:

> Pain has been, and pain is: no new sort of morals in Nature can remove pain from the past and make it pleasure for those who are its infallible estimators – the bearers thereof. And no injustice, however slight, can be atoned for by her future generosity, however ample, so long as we consider Nature to be, or to stand for, unlimited power.
>
> (*Life*, p. 315)

Because he rejected the idea of a God of love some people accused him of believing in the opposite. Hardy denied this emphatically:

> In connection with this subject it may be here recalled, in answer to writers who now and later were fond of charging Hardy with postulating a malignant and fiendish God, that he never held any views of the sort, merely surmising an indifferent and unconscious force at the back of things 'that neither good nor evil knows'. His view is shown, in fact, to approximate to Spinoza's – and later Einstein's – that neither Chance nor Purpose governs the universe, but Necessity.
>
> (*Life*, p. 337)

After the Great War, which destroyed a good many of his hopes for the future, he became more and more inclined to think that 'the never-ending push of the Universe was an unpurposive and irresponsible groping in the direction of the least resistance'. Some of his ideas about what this force might be can be found in the poem 'New Year's Eve'.

Mill and the idea of liberty

It is possible that John Stuart Mill had a deeper influence on Hardy than any other Victorian thinker. Hardy saw him only once, in 1865, when he was making an open-air speech as the Liberal candidate for Westminster – a speech pitched well over the heads of the crowd. He called him 'one of the profoundest thinkers of the last century' when he described this occasion over forty years later, and he was particularly impressed by Mill's essay *On Liberty*, 'which we students of that date knew almost by heart'. It was two or three years afterwards that he noted that the chapter on Individuality in this essay, along with Wordsworth's 'Old Leech-Gatherer', was his best 'cure for despair'.

Mill had an extraordinary life. His father, James, together with Jeremy Bentham (1748–1832), was responsible for working out the philosophy of Utilitarianism, based on the idea that 'it is the greatest happiness of the greatest number that is the measure of right and wrong'. They believed that human beings were motivated only by the desires of obtaining pleasure and avoiding pain. Together they founded the *Westminster Review*, a radical philosophical magazine, for which George Eliot was later to be a leading writer. The younger Mill was brought up strictly according to his father's ideas.

In his *Autobiography* (1873) Mill has recorded how his education began at the age of three: 'I never was a boy; never played at cricket.' He was taught Latin, Greek, mathematics and logic, but not English poetry. The Utilitarians tended to feel that nothing was valuable if it was not useful (an attitude which Dickens savagely sent up in *Hard Times*). As a young man Mill had some sort of nervous breakdown, and strangely enough what cured him was reading the poetry of Wordsworth. He began to feel that Utilitarianism left out too much of human experience and would have to be reappraised. In his essay *Utilitarianism* (1861) he argued that, while it was true that all human beings sought happiness, there were many different kinds of happiness, including the delight in doing good for its own sake. It was not true, as Bentham had said, that people were motivated only by self-interest. Human nature could not be viewed so mechanistically in the machine age. Human beings might be conscientiously compelled to sacrifice themselves for the general happiness of the human race.

Mill was perhaps the most enlightened and far-seeing thinker of the generation. He campaigned for women's rights, and for the rights of colonial peoples. He was interested in and sympathetic to the new Socialist ideas. But probably the most important thing he wrote was *On Liberty*. It is one of the two greatest arguments for freedom of speech in the English language (the other is Milton's *Areopagitica*) and its thesis is that if freedom is denied to the individual, the whole of society will suffer.

We know that Hardy had it 'almost by heart', particularly the third chapter on Individuality. He quotes from this chapter in *Jude the Obscure*, when Sue is trying to persuade her husband to let her leave him:

Sue continued: 'She, or he, "who lets the world, or his own portion of it, choose his plan of life for him, has no need of any

75

other faculty than the ape-like one of imitation". J.S. Mill's words, those are. I have been reading it up. Why can't you act upon them? I wish to, always.'

'What do I care about J.S. Mill!' moaned he. 'I only want to lead a quiet life!'

It is not a bad answer. But, starting from this point, Hardy shows how Phillotson eventually comes to realize that the kindest thing is to dissolve his marriage. There is a dreadful incompatibility between him and Sue which is intellectual as well as sexual: 'Her intellect sparkles like diamonds, while mine smoulders like brown paper.' Although he loves his wife and knows that society would support him in making her stay with him, he feels conscientiously forced to let her go. Hardy prefaces this part of the novel with a quotation from Milton: 'Whoso prefers either Matrimony or other Ordinance before the Good of Man and the plain Exigence of Charity, let him profess Papist, or Protestant, or what he will, he is no better than a Pharisee.'

It is clear that Hardy agreed with Mill and Milton that human happiness was more important than institutions. If a marriage makes either the husband or wife unhappy, then the marriage should go. It is true that Phillotson has to sacrifice himself to what Mill would have called the 'general good', but ultimately it would not make him happy, either, to go on exploiting another person. 'His mild serenity at the sense that he was doing his duty by a woman who was at his mercy almost overpowered his grief at relinquishing her.'

In fact, the whole of *Jude the Obscure* shows how deep the influence of *On Liberty* went. Mill's argument was that all human beings ought to have the fullest possible freedom of speech and action, so long as this did no harm to anyone else. A good many people would have argued at the time that it *did* do harm; that those who attacked religion, for example, or conventional morals would corrupt other people and might undermine the whole of civilization. The Victorians were very harsh with anyone who stepped out of line on these matters, and in some ways, Mill claimed, English society was actually tyrannical:

Society . . . practises a social tyranny more formidable than many kinds of political oppression, since, though not usually upheld by such extreme penalties, it leaves fewer means of escape, penetrating much more deeply into the details of life, and enslaving the soul itself. Protection, therefore, against the tyranny of the magistrate is not enough: there needs protection also against the tendency of society to impose, by other means than civil penalties, its own ideas and practices as rules of conduct on those who dissent from them; to fetter the development, and, if possible, prevent the formation, of any individuality not in harmony with its ways, and compel all characters to fashion themselves upon the model of its own . . . . In our times, from the highest class of society down to the lowest, everyone lives as under the eye of a hostile and dreaded censorship.

Jude the Obscure, which Hardy at first called *The Recalcitrants*, is all about this 'tyranny of the prevailing opinion and feeling'. The characters are all unconventional people who behave in unorthodox ways. Phillotson, as we have seen, agrees to his wife leaving him, and as a result gets persecuted and loses his job. Jude is a working-class boy with the wild dream of going to Oxford; Sue is an emancipated girl who laughs at religion and makes her own decisions on matters of sex. In the end, all three of them are defeated. Sue breaks down completely and forces herself to go back to Phillotson ('We must conform', she tells herself), Phillotson pretends to conform although his views have not really changed, and Jude dies. 'Our ideas were fifty years too soon to be any good to us,' he says near the end, and Hardy definitely seems to have felt that people who dissented from the received opinions were bound to suffer. In the story of Clym Yeobright, in *The Return of the Native*, he showed the same thing.

What frightened Mill about the tyranny of society was that this was bound to produce distorted human beings.

Its ideal of character is to be without any marked character; to maim by compression, like a Chinese lady's foot, every part of human nature which stands out prominently, and tends to make the person markedly dissimilar in outline to commonplace humanity.

This 'narrow theory of life' led to a 'pinched and hidebound type of human character':

Many persons, no doubt, sincerely think that human beings thus cramped and dwarfed, are as their Maker designed them to be; just as many have thought that trees are a much finer thing when clipped into pollards, or cut out into figures of animals, than as nature made them.

In fact this kind of repression was harmful to everybody, and particularly to the small but precious group of exceptional people, 'the salt of the earth', who were responsible for all the improvements in the human condition.

Genius can only breathe freely in an *atmosphere* of freedom. Persons of genius are . . . *more* individual than any other people – less capable, consequently, of fitting themselves, without hurtful compression, into any of the small number of moulds which society provides in order to save its members the trouble of forming their own character.

Perhaps unconsciously, Hardy took over several of these images when he came to write *Jude the Obscure*. Modern marriage was described in the Preface as 'the forced adaptation of human instincts to rusty and irksome moulds that do not fit them'. The same image, of a *mould*, comes up again when Sue says:

> 'I have been thinking . . . that the social moulds civilization fits us into have no more relation to our actual shapes than the conventional shapes of the constellations have to the real star-patterns. I am called Mrs Richard Phillotson, living a calm wedded life with my counterpart of that name. But I am not really Mrs Richard Phillotson, but a woman tossed about, all alone.'
>
> *(Jude, Part 4, Ch. 1)*

And later:

> 'I have only been married a month or two,' she went on, still remaining bent upon the table, and sobbing into her hands. 'And it is said that what a woman shrinks from – in the early days of her marriage – she shakes down to with comfortable indifference in half-a-dozen years. But that is much like saying that the amputation of a limb is no affliction, since a person gets comfortably accustomed to the use of a wooden leg or arm in the course of time.'
>
> *(Part 4, Ch. 2)*

It is the same idea that we find in *On Liberty*, that if people are forced to live in ways which they do not want then their whole personalities will become distorted. Just as Sue has to suppress the real, vital part of herself when she is married to Phillotson, so Jude, too, has to give up the dream of becoming a student which means almost everything to him:

> 'It is a difficult question . . . for any young man . . . whether to follow uncritically the track he finds himself in, without considering his aptness for it, or to consider what his aptness or bent may be, and re-shape his course accordingly, I tried to do the latter, and I failed . . . If I had ended by becoming like one of these gentlemen in red and black that we saw dropping in here by now, everybody would have said: "See how wise that young man was, to follow the bent of his nature!" But having ended no

better than I began they say: "See what a fool that fellow was in following a freak of his fancy!"'

(Part 6, Ch. 1)

Mill had written:

> The man, and still more the woman, who can be accused either of doing 'what nobody does', or of not doing 'what everybody does', is the subject of as much depreciatory remark as if he or she had committed some grave moral delinquency.

Because they try to live in the way that suits them best, Jude and Sue are avoided by other people for being 'peculiar'. Their attitude to marriage is particularly unconventional, for they both find it psychologically impossible to go through a legal ceremony. Jude says:

> 'The intention of the contract is good, and right for many, no doubt; but in our case it may defeat its own ends because we are the queer sort of people we are – folk in whom domestic ties of a forced kind snuff out cordiality and spontaneousness.'
>
> Sue still held that there was not much queer or exceptional in them: that all were so, 'Everybody is getting to feel as we do. We are a little before-hand, that is all.'

(Part 5, Ch. 4)

This echoes two ideas that we find in Mill. In the first place, he insisted that people had an absolute right to live as seemed best to them: 'If a person possesses any tolerable amount of common-sense or experience, his own mode of laying out his existence is the best, not because it is the best in itself, but because it is his own mode.' Thus, Jude thinks that marriage is suitable for most people but not for him and Sue because of their unusual temperaments: 'Customs are made for customary circumstances, and customary characters; and his circumstances or his character may be uncustomary.'

However, Sue believes that she and Jude are ahead of their time, and that in fifty or a hundred years everyone will feel as they do. Sue at the beginning of the novel, and Jude at the end, are both shown as people with enlightened ideas. Jude, speaking of the failure of his ambition, says: 'It takes two or three generations to do what I tried to do in one.' They are among the exceptional few whom Mill called 'the salt of the earth: without them, human life would become a stagnant pool'. Mill was very conscious of belonging to a tiny minority of thinkers whose position was always under attack from the prejudiced majority. Hardy, although he was a good deal younger, seems to have felt much the same. This is why he showed the characters in *Jude*, or Clym Yeobright in *The Return of the Native*, as lonely and misunderstood by other people. And after *Jude* had been denounced as the most immoral book of its generation, he apparently felt more strongly than ever that society was persecuting him for his beliefs.

The influence of Mill's great essay is particularly obvious in *Jude*, but it went further. It helped to determine Hardy's whole attitude to the problem of Victorian 'censorship', which we looked at in Chapter One, for this seemed to him a particularly blatant denial of his own freedom to think and write.

Hardy's politics

When Hardy's first novel, *The Poor Man and the Lady*, was turned down on account of its politics he professed to be surprised that 'he had written so aggressive and even dangerous a work almost without knowing it'. It certainly does seem to have been aggressive, to judge from his own account:

> The story was, in fact, a sweeping dramatic satire of the squirearchy and nobility. London society, the vulgarity of the middle class, modern Christianity, church restoration, and political and domestic morals in general, the author's views, in fact, being obviously those of a young man with a passion for reforming the world – those of many a young man before and after him; the tendency of the writing being socialistic, not to say revolutionary.
>
> (*Life*, p. 61)

It is only surprising that he was surprised when the publisher returned it. Yet throughout his life Hardy always was rather hurt when his books were attacked for being angry, immoral, or subversive. He always said that he was not trying to argue anything in his novels, but only to put down his impressions of life, and alongside his radicalism went a deep need to be approved of and accepted by other people. But at the age of eighty he told a visitor that 'my views on life are so extreme that I do not usually state them'.

He used to maintain that he was 'quite outside politics', but other people took it for granted that he would be on the progressive side. He was sometimes asked to sign the nomination papers for Liberal candidates, which he declined to do. During the crisis of 1911, when the Liberal Government had its great showdown with the House of Lords, Lloyd George threatened to create hundreds of Liberal peers to swamp it; among the names on his list was that of Thomas Hardy. This threat which finally broke the power of the Lords never had to be put into practice, so we cannot know whether Hardy would have taken a peerage or not. Probably not: he had earlier written in a private letter:

> I have always thought that any writer who has expressed unpalatable or possibly subversive views on society, religious dogma, current morals, and any other features of the existing order of things, and who wishes to be free and to express more if they occur to him, must feel hampered by accepting honours from any government – which are different from academic honours offered for past attainments merely.
>
> (*Life*, p. 327)

He did, however, accept the Order of Merit in 1910, perhaps because his novel-writing days were over and he felt that he would no longer be compromising himself. But he thought that he had 'failed in the accustomed formalities' when he met the King. Indeed, he always felt ill at ease when he was mixing in London high society, and he gave it up altogether after his first wife died. This was another of the many paradoxes in his life. After he became an established novelist he spent a few months every year in London, where he mixed on equal terms with statesmen and peers. Yet his diaries show that he was deeply out of sympathy with these people, however much he may have been flattered at being accepted into the 'best' society. 'These women!' he noted about some society beauties, 'If put into rough wrappers in a turnip-field, where would their beauty be?' (*Life*, p. 224). Other scribbled notes suggest that he was not as indifferent to politics as he liked people to think:

> The offhand decision of some commonplace mind high in office at a critical moment influences the course of events for a hundred years. Consider the evening at Lord Carnarvon's, and the intensely average conversation on politics held there by average men who two or three weeks later were members of the Cabinet. A row of shopkeepers in Oxford Street taken just as they came would conduct the affairs of the nation as ably as these.
>
> (*Life*, p. 172)

On another occasion he noted that

> the talk was entirely political – of when the next election would be – of the probable Prime Minister – of ins and outs – of Lord This and the Duke of That – everything except the people for whose existence alone these politicians exist. Their welfare is never once thought of.
>
> (*Life*, p. 238)

This feeling went very deep in Hardy, and kept him from having much respect for either of what were then the two big parties.

Though he never formulated any clear political principles he was usually, like Dickens, on the side of the people against the government.* His major novels are all about the ordinary people of Dorset, the men and women who do a real job of work, as opposed to the Mrs Charmonds and Alec Stoke-d'Urbervilles. We have laid a great deal of emphasis on the ways in which Hardy was different from other people – an unconventional thinker very conscious of being in a minority in his own time. But in fact he was always stressing the *representative* quality of his heroes and heroines. Tess, in her sufferings, is like 'some few millions of others'; Jude is faced with a question 'which thousands are weighing at the present moment in these uprising times', and Sue Bridehead is a representative of the new kind of woman 'who was coming into notice in her thousands every year – the woman of the feminist movement'. Hardy identified himself with these struggling masses of people, and, in his own way, tried to speak for them. One of his comments on his critics in the Preface to *Tess* was that they 'could not endure to have said what everybody nowadays thinks and feels'.

One subject on which he never hid his feelings was his hatred of war, and this for many years before 1914. The growing nationalism and xenophobia of these years deeply worried him, as we can see from a note which he wrote for a German professor in 1909:

> We call our age an age of Freedom. Yet Freedom, under her incubus of armaments, territorial ambitions smugly disguised as patriotism, superstitions, conventions of every sort, is of such stunted proportions in this her so-called time, that the human race is likely to be extinct before Freedom arrives at maturity.
>
> (*Life*, p. 347)

During the Great War he was abused by the Jingoists for a poem in which he wrote that the German and English peoples had the same interests at heart. Yet he did support the war, though never in a bigoted way, seeing it as a crusade against Great Power aggression. He hoped to see an international League of Peace set up to prevent future wars, in which context he wrote:

> Nothing effectual will be accomplished in the cause of *Peace* till the sentiment of *Patriotism* be freed from the narrow meaning attaching to it in the past (still upheld by Junkers and Jingoists) and be extended to the whole globe.
>
> (*Life*, p. 375)

* Dickens once said: 'My faith in the people governing is, on the whole, infinitesimal; my faith in the People governed, on the whole, illimitable.'

The kind of patriotism which meant affection for one's own country or region, and a feeling for human solidarity, came instinctively to Hardy. The kind which meant invading or bullying other nations he as instinctively loathed. He was not a pacifist, but when the aged Tolstoy published a sermon denouncing war and was attacked for it he responded at once in a letter to *The Times*:

> The sermon may show many of the extravagances of detail to which the world has grown accustomed in Count Tolstoy's later writings. It may exhibit, here and there, incoherence as a moral system . . . But surely all these objectors should be hushed by his great argument, and every defect in his particular reasonings hidden by the blaze of glory that shines from his masterly general indictment of war as a modern principle, with all its senseless and illogical crimes.
>
> (*Life*, p. 322)

Hardy did not, like Tolstoy, work out a clear political philosophy. But he did question almost all the common assumptions of his century, and he found himself in a very lonely and exposed position as a result. One of the great forces which shaped his art was his compelling need to seek out the truth, however uncomfortable or painful; the other was his passionate hatred of suffering. 'What are my books,' he said, 'but one long plea against "man's inhumanity to man" – to woman – and to the lower animals? Whatever may be the inherent good or evil of life, it is certain that men make it much worse than it need be' (*F.B. Pinion, A Hardy Companion*, p. 178). The cruelty of man and society; the immeasurable value of each human being and the tragic waste of human potential; these are the great themes of Hardy's writings, and in this sense it is true to say that he is a novelist of protest.

Hardy and later novelists

A great, but little-known writer who worked in the regional tradition of Hardy was Lewis Grassic Gibbon, whose early death was a grievous loss to Scottish literature. In his trilogy, *A Scots Quair* (1932–4), he described a remote and old-fashioned community, speaking a different language from the King's English, its relationship with the enduring land and its eventual destruction by the Great War. He, however, had no successor, though there are contemporary 'regional' novels, such as Graham Swift's *Waterland* (1983) exploring the landscape and community of the Fen country.

Today, the novel is very different. There is a split between 'entertaining' novels which reach a mass audience and 'serious' novels for the intellectual elite; moreover, it is coming up to a century since Hardy's last novel was published and during that time human life in the developed countries has undergone greater and more irreversible changes than at any other time in history. One cannot imagine what he would make of the modern literary scene. But it is worth mentioning a remarkable novel by a living author, John Fowles's *The French Lieutenant's Woman* (1969), set in Victorian Dorset at the time Hardy was working there as a young architect and which echoes many Hardyesque themes and preoccupations. It is about a hopeless relationship, class differences between lovers, Darwinism versus religion, and much more. Just because Fowles was wrong about Tryphena, we should not ignore Hardy's influence on this extraordinary work.

However, Hardy's influence has also been a broader one. During the First World War D.H. Lawrence wrote a long essay, 'A Study of Thomas Hardy', which tells us less about its subject than it does about Lawrence himself. Like Hardy, he had come from a very ordinary background and begun his career by writing about a class and a region (in his case, Nottinghamshire and its miners) which had scarcely been mentioned in literature. He was interested too in exploring man's relationship to the natural world (a large part of his essay is about Egdon Heath) and to modern industrial society. He also recognized Hardy as one of the first English novelists to treat the relationship between the sexes with the seriousness it deserved. Lawrence's public was not far removed from that which had abused Hardy; two of his novels, *The Rainbow* and *Lady Chatterley's Lover*, were banned at one stage. If he read Hardy's 'Candour in English Fiction', he could only have sympathized. It is fascinating to see how he rewrote the plot of *Jude* in Lawrentian terms, ending up with something completely different. As Ian Gregor has written in *The Great Web*, 'where *Jude* ends, *The Rainbow* begins'.

Hardy inspired Lawrence as a fellow outsider, in his use of regional settings, his social realism and in the modernity of his treatment of sexual relationships. His poetry was to exert a similar influence in its realism on poets as diverse as Auden, Larkin and the Movement of the 1950s. Though he wrote in a tradition which had little in common with later experimenters like Joyce or Woolf, and which drew the patronizing attention of Henry James, many of his concerns were distinctively modern. His mature work expresses a darker vision of an uncertain and bleaker universe, no longer ordered by Victorian liberal notions of progress and a beneficent divine providence, but a more unknowable and arbitrary place. Such a consciousness paralleled the work of a writer like Conrad and prefigured the concerns of modernist writers. No doubt Hardy the outsider, who always distanced himself from the metropolitan literary establishment, would have been much amused by the thought.

Part Two
Critical Survey

4   The Hardy hero and his predicament

When Hardy began work on *The Poor Man and the Lady*, at the age of twenty-seven, he tells us that:

> He considered that he knew fairly well both West-country life in its less explored recesses and the life of an isolated student cast upon the billows of London with no protection but his brains – the young man of whom it may be said more truly than perhaps of any, that 'save his own soul he hath no star'. The two contrasting experiences seemed to afford him abundant materials out of which to evolve a striking socialistic novel – not that he mentally defined it as such, for the word had probably never, or scarcely ever, been heard of at that date.
>
> (*Life*, p. 56)

As we have already noted the hero was a young architect from an obscure home in Wessex who wants to marry an heiress. Her parents turn him down and he gets mixed up in left-wing politics; in the end he and the Lady decide to elope, but she dies. Other characters included an architect's mistress who works in a shop making religious symbols, and the whole novel was intended as a satire on 'the vulgarity of the middle class' and 'modern Christianity'. This novel is lost, but the radicalism persists, in a smouldering way, in most of the novels he wrote later on.

There were other themes that persisted too. Everybody knows that he wrote about 'West-country life in its less explored recesses'; what is not so obvious is that he very often took for his hero a young man who has been cast adrift, not necessarily in London, but in a moral and intellectual wilderness in which there are no fixed rules to guide him, only the promptings of his own soul. This is the central theme in *The Return of the Native*, *Tess of the d'Urbervilles* and *Jude the Obscure*. It forms what we can call the essentially *modern* part of his novels, while his descriptions of life in the remote parts of Dorset must have seemed almost as old-fashioned to his earliest readers as they do to us.

After *The Poor Man and the Lady* Hardy wrote a pot-boiler, *Desperate Remedies*; his next novel was *Under the Greenwood Tree*, or *The Mellstock Quire*. This is a very much better and more characteristic novel, for in it Hardy returned to the people and scenes he knew best. 'Mellstock' is Stinsford, the hamlet where he grew up, and the choir is based on the perished group of musicians which had included several members of his own family. Although, as Hardy said, the book is not to be taken too seriously, he did feel that the destruction of old-fashioned church choirs was a tragic symbol in its small way. This made him gently, but very definitely, critical of the pretty young organist, Fancy Day, who takes over from the choir, and of the Reverend Mr Maybold, who is a decent man but hardly able to communicate with ordinary people. When Fancy is forced to choose between him and young Dick Dewy, a member of the original choir, she is really having to choose between two ways of life. Dick is a little bit 'beneath' her, whereas Maybold is the sort of educated gentleman whom her father has always wanted her to marry. This is the kind of conflict which comes up over and over again in Hardy's novels, and although Fancy makes the right choice in the end there is a suspicion that she cares less for Dick than he does for her.

Although they are only sketched in lightly, the 'hero' and 'heroine' are both recognizable Hardy types. Their names are symbolic; Dick represents dewy-eyed innocence; Fancy is ruled by her whims. She is a flirtatious girl, like so many Hardy heroines, while Dick is the unpretentious warm-hearted hero who is to become more important in the later and greater works.

In many ways the love story is not the real heart of the novel. Hardy wanted the title to be *The Mellstock Quire*, and his deepest sympathies are with the choir which is in the process of being destroyed. It is these people who represent what is really valuable in the life of the community, in a way that Fancy can never do, and there is a constant quiet suggestion that they are keeping alive, not only the best of the village traditions, but also a sympathetic awareness of nature which cannot be understood by those who have grown up in towns. The young Hardy never wrote anything finer than the first pages of this book, which show the choir assembling in the dark lanes on Christmas Eve:

> To dwellers in a wood almost every species of tree has its voice as well as its feature. At the passing of the breeze the fir-trees sob and moan no less distinctly than they rock; the holly whistles as it battles with itself; the ash hisses amid its quiverings; the beech rustles while its flat boughs rise and fall. And winter, which modifies the note of such trees as shed their leaves, does not destroy its individuality.

> (*Under the Greenwood Tree*, Ch. 1)

We first meet Dick, the hero, walking through 'the darkness of a plantation that whispered thus distinctively to his intelligence'. It is only the first of many scenes in Hardy's novels where he shows people working or walking in the countryside in a total or partial darkness, with only their knowledge of the landscape to guide them. He is interested in more than the simple skill of distinguishing trees from one another (in a countryside without electricity) by sound rather than sight. This is only one example, he seems to be saying, of how people can develop a deeply intuitive relationship with their surroundings which can give meaning and purpose to their lives.

Gabriel Oak

Man is part of nature, in the Wessex novels, and also part of history. This is worked out much more fully in Hardy's next important novel, his first really good one, *Far from the Madding Crowd*. His description of the shepherd Gabriel Oak, watching his flock on the lonely down at midnight, is interesting enough to be worth quoting at length:

> The sky was clear – remarkably clear – and the twinkling of all the stars seemed to be but throbs of one body, timed by a common pulse. The North Star was directly in the wind's eye, and since evening the Bear had swung round it outwardly to the east, till he was now at a right angle with the meridian. A difference of colour in the stars – oftener read of than seen in England – was perceptible here. The sovereign brilliancy of Sirius pierced the eye with a steely glitter, the star called Capella was yellow, Aldebaran and Betelgueux shone with a fiery red.
>
> To persons standing alone on a hill during a clear midnight such as this, the roll of the world eastward is almost a palpable movement. The sensation may be caused by the panoramic glide of the stars past earthly objects, which is perceptible in a few minutes of stillness, or by the better outlook upon space that a hill affords, or by the wind, or by the solitude; but whatever be its origin the impression of riding along is vivid and abiding. The poetry of motion is a phrase much in use, and to enjoy the epic form of that gratification it is necessary to stand on a hill at a small hour of the night, and, having first expanded with a sense of difference from the mass of civilised mankind, who are dreamwrapt and disregardful of all such proceedings at this time, long and quietly watch your stately progress through the stars. After such a nocturnal reconnoitre it is hard to get back to earth, and to believe that the consciousness of such majestic speeding is derived from a tiny human frame.

This is similar in some ways to a famous passage from *The Rainbow*, where Lawrence, who as a young man had been strongly influenced by Hardy's work, writes:

But during the long February nights with the ewes in labour, looking out from the shelter into the flashing stars, he knew he did not belong to himself. He must admit that he was only fragmentary, something incomplete and subject. There were the stars in the dark heaven travelling, the whole host passing by on some eternal voyage. So he sat small and submissive to the greater ordering.

Both writers are expressing the sense of awe which is felt by a solitary person on looking at the stars. Many of us feel at these times, and Lawrence appears to be saying, that man is something small and insignificant; Hardy doesn't say this. On the contrary, he feels that the whole universe takes its meaning from man's presence – 'the consciousness of such majestic speeding is derived from a tiny human frame'.

But if Hardy is more humanist, more centred on man than Lawrence, he too feels that man 'does not belong to himself'. He has a vital relationship with the natural world, which he ignores at his peril, and he also depends on other human beings to keep him alive. Gabriel, the hero of this novel, has a profound understanding of nature which helps to make him the most admirable character in the book. In the chapter we have just been studying, we see him nursing the newborn lambs, and telling the time of night from the stars. Later, when the sheep under his care are struck down by disease, he is the only one who knows how to cure them, and when a whole harvest is threatened by rain he saves it by working in the darkness 'entirely by feeling with his hands'. But he is not merely a skilful farmer; he is also *morally* stronger and better than most people. Near the beginning of the story he says to Bathsheba, the rather flighty girl whom he is in love with: 'I shall do one thing in this life – one thing certain – that is, love you, and long for you, and *keep wanting you* till I die.' Bathsheba turns him down at first and marries the flashy Sergeant Troy, who is the opposite of Gabriel, a womanizer. This type reappears several times in Hardy's novels (he satirizes it in a notorious late work, *The Well-Beloved*), and although he was not without sympathy he obviously felt that this type of man was dangerous. Troy nearly ruins Bathsheba's life, and incidentally her farm as well, before the story works itself out and she is left free to settle down with Gabriel.

For the Hardy hero like Gabriel Oak there is no real 'predicament', because whatever disasters may hit him he will carry on, stoically and without self-pity, doing the work that lies to hand. Perhaps this type of man, based on the shepherds and small farmers of Dorset among whom Hardy had grown up, was the kind of 'hero' he most admired. But the Gabriel figure becomes less common in his later novels, because by this time Hardy was beginning to be obsessed by problems of a very different kind.

Diggory Venn and Clym Yeobright

We can see this happening in his next great novel, *The Return of the Native*. The people who live on barren Egdon Heath have the same feeling as Gabriel for the great underlying reality of nature, which is always there although human lives, and human civilizations, come and go. 'The sea changed, the fields changed, the rivers, the villages and the people changed', says Hardy in the first chapter, 'but Egdon remained'. In *Far from the Madding Crowd* Nature was a positive and on the whole a friendly force; in this novel, on the other hand, it is something you have to put up with. People who refuse to adapt to the heath will be broken. Hardy shows us two characters, Eustacia, who yearns for a life of luxury in Paris, and the gambler and compulsive flirt Wildeve, both of whom are forced to live on the heath, but hate it. In the end they both die, drowned in the flooded weir on a night of wind and storm. On the other hand, people who accept the heath and understand its moods can live on it without too much trouble. This is true of the sweet and unsophisticated Thomasin, who brings her baby out on to the heath quite happily, and the reddleman Diggory Venn. This weird character, although he appears to have come from a realm outside nature, is actually very much like Gabriel Oak. He is essentially kind and unselfish, devoted to the woman he loves even when there seems no hope of getting her, and, like Thomasin, thoroughly well adapted to life on the heath. At certain times, particularly in the remarkable scene where he plays dice with Wildeve by the light of glow-worms, we feel that he has powers which aren't quite human. Nature seems to work on his side, because he understands and knows how to relate to it, and, like Gabriel, he has his reward at the end of the novel, when most of the other characters are broken or die.

And yet the real hero of this novel is not Diggory, but – some would say – a much less admirable figure, Clym Yeobright. When we first meet him, nearly a third of the way through the novel, we are immediately made aware that Clym is different from other people – 'singular' is the word Hardy uses. 'Had Heaven preserved Yeobright from a wearing habit of meditation, people would have said, "A handsome man!" Had his brain unfolded under sharper contours they would have said, "A thoughtful man". But an inner strenuousness was preying upon an outer symmetry, and they rated his look as singular' (Ch. 2, p. 6).

Clym's physical health and good looks are fated to be shortlived because he worries too hard about himself, and about the whole human race. He has come back to the heath where he was born, throwing up a good career as a diamond merchant, because he wants to do something useful with his life. 'Can any man deserving the name waste his time in that effeminate way, when he sees half the world going to ruin for want of somebody to buckle to and teach them how to breast the misery they are born to?' His idea is to become a teacher to the heath workers' children, and he is content to live on Egdon because its roughness and wildness suit him: 'To my mind it is most exhilarating, and strengthening, and soothing. I would rather live on these hills than anywhere else in the world.'

Yet Clym has moved a long way away from the dwellers on the heath, who don't understand why he has come back to live there when he could be having a good time in Paris. His plans to start a school never work out, and although he is quite happy to cut furze on the heath when he can do nothing better, he cannot really go back to being a land worker when his whole life has made him, inescapably, an intellectual. He has no clearcut social position and is isolated from other people because, Hardy suggests, he is too far ahead of them. He has a 'typical countenance of the future', which means that, in the present, he is bound to look 'singular'. 'The rural world was not ripe for him. A man should be only partially before his time; to be completely to the vanward in aspirations is fatal to fame.'

But worse is to happen to Clym. Through a series of events over which he has very little control, he comes to feel responsible for the deaths of his mother and of his wife. By the end of the novel he is left a semi-invalid with a profound sense of guilt. 'It is I who ought to have drowned myself. Those who ought to have lived lie dead, and here am I alive!' There is nobody left who cares much about Clym as a person, but he does, in the end, rebuild his life by staying on the heath, as he planned, and becoming an unorthodox preacher:

> Yeobright had, in fact, found his vocation in the career of an itinerant open-air preacher and lecturer on morally unimpeachable subjects . . . He left alone creeds and systems of philosophy, finding enough and more than enough to occupy his tongue in the opinions and actions common to all good men. Some believed him, and some believed not; some said that his words were commonplace, others complained of his want of theological doctrine; while others again remarked that it was well enough for a man to take to preaching who could not see to do anything else. But everywhere he was kindly received, for the story of his life had become generally known.
>
> (Part 6, Ch. 4)

'I got to like the character of Clym before I had done with him,' Hardy wrote, when he re-read the novel many years afterwards. 'I think he is the nicest of all my heroes and *not a bit* like me.' Indeed there can hardly be any doubt, in this last paragraph, of his affectionate feelings towards his hero. Clym deserves kindness, because he has suffered so drastically, and his moral philosophy closely resembles Hardy's in being a simple system of ethics, divorced from theology. It is less obvious that Clym is 'not a bit like me'. In many ways Hardy does seem to have been very like Clym in his unconventional ideas, his doubting many received opinions, and his feeling that when life is cut off from its natural roots it will be unhappy. What is certain is that in his later work Hardy became more and more interested in this kind of hero, the lonely misfit, the intellectual who is thought of an an eccentric, the man with a haunting and indestructible feeling of guilt.

Over the next eight or ten years, one of Hardy's less productive periods, the themes of loneliness and self-sacrifice become increasingly important in his work. John Loveday, the hero of *The Trumpet-Major*, renounces the woman he loves to his brother and goes off to the Napoleonic wars to be killed. Viviette in *Two on a Tower* gives up her lover for the good of his career and in the end she dies too. In *A Laodicean* (perhaps his weakest novel) Hardy again shows a girl sacrificing herself for the good of her lover and eventually going into a convent. And *The Mayor of Casterbridge*, which is discussed more fully in the next chapter, shows the hero progressively breaking all his human and social ties until he is driven out of the community, to die almost alone on Egdon Heath.

Giles Winterborne

The Woodlanders, written ten years after *The Return of the Native*, has some things in common with it, but the tone is sadder, more resigned, much less confident about the power of new ideas to change the world. There is nobody in the woodland community at all like Clym Yeobright. Mr Fitzpiers, the 'very clever and learned young doctor' whose light Grace watches in fascination as it changes to blue, then violet, and then red, represents 'like a tropical plant in a hedgerow, a nucleus of advanced ideas and practices which had nothing in common with the life around'. But Fitzpiers has no idealistic dreams about reforming the world; he is dabbling in strange studies for his own amusement and he is also a cold-hearted philanderer who boasts that he has been infatuated with five women at once. Both he and Mrs Charmond, the rich landowner with whom he has an affair, dislike living in the woods and do not know their way round them, just as Wildeve and Eustacia feel lost on Egdon Heath. But Mrs Charmond actually owns the despised woods and can pull down houses and trees at her pleasure, and without really wanting to harm the woodland workers she exercises a casual tyranny over their lives. This has ramifications into other than property relationships: as Creedle says to Giles Winterborne, the real hero of the novel:

> 'Ye've lost a hundred load of timber well seasoned; ye've lost five hundred pound in good money; ye've lost the stone-windered house that's big enough to hold a dozen families; ye've lost your share of half-a-dozen good wagons and their horses – all lost! – through your letting slip she that was once yer own!'

What this means is that Giles has 'let slip' Grace, who later becomes the wife of Fitzpiers, because Mrs Charmond has turned him out of his house, and also because he is not thought good enough for a girl whose father has had her expensively educated. 'Learning is better than houses and lands', says Creedle, but in this novel the three go together, and cultivated upperclass people, the Charmonds and Fitzpierses of this world, have no difficulty in taking what they want from the ordinary people who work in the woods, like Giles, and the girl Marty South.

'On taking up *The Woodlanders* and reading it after many years I think I like it, *as a story*, the best of all,' Hardy said, and one is tempted to agree with him when one comes back to this beautiful and comparatively neglected novel – perhaps the most neglected of all his great works. Some of the things which we remember longest are the lyrical and lovely descriptions of the fertile country around the Hintocks, as in this passage:

> It was the cider country more especially, which met the woodland district some way off. There the air was blue as sapphire – such a blue as outside that apple-region was never seen. Under the blue the orchards were in a blaze of pink bloom, some of the richly flowered trees running almost up to where they drove along. At a gate, which opened down an incline, a man leant on his arms regarding this fair promise so intently that he did not observe their passing.
>
> 'That was Giles,' said Melbury, when they had gone by.
>
> 'Was it? Poor Giles,' said she.
>
> 'All that apple-blooth means heavy autumn work for him and his hands. If no blight happens before the setting the cider yield will be such as we have not had for years.'
>
> (*The Woodlanders*, Ch. 19)

Giles and his fellow-workers are not merely figures in a landscape; they actually *create* that landscape. He and Marty have an instinctive love and knowledge of nature which seems miraculous to people who don't work in the woods.

From the light lashing of the twigs upon their faces when brushing through them in the dark either could pronounce upon the species of the tree whence they stretched; from the quality of the wind's murmur through a bough either could in like manner name its sort afar off.

Of Giles we are told that 'he had a marvellous power of making trees grow . . . There was a sort of sympathy between himself and the fir, oak or beech that he was operating on; so that the roots took hold of the soil in a few days.' But these skills, the basis of life itself, are much less highly thought of than the possession of money, or an 'old' family name. In a famous passage, Marty says that the young trees sigh 'because they are very sorry to begin life in earnest – just as we be'. She is right, because life is intensely hard, even tragic, for people like Giles and herself. Unlike Gabriel Oak and Diggory Venn, whom he strongly resembles in some ways, Giles can find no fulfilment in the world of this novel. He sacrifices himself for Grace, and dies, to be forgotten by her in exactly eight months. She goes off to the Midlands with her husband, where, we suppose, they will lead a more or less unhappy married life, and we are left with the memory of Giles's goodness and the trees which will live on after his death.

This was the last time that Hardy wrote about this kind of hero. The men in his later novels are more complicated, less straightforwardly *good* than Giles is, and they don't share his close intimacy with the natural world. What happens to a girl of the same type as Marty South, when her values collide with the Victorian moral code, is shown in detail in *Tess of the d'Urbervilles*.

Angel Clare

Tess Durbeyfield is like Marty (and Gabriel and Giles) because she is happily adjusted to her environment. 'A fresh and virginal daughter of Nature' is what she first seems to Angel Clare. When she is working as a milkmaid at Talbothays Dairy Hardy emphasizes, in some marvellous passages, that she and Angel are leading a kind of life which is not only precious in itself, but essential:

They met continually; they could not help it. They met daily in that strange and solemn interval, the twilight of the morning, in the violet or pink dawn; for it was necessary to rise early, so very early, here. Milking was done betimes, and before the milking came the skimming, which began at a little past three . . . The spectral, half-compounded, aqueous light which pervaded the open mead, impressed them with a feeling of isolation, as if they were Adam and Eve . . . At that preternatural time hardly any woman so well endowed in person as she was likely to be walking in the open air within the boundaries of his horizon; very few in all England. Fair women are usually asleep at midsummer dawns. She was close at hand, and the rest were nowhere.

(Tess, Ch. 20)

Like Gabriel, watching his flock under the stars, Tess and Angel are awake and caring for the animals at a time when most people are in bed. Hardy makes the same point when they deliver milk to the London train, for 'strange people that we have never seen . . . who don't know anything of us, and where it comes from; or think how we two drove miles across the moor tonight in the rain that it might reach 'em in time'.

But Tess is not a simple character, a girl like Thomasin in *The Return of the Native* whose life is an open book. Angel doesn't know, perhaps because he doesn't understand the roughness of life in the English villages, that she has been seduced and had an illegitimate baby at the age of sixteen. And Tess is unable to be really happy at Talbothays, as all her instincts tell her to be, because she cannot forget that in the eyes of the world she is a fallen woman:

> Her face had latterly changed with changing states of mind, continually fluctuating between beauty and ordinariness, according as the thoughts were gay or grave. One day she was pink and flawless; another pale and tragical. When she was pink she was feeling less than when pale; her more perfect beauty accorded with her less elevated mood; her more intense mood with her less perfect beauty.

(Tess, Ch. 16)

This reminds one of the description of Clym Yeobright's face, where his natural good looks and cheerfulness are being undermined because he cannot stop worrying. Not that Hardy is arguing that people ought *not* to worry; on the contrary he seems to think that under the conditions of modern life they can hardly help it. For modern society is diseased, often cruel and inhuman, and the conventions it lays down are in many important ways *unnatural*. Tess has been 'made to break an accepted social law', but not any law that exists in nature. And it is the conflict between natural human feelings and social conventions which, in the end, destroys her, a conflict which is acted out in the mind of the man she loves, Angel Clare.

Angel is one of the most interesting heroes whom Hardy had so far attempted to draw. He has given up the faith of his father and brothers and become an advanced thinker, who wishes to use his education 'for the honour and glory of man'. Shut out from the university because of his agnosticism (like Hardy?) he comes to live at Talbothays to study farming. Like Clym, he has taken a step downwards from his own class by doing this, and the dairyman's wife treats him as a gentleman, making him eat at a different table from everyone else. Again like Clym, he finds that living close to nature makes him surprisingly cheerful:

> Unexpectedly he began to like the outdoor life for its own sake
> ... He became wonderfully free from the chronic melancholy which is overtaking the civilised races with the decline of belief in a beneficent Power.
> ... He grew away from old associations, and saw something new in life and humanity. Secondarily, he made close acquaintance with phenomena which he had before known but darkly – the seasons in their moods, morning and evening, night and noon, winds in their different tempers, trees, waters and mists, shades and silences, and the voices of inanimate things.
>
> (*Tess*, Ch. 18)

Together with this new awareness of nature goes a new awareness of human beings; he stops thinking of the dairy workers as comic yokels and begins to like and respect them as people – 'much to his surprise he took, indeed, a real delight in their companionship'. The change in his attitudes, brought about by working in the dairy, is responsible for his falling in love with Tess, who is obviously not the sort of girl his family wants or expects him to marry. What causes him to reject her is not his natural feelings, but the residue of prejudice left by his upbringing: 'With all his attempted independence of judgement this advanced and well-meaning young man, a sample product of the last five-and-twenty years, was yet the slave to custom and conventionality when surprised back into his early teachings' (*Tess*, Ch. 39).

This is one of the most tragic dilemmas in all Hardy's novels, and one which he was to explore still more deeply in *Jude the Obscure*. It is not an easy thing to be ahead of one's time, at any rate not in Victorian England; the most sincere convictions are liable to crack under a personal shock. Angel leaves Tess after she tells him about her past, even though he knows that she is at least as pure as he is, calling her with cruel snobbishness 'an unapprehending peasant woman'. Worse still, he lets her think that he has gone for good, until in despair she is forced back to her original seducer. By the end of the novel, after she has been hanged, he has been reduced, like Clym, to a 'mere yellow skeleton', who is to be haunted by guilt for the rest of his life.

Society, Hardy seems to be saying in the most bitter novel he had yet written, has its values turned upside down. Tess was abused as 'a little harlot' in many London drawing-rooms; in the book she is condemned as a murderess. Angel, on the other hand, has not done anything legally wrong. Yet in fact he knows himself to be much more guilty than she, perhaps even more guilty than Alec, and in the end he could easily have said, like Clym, 'My great regret is that for what I have done no man or law can punish me'.

Jude Fawley

Jude the Obscure, Hardy's last novel, is still more bitter. By this time he seems to have felt even more certain that something was deeply wrong with the society he lived in, and this feeling is expressed through the surprisingly modern parable of a young working man who wants to go to Oxford, and fails. Like Angel and Clym, Jude has left his own class without joining another but, unlike them, he is hoping to *rise* in the world. This is not only ambition, although that has something to do with it; it is much more the yearning for a life which is intellectually and morally *better* than the one he is expected to lead. Hardy makes it clear that no sensitive person could endure life in Marygreen. Nature is much grimmer here than in his earlier novels; Jude's job is scaring birds in a lonely ploughed field and when he lets himself show sympathy for them the farmer beats him. He has no parents and there are no village traditions (such as the Mellstock choir) to which he can attach himself, for the old landmarks have been pulled down and he knows next to nothing about his ancestors who are buried in the dismantled graveyard. One of the most moving passages in the entire novel comes near the end, when he goes into the ugly new church which has been raised on a different site from the old one: 'Everything was new, except a few pieces of carving preserved from the wrecked old fabric, now fixed against the new walls. He stood by these: they seemed akin to the perished people of that place who were his ancestors and Sue's' (Part 6, Ch. 8).

Jude's alienation has gone so far that the one light on the bleak horizon appears to be Christminster, the university city based on Oxford, on the extreme border of Hardy's Wessex:

> It had been the yearning of his heart to find something to anchor on, to cling to – for some place which he could call admirable. Should he find that place in this city if he could get there? Would it be a spot in which, without fear of farmers, or hindrance, or ridicule, he could watch and wait, and set himself to some mighty undertaking like the men of old of whom he had heard?
>
> (Part 1, Ch. 3)

Like all true Hardy heroes, Jude wants to find something greater than himself to which he can give himself totally. In earlier novels, this had meant productive work on the land; in others it meant the cause of progress or learning (the young hero of *Two on a Tower*, for instance, is committed to studying the stars). Jude belongs to a generation for whom work on the land has become irrelevant; instead he strains himself to the limit in the struggle to be a learned man who can find a home in the Christminster colleges. But the reality of Christminster, as he finds out when he actually gets there, is that of a bigoted, cruel and sordid city. The university establishment is satirized throughout the story. Colleges have names like Biblioll and Sarcophagus; horses are kicked in the stomach outside the college gates and there are 'two nations' inside the same city: the learned doctors and clergymen, and the ordinary people of Christminster who have no idea what it's all about. This means that the university is closed to those, like Jude, who could benefit most from it, because he was born into the wrong class. When he makes his moving speech to the Christminster crowd about the failure of his dream, Hardy emphasizes that Jude is more intelligent, and more moral, than the gentlemen in the university:

> 'Well preached!' said Tinker Taylor. And privately to his neigh-
> bours: 'Why, one of them jobbing pa'sons swarming about here,
> that takes the services when our head Reverends want a holiday,
> wouldn't ha' discoursed such doctrine for less than a guinea
> down! Hey? I'll take my oath not one o' 'em would! And then he
> must have had it wrote down for 'n. And this only a working
> man!'
>
> (Part 6, Ch. 1).

(Not surprisingly, the policeman in attendance tells Jude, 'Keep yer tongue quiet, my man'.)

When Jude first comes to Christminster he has, as he says himself, 'a neat stock of fixed opinions', but these are gradually eroded under the pressure of the life he leads and the influence of his cousin Sue, an extraordinarily bright and clever girl with whom he falls in love. These 'fixed opinions' were those of most conventional Victorians, and included respect for Oxford University in its contemporary form, the Anglican Church, the institution of marriage and so on. After Jude has realized that the University is closed to the working class, that the Church is indifferent to ordinary human problems and that marriage to the wrong person can be a torment, Hardy says that his experiences have 'enlarged his own views of life, laws, customs and dogmas'. The opposite happens to Sue. The girl whose intellect 'scintillated like a star' cannot hang on to her independence of mind when tragedy strikes her, and she goes back to the husband whom she should never have married, even forcing herself to do 'the ultimate thing'. Jude, dying of exposure and neglect in what was his holy city, Christminster, says:

> 'It takes two or three generations to do what I tried to do in one ... As for Sue and me ... when our minds were clear, and our love of truth fearless – the time was not ripe for us! Our ideas were fifty years too soon to be any good to us. And so the resistance they met with brought reaction in her, and recklessness and ruin on me!'
>
> (Part 6, Ch. 10)

Like another seeker for truth, Clym Yeobright, they were unfortunate in being born too far ahead of their time. It is not really surprising that Sue breaks and Jude dies, because, like Hardy, they are both ultrasensitive, and the pressures on them are more than most people could bear. Just as nobody can understand why the 'obscure' Jude wishes to go to Oxford, or why he and Sue cannot shake down with the people they marry, or why Phillotson refuses to do the proper thing when his wife wants to leave him, so the public couldn't understand what Hardy meant by writing a novel like *Jude*. The attacks on the book upset Hardy so much that he gave them as his reason for writing no more novels.

Jude has nothing to fall back on after Sue leaves him; not God, and not nature, which in many of Hardy's earlier novels was seen as a comforting and strengthening force. Indeed in this novel Hardy says that nature's law is 'mutual butchery', and comments sadly on 'the scorn of Nature for man's finer emotions, and her lack of interest in his aspirations'. And yet these emotions, and these aspirations, are still facts, and Jude is no less of a hero to Hardy because he has failed in almost everything that he set out to do.

5 *The Mayor of Casterbridge*

Hardy was at the height of his powers when he began work on *The Mayor of Casterbridge* at the age of forty-four. He had written ten novels up to then, but only one, *The Return of the Native*, written seven years before, was a masterpiece. Since that time, he had produced some inferior books. But by 1884, he could afford to have a house built in Dorchester, the town he called Casterbridge, and most of the novel was written there, as were *The Woodlanders*, *Tess of the D'Urbervilles* and *Jude the Obscure*.

It seems to have had a good effect on his work. *The Mayor of Casterbridge* is a magnificent novel, although Hardy himself was not entirely happy about it.

> It was a story which Hardy fancied he had damaged more recklessly as an artistic whole, in the interest of the newspaper in which it appeared serially, than perhaps any other of his novels, his aiming to get an incident into each week's part causing him in his own judgment to add events to the narrative somewhat too freely.
>
> (*Life*, p. 174)

The readers were not entirely happy either, for different reasons. Some felt (predictably) that it was less good than *Far from the Madding Crowd*. And it was nearly turned down by the publisher on the grounds that 'the lack of gentry among the characters made it uninteresting – a typical estimate of what was, or was supposed to be, mid-Victorian taste' (*Life*, 180).

Perhaps it is just because of its differences from Hardy's other novels that *The Mayor of Casterbridge* is so popular today. It would not have been easy to fit either Henchard or Farfrae into the last chapter, on Hardy's heroes. We saw there that Hardy usually wrote about men like Gabriel Oak, who represented his ideal of the countryman, or about men like himself, deeply troubled intellectuals like Clym Yeobright or Jude. Neither Henchard nor Farfrae is at all like this, and it is one of the triumphs of Hardy's art that he could write so convincingly about men so unlike himself. They are unlike each other, too; in fact the difference goes so deep that it leads to a struggle which can only end in death. Henchard is a giant with black whiskers and eyes 'which always seemed to have a red spark of light in them', a man of tremendous and sometimes frightening strength who can wrench a bull's head 'as if he would snap it off'. Farfrae is 'ruddy and of a fair countenance, bright-eyed, and slight

The Mayor of Casterbridge

by Thomas Hardy.

Author of "Far from the Madding Crowd", "A Pair of Blue Eyes", &c.

Chapter I.

One evening of late summer, before the present century had
reached its middle-age, a young man & woman, the
latter carrying a child, were approaching the large village
of Weydon-Priors on foot. They were plainly but not ill clad,
though the thick hoar of dust which had accumulated on their
shoes & clothing from an obviously long journey lent a disadvantageous
shabbiness

Opening page of The Mayor of Casterbridge *from the original
manuscript*

in build'. Henchard rushes from one extreme to another, in trade and in his emotional life; Farfrae has a cool scientific attitude to trade and to people. At the same time he charms everyone he comes into contact with: 'The curious double strands in Farfrae's thread of life – the commercial and the romantic – were very distinct at times. Like the colours in a variegated cord those contrasts could be seen intertwisted, yet not mingling.' (Ch. 23)

We see something of the basic differences between them when Henchard tells Farfrae about 'the gloomy fits I sometimes suffer from, on account o' the loneliness of my domestic life, when the world seems to have the blackness of hell, and, like Job, I could curse the day that gave me birth'. Farfrae replies, 'Ah, now, I never feel like it', and it is, and is meant to be, a significant point. Hardy *had* felt like that, and this is one reason for the deep sympathy and identification with Henchard which runs right through the book. Not that he glosses over his hero's faults; quite the opposite. Henchard is so *obviously* wrong, most of the time; Farfrae is so *obviously* blameless and sweetly reasonable. Yet there is no doubt at all about which man Hardy feels for. And such is the genius of his art that we begin to see unsuspected qualities of generosity and goodness in the Mayor, and something unpleasantly cold and scheming about his young rival.

The novel opens dramatically with the splendid scene in which Henchard sells his wife and child to the sailor. Hardy used to say that a novelist could not expect people to read him unless he told them something unusual enough to be worth hearing, and this first chapter is one of the most compelling he ever wrote. Strange though it may seem now, and did seem then to his London readers, it was not uncommon for poor and uneducated men to sell their wives, right up to the end of the nineteenth century. It was done in public, with a halter round the woman's neck, and most people firmly believed that it was legal. Susan Henchard does, and Hardy remarks that she was not the first or last woman to do so. Henchard is not so simple; he is a skilled labourer and a comparatively well-educated man (we first see him absorbed in reading a ballad-sheet) who only sells his wife because he is drunk. But before that he has already begun to resent her, not because he wants another wife but because she and the child are holding him back from getting on: 'I haven't more than fifteen shillings in the world, and yet I am a good experienced man in my line. I'd challenge England to beat me in the fodder business; and if I were a free man again I'd be worth a thousand pound before I'd done o't.' (Ch. 1). This is the introduction to one of the great central themes of the novel: ambition, and its effects on human relationships. Henchard wants to get rid of his wife and child because he thinks they are preventing him from making a fortune.

Later in the novel we meet another young man, Donald Farfrae, who has left Scotland because he is motivated by the same dream of getting some of 'the prizes of life'. And, in her own way, Elizabeth-Jane wants this too – her mother's main reason for going back to Henchard is to 'advance Elizabeth'. For, more than any other Hardy novel, *The Mayor of Casterbridge* is about the great Victorian myth of 'getting on'. In *The Return of the Native* he had shown how the idealistic Clym Yeobright deliberately chooses to go *back* in the world in order to help people; in this novel the ruthless materialist Henchard sacrifices his closest human ties to ambition. In Victorian terms, he is perfectly right. Not that the orthodox economic thinkers would have condoned actual wife-selling, but they would certainly have said that Henchard was very foolish to get married for love at eighteen. It was everywhere preached during the nineteenth century that if you were poor it must be your own fault. Anybody could become rich if he saved every penny, did not drink, and above all, did not encumber himself with dependants – the Reverend Thomas Malthus had preached that the working classes should abstain from having children, just as we are now told that people in the Third World are poor because they do not practise birth control. As always, there were just enough people who did rise from the depths and become millionaires to make this view of life plausible. Samuel Smiles' little book *Self-Help* (1859) is full of the stories of such people, and it became a kind of bible to many thousands who tried to do the same thing. But there was always another strand in Victorian thinking which sensed that this philosophy was destructive to the deepest human values. Dickens had explored its damaging effects in *Great Expectations*, and Hardy, in *The Mayor of Casterbridge*, did the same thing.

It was a paradox that he of all people should be critical of the idea of 'getting on in the world'. He himself had risen in the last twenty years from an obscure young architect to a famous novelist (and had put off marriage, for financial reasons, until he was thirty-four). This involved a good deal of writing and social mixing which he disliked, and it says in the *Life* that at this time he regarded his novels as 'mere journeywork'. When he was a very old man 'he said that if he had his life over again he would prefer to be a small architect in a country town, like Mr Hicks at Dorchester, to whom he was articled' (*Life*, p. 443). Perhaps he was in a unique position to sympathize with Henchard and yet to see that his ambition would not, in the end, bring him what he cared about most.

When we next see Henchard, some twenty years later, he has done exactly what he said. He has been a great success in 'the

This melodramatic scene appeared in the serialized version of The Mayor of Casterbridge, *but was not reprinted afterwards*: 'I don't drink now – I haven't since that night.'

fodder business' – the selling of oats, roots and corn. Now he is the Mayor of Casterbridge, complete with gold chain and diamond studs, and his wife first sees him through the window of the 'chief hotel' where he is presiding at a great public dinner. She is out in the street, with the rest of the people who haven't been invited, and there is a great contrast between the two groups. Hardy shows the dinner-guests 'searching for tit-bits, and sniffing and grunting over their plates like sows nuzzling for acorns', and finally drinking themselves into a stupor. Whereas the poor people outside the window have to live on the bad bread which Henchard has sold them, 'They can blow their trumpets and thump their drums, and have their roaring dinners, . . . but we must needs be put-to for want of a wholesome crust'. These are the people who shout back rudely at Henchard when he is making his speech at the grand dinner, and later on we are to hear much more about them. The tensions which are to destroy Michael Henchard exist already, for Casterbridge is by no means so pleasant a place as it seems. Our first impression is one of 'great snugness and comfort':

> The front doors of the private houses were mostly left open at this warm autumn-time, no thought of umbrella stealers disturbing the minds of the placid burgesses. Hence, through the long straight entrance passages thus unclosed could be seen, as through tunnels, the mossy gardens at the back, glowing with nasturtiums, fuchsias, scarlet geraniums, 'bloody warriors', snapdragons, and dahlias, this floral blaze being backed by crusted grey stone-work from a yet remoter Casterbridge than the venerable one visible in the street.

(Ch. 9)

But alongside this cosy picture Hardy shows us aspects of Casterbridge which are altogether more sinister. We hear from the talk of the Three Mariners that it is 'an old, hoary place of wickedness', and that 'when you take away from among us the fools and the rogues, and the lammigers, and the wanton hussies, and the slatterns, and such-like, there's cust few left'. We hear about the 'red-robed judge' who sentences sheep-stealers, about hangings, and about the grisly history of the Amphitheatre where a woman was burned to death. And gradually we get some idea of the precariousness of Henchard's position, which at first seemed so secure.

He is a lonely man, for all his wealth and power, and this is why he is so keen to get Farfrae to stay with him, for he has no real friends in the town. He begins to be undermined at a very early stage, after he has married his wife again (for the child's sake) and taken Farfrae on as his assistant. It is largely his own fault. We see him antagonize Farfrae by his callous treatment of Abel Whittle, even though, as we learn afterwards, he has 'kept Abel's old mother in coals and snuff all the previous winter', which shows his fundamental decency. But his uncontrollable temper drives Farfrae away from him, just as it had driven Susan away when he was young. After he has broken up their friendship 'his heart sank within him at what he had said and done'. His problem is that he craves for affection, but can only give it in bouts and spurts. When his wife has died he feels a passionate need for Elizabeth, only to turn against her when he finds out that she is the sailor's child. 'Being uncultivated himself' he is particularly sensitive to what he thinks is common about her behaviour, such as speaking the dialect or being kind to servants. He tells her that she will 'disgrace him to the dust'. Yet he could have learned from Farfrae that the best way to deal with people is by considering their feelings. It turns out that he has offended his colleagues on the Corporation and so is not to be kept on as an alderman, while at the same time, Farfrae is taken on to the Council.

What happens next is financial ruin. Hardy has already shown how the Mayor has entered into a 'war of prices' and 'mortal commercial combat' with Farfrae. This may seem an overdramatic way of describing the rivalry of two corn merchants in a small country town, but, in this novel, Casterbridge *is* the world of commerce, and the struggle between Henchard and Farfrae is just what was happening in the City of London on an infinitely larger scale. There is no room for human kindness in this atmosphere of fierce competition. Farfrae does not want to take away Henchard's customers, but he finds that he has to, in sheer self-defence. In the end his own recklessness and the changeable weather bring Henchard down. Hardy tells us in the Preface that the novel was partly inspired by events in 'the real history of the town called Casterbridge', including the uncertain harvests in the 1840s in which it is set. In those days, before the repeal of the Corn Laws, a bad harvest could mean starvation for the poor and ruin for those who traded in grain. Henchard finds that 'a man might gamble upon the square green areas of fields as readily as upon those of a card-room'. On the other hand Farfrae, the born capitalist, works out a strategy for dealing with the weather which makes him a handsome profit. This is the end of their 'war of prices'. The penniless young singer of the early chapters is all set to become the leading man in town, while the rich Mayor of Casterbridge is humbled to the dust.

Hardy points out more than once that Henchard is incapable of seeing that his best move would be to encourage Farfrae's interest in Elizabeth-Jane. She is obviously the ideal wife for him. They are both sensible, 'moderate' sort of people, eager to get on in the world and very, very respectable (they are both a little shocked by the hard-bitten types in the Three Mariners in Ch. 8). But this means that neither of them is likely to get carried away by a great passion. Elizabeth tries to stifle her feelings for Farfrae, because they seem 'one-sided, unmaidenly, and unwise', and Farfrae apparently has only a very mild liking for her: 'An exceptionally fortunate business transaction put him on good terms with everybody, and revealed to him that he could undeniably marry if he chose. Then who so pleasing, thrifty, and satisfactory in every way as Elizabeth-Jane?' (Ch. 23)

It is in this frame of mind that he meets and falls in love with Lucetta, the girl from Jersey who has compromised herself with Henchard before the real story begins. The chapters which deal with her and her two lovers are very much weaker than the rest of the book. It is not only that Hardy is vague about her past life; it is that whenever she appears the writing becomes slack, conventional, and at times melodramatic:

> 'I am greatly obliged to you for all that,' said she, rather with an air of speaking ritual. The stint of reciprocal feeling was perceived, and Henchard showed chagrin at once – nobody was more quick to show that than he.
>
> 'You may be obliged or not for't. Though the things I say may not have the polish of what you've lately learnt to expect for the first time in your life, they are real, my lady Lucetta.'
>
> 'That's rather a rude way of speaking to me,' pouted Lucetta, with stormy eyes.
>
> (Ch. 25)

This is infinitely less convincing than the speech of the corn merchants and agricultural workers of Casterbridge, which Hardy gives in so much loving detail. He was far less interested in society women, although he knew the type well enough from his visits to London. Lucetta's story is never really integrated with the rest of the novel, and this is its one major flaw.

She is an obvious *femme fatale*, with none of the quiet integrity of Henchard's dead wife, whom she patronizes: 'Poor woman, she seems to have been a sufferer, though uncomplaining, and although weak in intellect not an imbecile'. Although she seems to have an instantaneous effect on every man she meets, cutting Elizabeth out, there is little in her beneath the attractive surface. 'How folk do worship fine clothes!' says one of the townspeople, during the royal visit, making the point that Elizabeth is, in fact, the better-looking woman. At quite an early stage Hardy suggested that Lucetta's personality is, to a great extent, created by *clothes*:

> Entering her friend's bedroom Elizabeth saw the gowns spread out on the bed, one of a deep cherry colour, the other lighter – a

glove lying at the end of each sleeve, a bonnet at the top of each neck, and parasols across the gloves, Lucetta standing beside the suggested human figure in an attitude of contemplation.

'I wouldn't think so hard about it,' said Elizabeth, marking the intensity with which Lucetta was alternating the question whether this or that should suit best.

'But settling upon new clothes is so trying,' said Lucetta. 'You are that person' (pointing to one of the arrangements), 'or you are that totally different person' (pointing to the other), 'for the whole of the coming spring; and one of the two, you don't know which, may turn out to be very objectionable'.

It was finally decided by Miss Templeman that she would be the cherry-coloured person at all hazards.

(Ch. 24)

In the short term Lucetta is a great success. Farfrae marries her, and Henchard is forced to accept the fact that he has lost to the Scotsman all along the line. This is when we first see him standing on the remoter of the two bridges, with the thought of suicide beginning to shape in his mind. Their old positions have been reversed now: 'Here be I, his former master, working for him as man, and he the man standing as master, with my house and my furniture and my what-you-may-call wife all his own' (Ch. 32).

This marriage is broken up by a group we have heard of already, the poorest and most degraded of the people of Casterbridge. Earlier we saw them outside the windows of the King's Arms, where the Mayor and Corporation were dining, complaining about Henchard's bad bread. We've also caught some idea from the conversation in the Three Mariners (which caters for a slightly lower class of people) of the toughness of Casterbridge life, with its 'hard winters, and so many mouths to feed, and God-a'mighty sending his little taties so terrible small to fill 'em with'. In chapter 36 we are introduced to a third inn, Peter's Finger, which 'bore about the same social relation to the Three Mariners as the latter bore to the King's Arms', and which he describes as the *church* of Mixen Lane. This lane (Mill Lane, in reality) was one of the worst parts of old Dorchester, and the scene of one of the last cholera epidemics in England in 1854. Hardy calls it 'a mildewed leaf in the sturdy and flourishing Casterbridge plant', and hints that it has been the scene of vice, theft and slaughter. Some people in the slum are poachers, some are prostitutes, others have drifted from the countryside after losing their livelihood, like the old furmity-woman who commits a 'nuisance' against the church wall. All of them are delighted to have the chance of getting at Lucetta, as 'one that stands high in this town'. And Farfrae has also grown less popular since he went up in the world.

As the Mayor and man of money, engrossed with affairs and ambitions, he had lost in the eyes of the poorer inhabitants something of that wondrous charm which he had had for them as a light-hearted penniless young man, who sang ditties as readily as the birds in the trees.

The skimmity-ride is planned for the evening after a certain Royal Personage has paid a flying visit to Casterbridge, 'As a wind-up to the royal visit the hit will be all the more pat by reason of their great elevation today'. This visit is based on historical facts (Prince Albert had passed through Dorchester in 1849) but Hardy has integrated it skilfully with the novel's main theme of rising in the world. There is a strong implication that the whole affair is ridiculous, an absurd waste of energy and emotion over a person who only stays in the town for a few minutes. While the Council prepare to have an impressive ceremony,

Solomon Longways, Christopher Coney, Buzzford, and the rest of that fraternity, showed their sense of the occasion by advancing their customary eleven o'clock pint to half-past ten; from which they found a difficulty in getting back to the proper hour for several days.

Everybody 'shone in new vesture according to means' except Henchard, and for this reason Lucetta pretends not to see him 'as gaily dressed women will too often do on such occasions'. She is absorbed in Farfrae, who is wearing 'the official gold chain with great square links, like that round the royal unicorn'; she even dreams that he may get knighted. Yet already the plot is being hatched which will pull down Lucetta, and show up the emptiness of her social pretensions. 'I do like to see the trimming pulled off such Christmas candles,' as one of the Casterbridge women remarks.

This helps us to understand Hardy's instinctive sympathy when Henchard staggers on to the scene, half-drunk, shabbily dressed, and waving his home-made Union Jack at the Illustrious Personage. For what Henchard desperately needs is some sort of recognition of his own importance, and this is coldly refused him by Farfrae and Lucetta. 'She has supplicated to me in her time, and now her tongue won't own me or her eyes see me!' When Farfrae pushes him out of the way of the royal carriage 'he could hardly realize such an outrage from one whom it had once been his wont to treat with ardent generosity'. Farfrae is shocked that Henchard should have 'insulted Royalty', whereas Henchard is concerned with the much deeper human outrage against his feelings from the people he has loved. 'Royalty be damned', as he says. This is what leads to his crazy assault on Farfrae, with one arm tied 'to take no advantage'. But it is obvious that he will never be able to kill him; when Farfrae appears, singing a song about *friendship*, he weakens: 'Nothing moved Henchard like an old melody. He sank back. "No; I can't do it!" he gasped. "Why does the infernal fool begin that now?"' And afterwards, when he has Farfrae in his power:

> Henchard looked down upon him in silence, and their eyes met. 'O Farfrae! – that's not true!' he said bitterly. 'God is my witness that no man ever loved another as I did thee at one time . . . And now – though I came here to kill 'ee, I cannot hurt thee. Go and give me in charge – do what you will – I care nothing for what comes of me!'
>
> (Ch. 38)

It is the events of this day and the next night and morning which at last bring about a moral crisis in Henchard. Up till now he has constantly been wavering between the best and the worst in his own nature; threatening to ruin Lucetta, and then finding that after all he can't do it; rejecting Elizabeth-Jane, and then softening. After he has threatened to kill Farfrae, he has one of these violent revulsions of feeling and tries to bring him back to see Lucetta before it is too late. But nobody will believe him now, and Lucetta dies:

> Besides the watchman who called the hours and weather in Casterbridge that night there walked a figure up and down Corn Street hardly less frequently. It was Henchard's, whose retiring to rest had proved itself a futility as soon as attempted; and he gave it up to go hither and thither, and make inquiries about the patient every now and then. He called as much on Farfrae's account as on Lucetta's, and on Elizabeth-Jane's even more than on either's. Shorn one by one of all other interests, his life seemed centring on the personality of the stepdaughter whose presence but recently he could not endure. To see her on each occasion of his inquiry at Lucetta's was a comfort to him.
>
> The last of his calls was made about four o'clock in the morning, in the steely light of dawn. Lucifer was fading into day across Durnover Moor, the sparrows were just alighting into the street, and the hens had begun to cackle from the outhouses. When within a few yards of Farfrae's he saw the door gently opened, and a servant raise her hand to the knocker, to untie the piece of cloth which had muffled it. He went across, the sparrows in his way scarcely flying up from the road-litter, so little did they believe in human aggression at so early a time.
>
> 'Why do you take off that?' said Henchard.
>
> She turned in some surprise at his presence, and did not

answer for an instant or two. Recognising him, she said, 'Because they may knock as loud as they will; she will never hear it any more.'

(Ch. 40)

This marvellous passage shows the beginning of a profound change in Henchard. Lucetta has faded out of life, almost as swiftly and silently as Susan did earlier; Farfrae is hopelessly alienated, and Elizabeth is the only channel for his affection, though this may not last, as her real father wants her back. It is after he has told his futile lie to Newson that he goes out to drown himself in Ten Hatches Weir. Then it seems as if an 'appalling miracle' has been worked to save him; he sees his own effigy floating in the water and this shocks him out of his plan, although it is only an accident:

Despite this natural solution of the mystery Henchard no less regarded it as an intervention that the figure should have been floating there. Elizabeth-Jane heard him say, 'Who is such a reprobate as I? And yet it seems that even I be in Somebody's hand!'

(Ch. 41)

Of course, as Hardy says, this is not the real answer: 'The emotional conviction that he was in Somebody's hand began to die out of Henchard's breast as time slowly removed into distance the event which had given that feeling birth'. It is human, not divine love which Henchard wants, and he gets this for a short time and in a watered down form from Elizabeth-Jane. It cannot be more than that, for he has 'frozen up her precious affection when originally offered'. Economically things improve for him; his little seed and root shop is making a profit. But he doesn't want the shop without Elizabeth, and when he knows that she is about to find him out he leaves Casterbridge, dressed in working clothes as he was when he came there 'for the first time nearly a quarter of a century before'. Yet even after that he cannot keep far away from Elizabeth: 'O you fool! All this about a daughter who is no daughter of thine!'

At the same time that he has become conscious of his love for a girl who is, strictly speaking, nothing to him, he has lost his ambition. The world has become a 'mere painted scene to him', one he would not be sorry to leave:

Very often, as his hay-knife crunched down among the sweet-smelling grassy stems, he would survey mankind and say to himself: 'Here and everywhere be folk dying before their time like frosted leaves, though wanted by their families, the country, and the world; while I, an outcast, an encumberer of the ground, wanted by nobody, and despised by all, live on against my will!'

(Ch. 44)

Hardy is here using the traditional biblical images of leaves and grass to express the vulnerability of human beings. Henchard is reaping the grass before its time, and death, too, has been visualized throughout the centuries as a Reaper who cuts off human lives in the same meaningless way. Henchard feels that he cannot die, because of the irony of things. But he does die before his time, and without any obvious reason: perhaps the truth is that he dies of a broken heart. When he comes back for Elizabeth's wedding he is made to feel, more than ever, that he is not wanted. Just as she and Farfrae once looked in from the outside at him, when he was the Mayor of Casterbridge and presided at dinners in the King's Arms, so he is now the outsider looking in at them. Elizabeth's cold words are all he needs. Frozen out of Casterbridge, he goes out on to Egdon Heath, 'that ancient country whose surface never had been stirred to a finger's depth, save by the scratchings of rabbits, since brushed by the feet of the earliest tribes'. Once he is cut off from civilization, he dies.

Throughout the novel Hardy seems to be making the point that the only way to live in a community is not to ask for too much from it. Farfrae and Elizabeth-Jane can be happy because they have the knack of 'making limited opportunities endurable', through 'the cunning enlargement of those minute forms of satisfaction that offer themselves to everybody not in positive pain'; Henchard dies because he has no idea how to do this. Yet the community which elects Farfrae as Mayor seems, like Farfrae himself, cold and narrow. In the end, the most compassionate person in Casterbridge is not Elizabeth but a half-witted labourer, Abel Whittle, and the way in which he cares for Henchard in the last days of his life shows up, though he doesn't know it, Elizabeth's moral failure.

Hardy constantly stresses that man, like the leaves and grass, has only a short time on earth, and that everything he has worked for can be destroyed in a moment. In a cancelled passage, he shows the dying Mrs Henchard sitting in an avenue of trees on an autumn day, and talking to Lucetta.

Old Solomon Longways, with a long white wooden rake, was scraping together the yellow, brown, and green leaves which had fallen, and heaping them into a deep wheelbarrow; they were insinuating visitors, those autumn leaves, sailing down the air into chimneys, green-houses, and roof gutters, even finding their way in some mysterious manner, as far as the Town Pump . . .

Upon her shoulders, as upon his wife's, an occasional red leaf rested as it floated down.

The leaves symbolize the fragility of Mrs Henchard's life, even though they are real leaves, and realistically observed. And Henchard's commercial empire is equally fragile.

Afterwards she was passing by the corn-stores and haybarns which had been the headquarters of his business. She knew that he ruled there no longer; but it was with amazement that she regarded the familiar gateway. A smear of decisive lead-coloured paint had been laid on to obliterate Henchard's name, though its letters dimly loomed through like ships in a fog. Over these, in fresh white, spread the name of Farfrae.

(Ch. 31)

The same theme of the blotting out of names is taken up again in Chapter 33, when Henchard makes the choir sing a psalm aimed at Farfrae:

> A swift destruction soon shall seize
> On his unhappy race;
> And the next age his hated name
> Shall utterly deface.

This is adapted from the Authorised Version: 'Let his posterity be cut off; and in the generation following let their name be blotted out' (Psalm 109:13). It is exactly what happens to Henchard, for he leaves no posterity and his last wish is that his own name shall be forgotten:

'That Elizabeth-Jane Farfrae be not told of my death, or made to grieve on account of me.
'& that I be not bury'd in consecrated ground.
'& that no sexton be asked to toll the bell.
'& that nobody is wished to see my dead body.
'& that no murners walk behind me at my funeral.
'& that no flours be planted on my grave.
'& that no man remember me.'

(Ch. 45)

In this Last Will and Testament, Henchard clearly rejects the pomp and ceremony which surround a mayor's funeral. And in doing this, he also rejects the ambition to which he has given twenty years of his life. In a world where life is necessarily short, and which is dominated by the values of industrial capitalism, Hardy suggests that the one thing which really matters is solidarity between people. Henchard knows that it is not enough to be a property owner,

Justice of the Peace, and Mayor of Casterbridge; morally he is a changed man when he dies. And, strangely enough, the sailor's bastard daughter becomes the wife of the next Mayor. Elizabeth, narrow and rather prudish in the beginning, has also learned a good deal by the end of the novel, and it is only because of this, Hardy feels, that she has the right to be happy. For, in the future, she will be more compassionate than she was to Henchard. 'Her strong sense that neither she nor any human being deserved less than was given, did not blind her to the fact that there were others receiving less who had deserved much more.'

6 The short stories and *The Dynasts*

Short stories

During his career as a novelist Hardy wrote around fifty short stories, the best of which are collected in *Wessex Tales* (1888) and *Life's Little Ironies* (1894). Although they have generally been overlooked in favour of his longer work, some are superb. A few ('Fellow-Townsmen') read like a miniature Hardy novel; others ('The Three Strangers' is the best example) perform the story-teller's traditional function, to highlight a memorable or striking event.

'Memorable' and 'striking' are the key words. Hardy insisted – referring to Coleridge's ballad, 'The Ancient Mariner' – that:

> a story must be exceptional enough to justify its telling. We tale-tellers are all Ancient Mariners, and none of us is warranted in stopping Wedding Guests (in other words, the hurrying public) unless he has something more unusual to relate than the ordinary experience of every average man and woman. The whole secret of fiction and the drama – in the constructional part – lies in the adjustment of things unusual to things eternal and universal. The writer who knows how exceptional, and how non-exceptional, his events should be made, possesses the key to the art.
>
> (*Life*, p. 252)

Some stories, we shall see, are based on fact, and it is tempting to relate others to Hardy's experiences. 'An Imaginative Woman' (1893), not one of the better ones, contains some revealing stuff about young writers who try to get their poetry published and who wince under bad reviews. Again, we may suspect that the wife in 'Fellow-Townsmen', socially superior to her husband and the townspeople but impossible to live with, has something in common with Emma. But there is no doubt that one of the earliest stories, 'The Distracted Preacher' (1879) is not only partly true but is affected by the fact that Hardy's family had been involved in smuggling.

This fact colours his sympathies. Lizzy, the female smuggler, and the Nonconformist minister Stockdale who is in love with her, are convincing examples of two people who are attracted but whose values are incompatible. Stockdale takes the view that the law, even if it is an ass, must be obeyed. But Lizzy argues with conviction that she and her friends have done nothing wrong (the brandy is paid for and there is no serious violence), 'and if a king who is nothing to us sends his people to steal our property, we have a right to steal it back again'. Later she reveals that she and her mother must smuggle to survive:

> 'My conscience is clear. I know my mother, but the king I have never seen. His dues are nothing to me. But it is a great deal to me that my mother and I should live.'

This reminds us of Henchard's 'Royalty be damned'. Behind Lizzy is a whole community of cheerful smugglers who pit their wits against the system with some success, and are driven by hard poverty. The customs officer and the parson are isolated figures, and while the former soon gives up ('you may serve your government at too high a price'), Stockdale's religion will not let him compromise, and he and Lizzy are driven apart. Here as elsewhere Hardy suggests that the Church has failed to come to terms with the pressures of ordinary life.

The story strongly suggests that Lizzy and the minister are incompatible. But Hardy wrote an unconvincing ending, in which Lizzy 'owns that we were wrong', saying thirty years later that this 'was almost *de rigueur* in an English magazine at the time'. The historical ending (the real Lizzy married a fellow smuggler) was, he said, the one he would have preferred.

'Fellow-Townsmen' (1880) is basically, like so many Hardy stories (including nearly all the Wessex Novels), about two people who fail to grasp their happiness when they have the chance. But it contains one moment of high moral tension (the episode most likely to stick in our minds) when the hero's wife has apparently been drowned. He knows that he can only marry the woman he loves if she is dead; moreover she has already been pronounced dead so neither the law nor public opinion could touch him if he allowed her to die. Nevertheless his conscience forces him to resuscitate her. Barnet is more refined than his friend Downe (who takes what he wants without much hesitation); he is also the last of a long-established family. Unlike his forebears (and like Hardy?) he does nothing that they would recognize as work and gradually drops out of the life of the town. Eventually he goes away for good, not knowing that Lucy would marry him if he made one more effort. The suggestion is that the man who is more sensitive than his fellows is unlikely to succeed in any area of life. It reminds us of Clym, Giles Winterborne, Angel Clare and Jude.

There is no shortage of the 'exceptional' in three of the finest stories, all written in the 1880s – 'The Three Strangers', 'The Withered Arm', and 'The Melancholy Hussar'. All of them powerfully involve the reader's feelings, for all are dominated by the death penalty and appeal to the deep human instinct which wants to see a hunted creature go free. Hardy, as has been noted, actually saw two hangings, one of which gave him the germ of the idea for *Tess*. He was also haunted by an execution which happened before he was born:

> My father saw four men hung for *being with* some others who had set fire to a rick. Among them was a stripling of a boy of eighteen. Skinny. Half-starved. So frail, so underfed, that they had to put weights on his feet to break his neck. He had not fired the rick. But with a youth's excitement he had rushed to the scene to see the blaze. . . . Nothing my father ever said to me drove the tragedy of Life so deeply into my mind.

The details reappear in two stories, 'The Withered Arm' and the shorter 'The Winters and the Palmleys'. Hardy never formally condemned capital punishment, but invariably, in his imaginative work, he takes the victim's side.

'The Three Strangers' (1883) opens with a modest celebration in a shepherd's hut the night before a hanging. Tension mounts as the party is joined first by the hangman's intended victim and then by the hangman himself. These facts are not given to us at once and, like the partygoers, we are misled when the third stranger (who turns out to be the victim's brother) appears and then runs away. But although the surprise ending has a great impact, the story is not to be discarded like the average detective novel once we know the plot. It is strong enough to bear repeated re-readings.

Like the church-going smugglers in 'The Distracted Preacher' this community, on the surface, behaves correctly, joining in the hunt for the condemned man when they are forced. But instinctively they recoil from the hangman and turn a blind eye to let the fugitive escape. We are reminded that he has broken the law only to feed his family and has shown 'marvellous coolness and daring' (like Lizzy). As in the earlier story, the legal establishment is contrasted unfavourably with, and defeated by, the natural morality of the poor.

A hanging provides a devastating climax to 'The Withered Arm' (1888). But this long story has several other themes, including the double standard, and class. There is a social gulf between Farmer Lodge and the woman and child he has abandoned. Farmers are often oppressive figures in the Wessex novels (Groby in *Tess*, Troutham in *Jude*) and although he has a change of heart at the end, Lodge for most of the time is a selfish man. While he is a gentleman, Rhoda and her son are labourers, they live in a mud hut and eke out their food by poaching, and the son is eventually hanged for taking part in an agricultural riot.

There is also a gulf between the expectations of men and women. At the beginning of the story Lodge is about forty, Rhoda thirty (and already 'fading'), Gertrude nineteen. The chosen and the rejected woman, married lady of leisure and unmarried working mother, appear to occupy different worlds. Rhoda is maddened when she dreams of Gertrude flaunting her wedding ring. But as Gertrude's looks fade, so does her husband's love, and we realize that they are both victims of the same man. For a time it looks as if they could be friends, but in their situation this is impossible. The final break (Rhoda calling her 'Hussy') comes when we realize that Gertrude has tried to benefit from the death of Rhoda's child. This is another shattering, unexpected ending.

The story is realistic and yet hinges on Rhoda having cast an evil spell on Gertrude, a phenomenon that seems grotesque. This worried Leslie Stephen; 'Either I would accept the superstition altogether and make the wizard a genuine performer . . . or I would leave some opening as to the withering of the arm, so that a possibility of explanation might be suggested'. But Hardy maintained that 'a story dealing with the supernatural should never be explained away'.

What he is saying is not that witchcraft exists, but that evil actions have unforeseeable results. The evil in Lodge's treatment of Rhoda and her child has somehow to work its way out; in realistic terms (the boy is neglected and comes to a bad end) and also non-realistic (his childless marriage, his wife's withered arm). Gertrude has 'longed for the death of a fellow-creature'. This is understandable but it is still evil and it rebounds on her; her blood is 'turned' too far and she dies.

The withered arm is not the only mysterious physical phenomenon in this story. Gertrude dies, apparently, of pure shock; Farmer Lodge committed suicide in the original script but Hardy altered this to death from 'a painless decline'. They would seem to be destroyed by guilt for their indirect share in the young man's unnatural death. Knowing as we now do that there is a real relationship between the health of mind and body (recall John South in *The Woodlanders*), we need not think 'The Withered Arm' is utterly fantastic.

'The Melancholy Hussar' (1890) is another story which climaxes in an execution. As Hardy indicates on the last page, it really happened; the two young desserters were victims of the European wars just as Rhoda's son is a victim of agricultural poverty and riot.

Phyllis is a victim too, of a society which will not let her move about or choose a husband freely.

Like Barnet in 'Fellow-Townsmen' (but this story is much more painful) the two lovers are too idealistic to seize what they want and are united only in death. The hussar is 'virtuous and kind; he treated her with a respect to which she had never before been accustomed', and certainly Hardy does not feel that he was wrong to desert. Phyllis believes she has done wrong by breaking social conventions, but again, Hardy clearly does not. The bitterest irony is that she sacrifices herself because of her promise to Humphrey Gould, who has had no qualms about breaking his promise to her. It is obviously the Humphreys of this world who live and thrive; again, as we are told in *Jude*, the selfish come off best.

'A Tragedy of Two Ambitions' (1888) hinges on the two brothers' decision to let their father drown because they feel, with some justification, that he is ruining their lives. The drowning, like the one in 'Fellow-Townsmen' (where again there is a choice between doing nothing and making positive efforts to save a life), is a moral test. But while Barnet's decision prevented him from being completely happy, the Halboroughs's opposite choice will haunt them all their lives. The story is told in such a way that we can sympathize with them, especially as they are more concerned for their sister than themselves. But in the end it looks as if the secret will drive them to suicide and that Rosa will be damaged too. Hardy does not condone what he called elsewhere 'a cold blooded murder'.

Like *Jude*, the novel he was planning at the time, 'A Tragedy of Two Ambitions' is about the established church and about class. Like the young Hardy, the brothers have had to abandon their dream of going to university and are studying the classics in their spare time with the idea of going into the church. Unlike him, they take the final step and become clergymen. In a well-known passage, Joshua says bitterly that Christianity is the least important thing for a cleric and that what matters is to appear a 'gentleman'. To do this the Halboroughs must conceal embarrassing facts about themselves, as Hardy has been accused of doing, and they are also aware of the importance of marriage (their sister's) as a means of rising in the world. The cruel and rigid class barriers are real ones (Rosa's future husband discusses them quite coolly, saying 'Her lack of influential connections limits her ambition'), and if they had not existed there would have been no murder. Joshua eventually feels that he would have done better not to get caught up in the system, 'A social regenerator has a better chance outside. . . . I would rather have gone on mending mills, with my crust of bread and liberty'. ('To Please his Wife', written in 1891, has the theme of a woman who destroys her family by her ambition.)

Like this story, 'Barbara of the House of Grebe' (1890) and 'The Son's Veto' (1891) are dominated by class, and also by a woman's weakness. 'Barbara' is memorable and horrific. Many critics have attacked it for its depiction of sadism ('man's inhumanity to woman', as Hardy called it), and it certainly is not pleasant to read. Yet as sadism does exist, particularly within the home, it is difficult to see why Hardy should be blamed for recognizing the fact.

The tragedy happens because Barbara's husband is not considered good enough for her and is sent abroad to be made more presentable. Worse still, she has internalized her parents' prejudices and 'admitted to herself that a man whose ancestor had run scores of Saracens through and through in fighting for the site of the Holy Sepulchre was a more desirable husband, socially considered, than one who could only claim with certainty to know that his father and grandfather were respectable burgesses'. The image suggests that the aristocracy are only good for fighting, and for an object – the Holy Sepulchre with its connotations of death and superstition – which Hardy certainly does not value.

Lord Uplandtowers, whose ancestors distinguished themselves in this way, is probably the most evil character in Hardy's fiction. Yet Barbara, a 'tender but somewhat shallow lady', has a 'sweet-pea' nature which makes her neurotically dependent on her husband – 'obsequious amativeness towards a perverse and cruel man'. It is because she cannot take on adult responsibilities – such as standing by her first husband when he is injured, or refusing to be bullied by her second husband – that she is destroyed. Other Hardy women, like Grace Melbury and Sue, show the same kind of weakness, and still others, like Lucetta in *The Mayor of Casterbridge*, die because they have not the strength to live.

'The Son's Veto' is the story which Hardy considered his best. Like 'A Tragedy of Two Ambitions', it is written in the shadow of *Jude*; class barriers and the established church, which are inextricably connected, press cruelly on ordinary people. We should be in no doubt that these barriers were real ones. The Reverend Mr Twycott has 'committed social suicide' by marrying Sophy, despite her 'spotless character'. Their son is educated to be a replica of his father and learns to despise his mother; we first see him correcting her grammar (like Henchard with Elizabeth-Jane) and he goes on to become one of the public school young men who, in *Jude*, have taken over the university. Because he is so much better educated than Sophy and believes in his natural right to rule she is utterly intimidated.

Sophy's involvement with the vicar, when she could have married a man of her own age and background, has all sorts of evil results. It is through being a servant in his house that she suffers the injury which cripples her. Through the imagery he uses, Hardy gives us clearly to understand that the marriage is unnatural. The ill-suited couple have to move to London, 'abandoning their pretty country home, with trees and shrubs and glebe, for a narrow dusty house in a long, straight street'. Sophy's 'apple cheeks' (this sounds like a cliché but the apple is a universal symbol of natural goodness) wane 'to pink of the very faintest'. Her artificial situation, as a widow kept from too much contact with her child, is expressed through her wasting hours in elaborately braiding her hair.

The market-gardener Sam, who brings 'fresh green-stuff' to London, stands for an entirely different set of values. The vegetables on his cart are described almost lyrically, 'green bastions of cabbages . . . masses of beans and peas . . . pyramids of snow-white turnips'. He even seems to bring fine weather into the city; when Sophy is alone we hear only of the 'feeble sun', but when she rides with him to Covent Garden 'the air was fresh as country air at this hour, and the stars shone'. Sophy is almost cured by his sympathetic presence and the reminiscences of her old life; at first 'depression and nervousness' stop her sleeping, but after the surreptitious ride 'her cheeks were quite pink – almost beautiful'.

All this – the lovers meeting before dawn, food being brought to London, the goodness of farm produce – is very reminiscent of the Talbothays scenes in *Tess*. Well before Lawrence, Hardy was aware of man's need to keep in touch with the natural world and his own instincts. His cure for 'the chronic melancholy which is taking hold of the civilized races' (*Tess*) is constructive work, preferably on the land. The healthy cabbages and turnips have the same function as the city-dweller's box of geraniums; contact with growing things, in any form, is therapeutic. Hardy may well have been remembering how his own years in London damaged his health and how 'residence in or near a city tended to force mechanical and ordinary productions from his pen'.

The natural affection between Sophy and Sam is contrasted with Randolph's perversion of Christianity, culminating in the medieval-type scene where he makes her kneel and swear to give up what could have been 'an idyllic life'. She is too overawed by him to refuse or to break the oath once sworn, and eventually dies. Like the much more intelligent Sue Bridehead, she is completely broken, and religion plays a part in this.

Religion, though, is less important than class. Randolph has lost the natural sympathies he was born with and becomes like Angel Clare's brothers, interested in only 'a few thousand wealthy and titled people'. To Hardy, these artificial barriers spelled death, and 'The Son's Veto' is a moving attack on the system and a statement of solidarity with ordinary people, who seem helpless to fight it.

There remains 'The Fiddler of the Reels' (1893), which many consider Hardy's best short story. It is certainly quite different from the rest. Beginning with the Great Exhibition of 1851, the big event of his childhood, it ranges over forty years and is dominated by a sense of history. Old and new are continually set side by side – walking from Dorset to London with excursion-trains, staying in one place all one's life with emigration to America, a settled community with a man from nowhere. The final sentence reminds us that the young grow old. But it is part of Mop's glamour that we never see him ageing; instead, in true Romantic tradition, he disappears.

Mop belongs to a time just after the village musicians, whose passing was described regretfully by Hardy in *Under the Greenwood Tree*. While the choir held a balance between sacred and secular, Mop plays only 'devil's tunes'. Having been to several 'wedding-randies' as a child with his violinist father, Hardy knew all about the erotic effects of music. He relates in 'The History of the Hardcomes' how two couples choose the wrong partners 'under the hot excitement of that evening's dancing', and in this story he shows how Mop's presence and playing reduces the weak and silly Car'line to hysteria.

Mop is a curiously modern figure, reminding us of the pop star with his luxuriant 'mop' of hair who dominates a screaming, and largely female crowd. We are told that he is repellent to men but fascinating to women, making them do things which they afterwards regret. Possibly he owes something to the figure of Byron, who dominated the popular imagination for most of the nineteenth century, and who was renowned for his effect on women and for cruelly taking away his mistress's child. He inhabits a world of intense emotions, impulsive action, unfulfilled genius – everything which is opposed to common sense and a quiet life.

The story of Car'line and her husband Ned demonstrates how lives can be laid waste by the demonic forces which Mop summons up. Car'line achieves a modest degree of happiness – by the standards of her time, she is lucky to get it. But the bond is a weak one, kept in being by Ned's affection for the child and her desire for a home. It has no chance against the wild ecstasy and 'blissful torture' of the dance. This respectable married woman, who wanted to impress her neighbours, ends up drunk, senseless on the floor and incapable of protecting her child (who apparently yields to Mop's fascination like everyone else).

'She thus continued to dance alone, defiantly as she thought, but in truth slavishly and abjectly', Hardy writes. This makes it clear that he is not treating the theme in the same way as Lawrence, who would certainly have admired her and the fiddler for giving way to their instincts and perhaps made them go off together. Hardy is clear that Car'line is a woman who has failed to grow up. Moreover, the rational man in him distrusted everything about Mop – his aversion to work, his casual treatment of others – and he describes him with cool detachment. His oily hair and half-closed eyes make him 'come across' vividly, but do not sound attractive. Yet, unlike some Victorians, Hardy fully recognised the power of desire and instinct. Sometimes, as in 'The Son's Veto', he feels that instincts are a good guide to action and that it is unwise to suppress them. At other times they clearly bring disaster.

It is his neutral attitude which makes 'The Fiddler of the Reels' so impressive. Mop is bad but fascinating, Ned good but perhaps not a satisfactory husband, and our feelings for Car'line must be a mixture of sympathy and impatience. In the end, we are left with a mystery. Mop and the child disappear, the onlookers make cynical remarks, and Hardy feels no need to tell us the ultimate fate of the characters. It is a typically twentieth-century, 'open' ending. Yet we feel that it is a rather better story than others in which his emotions are more obviously involved.

The Dynasts

The Dynasts is the great white elephant of Hardy studies. He spent far more time on it than on any other creative work; compared to earlier publications, it was received respectfully, and he seems to have thought it was his finest achievement (the young poets who admired him and who had been through the Great War certainly did). Yet few people have read it, those who have, agree that much of it is poor and it is unlikely ever to become popular.

The Victorians had an idea that the very long or 'epic' poem was the highest art-form. They revered Milton's *Paradise Lost* (which came under attack from Eliot a few generations later), and Tennyson's *Idylls of the King* was among the most famous of many book-length works dealing with a 'great' subject in blank verse. Hardy comes almost at the end of this tradition. Today when any poem over fifty lines is called long, a poem of five hundred pages is too much for most readers to face.

Not that *The Dynasts* is all poetry. It is a drama in three parts, nineteen acts and one hundred and thirty scenes, mostly in blank verse but containing prose conversations (as in Shakespeare), lengthy stage-directions, some of which are remarkable pieces of writing, and several 'choruses' in rhyming verse. It is in these choruses that we find the best poetry. Hardy said that it was 'intended simply for mental performance', although an abridged version was performed in his lifetime, and it has also been broadcast. Apparently, both experiments worked well.

The subject is the vast upheavals in Europe in the early years of the nineteenth century, beginning with England's decision to go to war against Napoleon and ending with the battle of Waterloo. Historically, these wars were very close to Hardy, as the First or Second World War (according to our age) might be to us. He did not remember them himself but he had talked to old men who had fought in them, and nothing of equal magnitude had happened in his own time. They would have seemed like a heroic age still in the recent past. There was also a local connection; George III and his ministers had been at Weymouth in the summer of 1801, there had been rumours that the French were about to invade Dorset and preparations to fight them, and he liked to think that he was related to Nelson's friend, Admiral Hardy, who appears in Part First.

Other great novelists of the nineteenth century had brooded on the significance of Napoleon, notably Stendhal, Dostoevsky and Tolstoy (occasionally we have the uneasy feeling that Hardy is adapting a scene from *War and Peace*). Like Tolstoy, Hardy eventually comes down against Napoleon, not only because his country, district and family had been on the other side but also because he thought that the Emperor was willing to sacrifice any number of lives. Therefore he stresses England's role in his downfall and shows some sympathy for those like Nelson, Pitt and Wellington who had actually fought him. But he has no liking for the anti-Napoleonic 'dynasties' – Russia, the Holy Roman Empire, the Bourbons – and constantly stresses the horror and waste of war. His attitude was much the same as it would be when he had a friendly meeting with German prisoners of war in 1917, '. . . it does fill one with indignation that thousands of such are led to slaughter by the ambitions of Courts and Dynasties'.

Following Tolstoy, he sees Napoleon as a man of no great importance in himself, as a puppet of history:

> You'll mark the twitchings of this Bonaparte
> As he with other figures foots his reel,
> Until he twitch him into his lonely grave
>> (Part 1, Fore Scene)

He is known to the English by the reductive name 'Boney'; his figure when he takes the historic decision to invade Russia is 'diminished to the aspect of a doll'. But while Tolstoy's emperor is dwarfed by the extremely vivid, complex characters who fill the foreground of the novel, Hardy's Napoleon, though on stage a lot of the time, never really comes to life and is surrounded by hordes of minor figures with no more personality than himself. Compared to any of the novels which Hardy had now stopped writing, the characters are uninteresting and flat.

125

This is partly because he felt that they were merely playing the parts laid down for them and that individual personalities counted for little. Behind the human actors (the Tsar, Napoleon and his wives, ordinary people of Dorset) is a chorus of Spirits who comment on the events as they unfold. This seems strange to moderns but is derived from the Greek plays he had studied as a young man, and educated readers would have found it natural. It includes the 'Ancient Spirit of the Years' or force of history, spirits of the earth and of rumour, and – most interesting – the Spirit of the Pities and Spirits Sinister and Ironic.

The senior spirit and his chorus explain that cataclysmic events are caused not by humans but by the 'Immanent Will' or life force working blindly:

> The Immanent, that urgeth all,
> Rules what may or may not befall!
>
> Ere systemed suns were globed and lit
> The slaughters of the race were writ,
>
> And wasting wars, by land and sea,
> Fixed, like all else, immutably!

(Part I, V. ii)

To this the Spirit Sinister replies, 'War makes rattling good history; but Peace is poor reading. So I back Bonaparte'. He and the Spirit of the Pities, while remaining total opposites, comment on the events from a human perspective:

> CHORUS OF THE PITIES:
> Each for himself, his family, his heirs;
> For the wan weltering nations who concerns, who cares?
> CHORUS OF IRONIC SPIRITS:
> A pertinent query, in truth! –
> But spoil not the sport by your ruth:
> 'Tis enough to make half
> Yonder zodiac laugh
> When rulers begin to allude
> To their lack of ambition,
> And strong opposition
> To all but the general good!

(Part I, VI. v)

Hardy obviously has much in common with the Spirit of the Pities, who continually mourns the slaughter and questions the need for it. But the Sinister and Ironic Spirit speaks for another side of him. He appears to enjoy war; he is not at all unlike the Hardy who appreciated life's little ironies, including grim ones. But his real function is to point out the meanness and cynicism of the men who think they are titans when in fact, like Shelley's Ozymandias, they are instantly forgettable.

Napoleon bestowing crowns on his family is one example of human vaingloriousness – 'ephemeral at the best all honours be'. Another is the parade of emperors and kings at the London opera, who bow without knowing why – 'we were supposed to rise to the repeated applause of the people'. Then there is the Prince Regent with his two wives and the mad King George who is baffled when informed that he has won a 'glorious victory':

> He says I have won a battle? But I thought
> I was a poor afflicted captive here,
> In darkness lingering out my lonely days.
>
> (Part 2, VI. v)

As in *King Lear*, it is the madman who is intermittently sane. Most striking is the story of Napoleon's marriage in Part Second. This looks like costume drama, but it happens to illustrate Hardy's point particularly well because royal women, notoriously, are not allowed to display any human personality. Napoleon divorces his wife Josephine because she fails to bear him an heir. His new choice is Marie Louise of Austria, a young girl who has been taught to think of him as the arch-enemy but is now told that he is to be her husband. There is a pretence of letting her make up her own mind but, as Metternich notes cynically, 'what she must do she will; nought else at all'. Their marriage is celebrated with a crude street-ballad, 'First 'twas a finished coquette/ And now it's a raw ingenue/ Blonde instead of brunette/ An old wife doffed for a new', and the expected baby soon appears. The girl is allowed one brief protest, 'Why should I be tortured even if I am but a means to an end?', but this is drowned in a chorus of thanksgiving, with Napoleon's son hailed as the new Messiah. The Ironic Spirits comment in a biting little poem which is one of the high points of the drama:

> The Will Itself is slave to him,
> And holds it blissful to obey! –
> He said, 'Go to, it is my whim
>
> 'To bed a bride without delay,
> Who shall unite my dull new name
> With one that shone in Caesar's day.
>
> 'She must conceive – you hear my claim? –
> And bear a son – no daughter, mind –
> Who shall hand on my form and fame

> 'To future times as I have designed;
> And at the birth throughout the land
> Must cannon roar and alp-horns wind!'
>
> The Will grew conscious at command,
> And ordered issue as he planned.
>
> (Part 2, VI. iii)

Hardy does not overdo the irony by noting that the long-awaited son never achieved anything (a point made by Shakespeare at the end of *Henry V*, about Henry VI). He merely reports, deadpan, how the normal event of a healthy young woman giving birth is greeted with hysteria because the child's father is Napoleon, who is arrogant enough to think he can command 'the Will'. By Part Third everything has changed; Marie Louise has gone back to her family and the child is not 'going to trouble us much'. Marriages and military alliances form and dissolve with bewildering speed, as in Orwell's *Nineteen Eighty-Four* (1949). The thoughtful observer can only record the cynicism.

The Dynasts' subject is a grand one. Yet it is generally agreed that its language, with a few exceptions, is commonplace and uninspiring. Hardy's prose passages, in which he describes the convulsions from a great height, have often been admired. One is the picture of Europe as 'a prone and emaciated figure, the Alps shaping like a backbone, and the branching mountain-chains like ribs. . . . The peoples, distressed by events which they did not cause, are seen writhing, crawling, heaving, and vibrating in their various cities and nationalities'. Another, which repeats the insect-imagery, is the description of Napoleon's retreat from Russia:

> The caterpillar shape still creeps laboriously nearer, but instead of increasing in size by the rules of perspective, it gets more attenuated. . . . Pines rise mournfully on each side of the nearing object; ravens in flocks advance with its overhead, waiting to pick out the eyes of strays who fall. The snowstorm increases, descending in tufts which can hardly be shaken off. The sky seems to join itself to the land. The marching figures drop rapidly, and almost immediately become white grave-mounds.
>
> (Part 3, I. ix)

Coming from a man who had never been in an aeroplane or seen a moving picture, these are remarkable; if Hardy had watched the colour films and TV wars of our own day they would no doubt have inspired good poems. But the greater part of *The Dynasts* is written in 'Shakespearean' blank verse, which, in most people's hands, becomes lifeless. Here is a fairly typical example:

MINISTER:
Well; by the terms. There are among them these:
Five hundred thousand active men in arms
Shall strike (supported by Britannic aid
In vessels, men and money subsidies)
To free North Germany and Hanover
From trampling foes; deliver Switzerland,
Unbind the galled republic of the Dutch,
Rethrone in Piedmont the Sardinian King,
Make Naples sword-proof, un-French Italy
From shore to shore; and thoroughly guarantee
A settled order to the divers states;
Thus rearing breachless barriers in each realm
Against the thrust of his usurping hand.
SPIRIT OF THE YEARS:
They trow not what is shaping otherwhere
The while they talk thus stoutly!

(Part 1, I. v)

All the sonorous names do not convince us that we are in the presence of vast historical forces. The language is of no great interest (Hardy sometimes rewrote Parliamentary speeches in blank verse, and it shows) and the Spirit's 'ho ho, little do they know' comment nudges the reader too obviously. Then there is the unnecessary use of strange or archaic expressions, such as 'un-French', or 'trow'. There are great stretches of this sort of blank verse, which only comes to life occasionally, as in Captain Hardy's words to the dying Nelson:

Thoughts all confused, my lord: – their needs on deck,
Your own sad state, and your unrivalled past;
Mixed up with flashes of old things afar –
Old childish things at home, down Wessex way,
In the snug village under Blackdon Hill
Where I was born. The tumbling stream, the garden,
The placid look of the grey dial there,
Marking unconsciously this bloody hour,
And the red apples on my father's trees,
Just now full ripe.

(Part 1, V. iv)

It was the local details, such as the stream and apples, which stimulated Hardy's imagination, and the idea of calm normality going on at the same time as battles would inspire his poem 'In Time of "The Breaking of Nations"'. 'Marking unconsciously this bloody hour' is a great line; showing the clock to be an inanimate object on which men impose their own meanings. But *The Dynasts* only becomes great when Hardy stands at some distance from his characters and reflects on their place in the entire scheme of things.

It also looks as if he had no gift for blank verse, since a fine passage like this one is very unusual indeed. He needed the discipline of rhyme to write strong, effective poetry, like the lines on Napoleon's son. So we find that the passages from *The Dynasts* which we remember best tend to be the choruses, like the one before the battle of Waterloo which concentrates on the animals:

> The mole's tunnelled chambers are crushed by wheels,
> The lark's eggs scattered, their owners fled . . .
> The worm asks what can be overhead,
>
> And wriggles deep from a scene so grim,
> And guesses him safe; for he does not know
> What a foul red flood will be soaking him!

> (Part 3, VI. viii)

Hardy's fascination with animals, their vulnerability and ignorance of why men disrupt their world, gives rise to some of his best poetry. It is in the same tradition as John Clare's bird poems, and can be paralleled in our own time by Miroslav Holub's 'The Fly' and Richard Adams's 'Watership Down' (1972). Less well-known, but also good, is the Chorus of Pities in Part Second which comes over as a song of the dead. Hardy places his forgotten army on a marshy island, full of 'sour grasses' and 'strange fishy smells', where they are dying ingloriously of fever:

> We who withstood the blasting blaze of war
> When marshalled by the gallant Moore awhile,
> Beheld the grazing death-bolt with a smile,
> Closed combat edge to edge and bore to bore,
> Now rot upon this Isle!
>
> The ever wan morass, the dune, the blear
> Sandweed, and tepid pool, and putrid smell,
> Emaciate purpose to a fractious fear,
> Beckon the body to its last low cell –
> A chink no chart will tell.
>
> O ancient Delta, where the fen-lights flit!
> Ignoble sediment of loftier lands,
> Thy humour clings about our hearts and hands
> And solves us to its softness, till we sit
> As we were part of it.
>
> Such force as fever leaves is maddened now,
> With tidings trickling in from day to day

Of others' differing fortunes, wording how
They yield their lives to baulk a tyrant's sway –
Yield them not vainly, they!

In champaigns green and purple, far and near,
In town and thorpe where quiet spire-cocks turn,
Through vales, by rocks, beside the brooding burn
Echoes the aggressor's arrogant career;
And we pent pithless here!

Here, where each creeping day the creeping file
Draws past with shouldered comrades score on score,
Bearing them to their lightless last asile,
Where weary wave-wails from the clammy shore
Will reach their ears no more.

We might have fought, and had we died, died well,
Even if in dynasts' discords not our own;
Our death-spot some sad haunter might have shown,
Some tongue have asked our sires or sons to tell
The tale of how we fell;

But such bechanced not. Like the mist we fade,
No lustrous lines engrave in story we,
Our country's chiefs, for their own fames afraid,
Will leave our names and fates by this pale sea
To perish silently!

(Part 2, IV. viii)

Coming halfway through *The Dynasts*, this casts a cold shadow over what follows; evoking the underside of war, the multiple nameless, unpraised victims. Hardy's memories of the South African war (where more soldiers had died of fever than in battle), his liking for graveyards and his interest in obscure people and their place in history, combine to make this a memorable poem. It has a ghostly reality which the parliamentary debates and conclaves of kings do not possess.

7 Selected poems

'It is impossible to understand why the bulk of this volume was published at all,' wrote a reviewer of *Wessex Poems* in 1899. Having got used to Hardy the novelist, the public with its usual conservatism took a long time to come to terms with Hardy the poet. Today, though, his work is valued highly. Poets as different as Sassoon, Pound, Auden, Dylan Thomas, Graves and Larkin have all expressed deep admiration for him. 'There have been relatively few poet-novelists in English literature', wrote the editor of the 1960 Penguin Poets edition, '. . . the only authentic double-firsts in this field are, I believe, Hardy and D.H. Lawrence'.

Hardy himself commented in the *Life*, 'The change, after all, was not so great as it seemed. It was not as if he had been a writer of novels proper . . . that is, stories of modern artificial life and manners showing a certain smartness of treatment. He had mostly aimed at keeping his narratives close to natural life and as near to poetry in their subject as the conditions would allow.' A passage from his notebook says:

> Poetry. Perhaps I can express more fully in verse ideas and emotions which run counter to the inert crystallized opinion – hard as a rock – which the vast body of men have vested interests in supporting. To cry out in a passionate poem that (for instance) the Supreme Mover or Movers, the Prime Force or Forces, must be either limited in power, unknowing or cruel – which is obvious enough, and has been for centuries – will cause them merely a shake of the head; but to put it in argumentative prose will make them sneer, or foam, and set all the literary contortionists jumping upon me, a harmless agnostic, as if I were a clamorous atheist, which in their crass illiteracy they seem to think is the same thing. If Galileo had said in verse that the world moved, the Inquisition might have let him alone.
>
> (*Life*, p. 284)

Clearly, this is not the whole story. Yet it is true that poems cause less controversy than novels, partly because we do not confuse them with real life and partly because they are read by fewer people; Hardy was only able to devote himself to poetry after he had made enough money to retire. His readers were disappointed, and would have liked to see more Wessex novels. But he insisted for the rest of his life that he was primarily a poet.

Our own generation is well aware of his importance. Donald

Thomas Hardy in old age, photographed by Wheeler of Weymouth

Davie in *Thomas Hardy and British Poetry* (1973) wrote, 'In British poetry of the last fifty years . . . the most far-reaching influence, for good and ill, had been not Yeats, still less Eliot or Pound, not Lawrence, but *Hardy*'. Walford Davies describes him as 'the poet who most successfully relayed the native English tradition of the nineteenth century into the twentieth', influencing, for example, Philip Larkin and the poets of the Movement in which Davies himself was involved. His contemporaries thought him a 'prosaic' poet, compared with the enormously popular Tennyson. This was deliberate; 'for as long as I can remember,' he wrote in 1919, 'it has been my instinctive feeling to avoid the jewelled line in poetry, as being effeminate'. It was a welcome shift towards realism. But in the 1920s he was the one who seemed old-fashioned, as poets like Eliot (who was extremely and unreasonably hostile to him) became influential.

'I suppose I am too old to do it justice,' Hardy wrote to Amy Lowell about 'free verse', '. . . do you mind my saying that it too often seems a jumble of notes containing ideas striking, novel or beautiful as the case may be, which could be transfused into poetry, but which, as given, are not poetry?' 'Literature is getting too slovenly for words in these days of rhymeless, rhythmless poets', he complained during the war. And again:

> It is unfortunate for the cause of present-day poetry that a fashion for obscurity rages among young poets, so that much good verse is lost by the simple inability of readers to rack their brains to solve conundrums. They should remember Spencer's remark that the brain power spent in ascertaining a meaning is so much lost to its appreciation when ascertained.
>
> (Letter to Sydney Cockerell, 4th August 1918)

He would have been quite out of sympathy with Eliot's view that poetry in our time 'must be *difficult*'. As with his novels, he believed that readers could not be expected to spend time on him unless he took some trouble for them, a profoundly democratic attitude.

The war killed off a rising generation of poets: Edward Thomas (whose affinities with Hardy are obvious), Owen, Rosenberg, Sorley. There followed a sharp break with tradition and the domination of English poetry by the American Eliot, whom Hardy called 'a poet of the vers libre school'. Rhyme became unfashionable. Serious poetry became almost incomprehensible to the ordinary reader.

It is not necessary to agree with Hardy that 'vers libre', as he called rhymeless poetry, is suspect. But it is important to say that, for all his efforts to sound like an old fogey, the sensibility in his carefully-crafted, rhyming poetry is a modern one. Take 'Midnight on the Great Western', which is related to a scene in *Jude the Obscure*:

> In the third-class seat sat the journeying boy,
> And the roof-lamp's oily flame
> Played down on his listless form and face,
> Bewrapt past knowing to what he was going,
> Or whence he came.
>
> In the band of his hat the journeying boy
> Had a ticket stuck; and a string
> Around his neck bore the key of his box,
> That twinkled gleams of the lamp's sad beams
> Like a living thing.
>
> What past can be yours, O journeying boy
> Towards a world unknown,
> Who calmly, as if incurious quite
> On all at stake, can undertake
> This plunge alone?

Third-class seats, oil-lamps, hats, boxes – all these sound dated. But we immediately respond to the image of the child in transit between one unknown place and another (in our own day we would guess him to be travelling between estranged parents, and the boy in *Jude* is doing just that). The ideas of journeys, of rootlessness, of man being hurled towards an unpredictable destination, all strike profound chords with modern readers. Sue Bridehead describes the railway station as 'the centre of the town life now. The cathedral has had its day.' Time has moved on again since then, but the child's predicament remains universal although today he would probably be travelling by car or plane. He is a symbol of alienation.

This is just one poem, not among the greatest, which could be called, in Hardy's own words, a 'moment of vision'. Apart from *The Dynasts*, he left more than nine hundred, some written when he was very young and many others when he was over eighty. They range over several subjects and try out an extraordinary number of verse-forms. Some critics think that only about a dozen are among the greatest, others, like Philip Larkin, that all have some value. I have offered a cross-section of the most interesting.

Early Poems

Like most young poets, Hardy began by imitating other people. His earliest surviving piece, 'Domicilium', a description of his father's cottage, was written when he was sixteen in quite competent Wordsworthian blank verse. Other poems, including 'Shakespearean' sonnets, survive from his London years. But the first really amazing poem, probably turned down with the rest by magazine editors, was 'Neutral Tones'.

Neutral Tones

We stood by a pond that winter day,
And the sun was white, as though chidden of God,
And a few leaves lay on the starving sod;
 – They had fallen from an ash, and were gray.

Your eyes on me were as eyes that rove
Over tedious riddles of years ago;
And some words played between us to and fro
 On which lost the more by our love.

The smile on your mouth was the deadest thing
Alive enough to have strength to die;
And a grin of bitterness swept thereby
 Like an ominous bird a-wing . . .

Since then, keen lessons that life deceives,
And wrings with wrong, have shaped to me
Your face, and the God-curst sun, and a tree,
 And a pond edged with grayish leaves.

DATE 1867, but not published until thirty years afterwards.

STYLE This poem stands out from a mass of undistinguished early lyrics. The twenty-seven-year-old author handles rhyme expertly and his word-pictures in the first and last verses are stark and memorable. The slow movement of the lines creates an atmosphere of doom and some very ordinary images – pond, leaves, winter sun – somehow feel sinister. 'Ash' is a tree but also suggests dead, grey ashes; the sun is white and weak as if it had permanently exhausted its strength. The powerful word 'starving' for barren winter soil reinforces the impression of something that is alive, but only just. In many future poems and novels, Hardy will represent nature as 'neutral', indifferent to human suffering.

SUBJECT From the references to God having cursed the sun, we infer that the two actors in this scene have suffered a major disaster. The notorious *Providence and Mr Hardy* suggests that it describes the end of his relationship with Tryphena; more reliable writers think it was written in his London period. In fact we do not know who the woman was, nor if the pond was on Egdon Heath or somewhere else, and this does not greatly matter. The poem describes a love affair which has almost run its course, leaving bitterness and exhaustion, and we get the impression that this was not in 1867 but some years before. It is based on a very common experience; places, colours and objects which are associated with a painful event continue to depress us long after the worst of the pain has died. As George Eliot would write a few years later in *Middlemarch*, 'our moods are apt to bring with them images which succeed each other like the magic-lantern pictures of a doze; and in certain states of dull forlornness Dorothea all her life continued to see the vastness of St Peter's, the huge bronze canopy . . . and the red drapery which was being hung for Christmas spreading itself everywhere like a disease of the retina'.

The two middle verses (particularly the 'ominous bird a-wing') are less striking than the first and last. But it is clear that the young Hardy was already a poet of great power.

Standing by the Mantelpiece
(*H.M.M., 1873*)

This candle-wax is shaping to a shroud
Tonight. (They call it that, as you may know) –
By touching it the claimant is avowed,
And hence I press it with my finger – so.

Tonight. To me twice night, that should have been
The radiance of the midmost tick of noon,
And close around me wintertime is seen
That might have shone the veriest day of June!

But since all's lost, and nothing really lies
Above but shade, and shadier shade below,
Let me make clear, before one of us dies,
My mind to yours, just now embittered so.

Since you agreed, unurged and full-advised,
And let warmth grow without discouragement,
Why do you bear you now as if surprised,
When what has come was clearly consequent?

Since you have spoken, and finality
Closes around, and my last movements loom,
I say no more: the rest must wait till we
Are face to face again, yonside the tomb.

And let the candle-wax thus mould a shape
Whose meaning now, if hid before, you know,
And how by touch one present claims its drape,
And that it's I who press my finger – so.

DATE   Although obviously inspired by Horace Moule's suicide in 1873, this poem was not published until 1928, in the posthumous *Winter Words*. We have no way of knowing if it is an early work, held back for over fifty years for the sake of Moule's family, or if Hardy in old age was still creating poetry from an intense early experience. And that is just one of the mysteries.

STYLE   Whatever the date, the poem seems to belong with 'Neutral Tones', which is equally intense and doom-laden. Both are about a close relationship in which love and trust have gone sour. Moule is speaking, in the knowledge that he is soon to die, and the poem moves in a circle, the first and last verses using almost identical words shaped into different patterns. The tone is conversational ('as you may know'), but certain key-words are constantly repeated ('tonight', 'shade', 'know', 'so') giving the speech an obsessive quality. The images of wintertime and June, in the second verse, are hackneyed, but that of the candle is very powerful (it is worth reminding ourselves of the enormous symbolic importance of candles before the coming of electric light). Hardy apparently said that when he and Moule had their last conversation, in the room where he would kill himself three months later, Horace talked far into the night, 'standing by the mantelpiece', with the burned-out candle forming a 'shroud' behind him. Steeped in folklore as he was, he knew that this traditionally forecast a death. By touching it, the victim accepted his fate.

SUBJECT   The speaker is Moule, but who is the person addressed? One would naturally assume it to be Hardy, and the third and fourth verses suggest they quarrelled. But his own account of the visit to Cambridge states that it was a cheerful one. Perhaps the second person is (as one tradition says) the unnamed woman who had been engaged to Horace and who, his family had hoped, might save him. And how are we to interpret the phrases 'let warmth grow' and 'what has come'? *Providence and Mr Hardy* suggests that Moule had come between Hardy and Tryphena; Michael Millgate that he had made an unexpected and unwelcome homosexual approach to Hardy himself. The situation remains mysterious.

It is obvious, though, that the poem was written with hindsight; the precise sequence of events in it never took place. Hardy is weaving together his memories of their last meeting and his knowledge of what came afterwards (the 'meaning', 'hid before'). We shall not understand the poem without knowing the outlines of Horace Moule's story, but the details do not really matter. 'Standing by the Mantelpiece', like 'Neutral Tones', works through invoking deep feelings of guilt and loss.

Hardy's black period

During his years as a novelist Hardy went on writing poems, but few of them are among his greatest. In the black period which followed the publication of *Jude the Obscure* he turned exclusively to poetry again, and the bitterness of the years 1895–6 is crystallized in two of the longer poems, 'In Tenebris' and 'Wessex Heights'. The first of these is a group of three poems, apparently loosely related, but sharing a common feeling of pain, loneliness and deprivation.

In Tenebris

'Percussus sum sicut foenum, et aruit cor meum'.

Wintertime nighs;
But my bereavement-pain
It cannot bring again:
　Twice no one dies.

Flower-petals flee;
But, since it once hath been,
No more that severing scene
　Can harrow me.

Birds faint in dread:
I shall not lose old strength
In the lone frost's black length:
　Strength long since fled!

Leaves freeze to dun;
But friends can not turn cold
This season as of old
　For him with none.

Tempests may scath;
But love can not make smart
Again this year his heart
　Who no heart hath.

Black is night's cope;
But death will not appal
One who, past doubtings all,
　Waits in unhope.

DATE　This was probably written in 1895, but was not published until 1902.

STYLE　This is one of Hardy's most perfect lyrics, in spite of the fact that it is so dark in feeling. The very short lines emphasize the feeling of starkness (what could be more abrupt and factual than 'Wintertime nighs'?) which is powerfully brought home in the last line of each verse. Hardy seems to be raising a series of moderately hopeful images, only to dash them. He will not lose his strength or his friends because he no longer has any; he does not suffer from doubt because he has no hope. Each verse is a self-contained unit which goes through a dialectical process; nature is bleak; this does not frighten the poet, because, and here the shock comes, things are bleaker within his own soul.

IMAGERY 'In Tenebris' means 'in the darkness', and the Latin motto from Psalm 102 means, 'My heart is smitten, and withered like grass'. These images of darkness and of the death of nature are repeated all the way through the poem. Frost, and of course night, is 'black'; flowers and leaves die and birds 'faint in dread'. And, as argued in the chapter on *The Mayor of Casterbridge*, leaves and grass are a symbol of the frailty of human beings; Hardy tells us in the first verse that someone has died and the 'severing scene' in the next verse may be the same thing, or may refer to his estrangement from his wife.

CONCLUSION There seems to be no chink of hope in this poem, and indeed the climactic word 'unhope', one of the eccentric constructions which Hardy was fond of, deliberately rules it out. The speaker is only not suffering because his heart is dried up and he can suffer no more. But to print this poem in isolation, as is sometimes done, gives a wrong impression. It has to be seen as part of the whole cycle.

In Tenebris II

'Considerabam ad dexteram et videbam; et non erat qui cognosceret me.
Non est qui requirat animam meam.'

When the clouds' swoln bosoms echo back the shouts of the many and strong
That things are all as they best may be, save a few to be right ere long,
And my eyes have not the vision in them to discern what to these is so clear,
The blot seems straightway in me alone; one better he were not here.

The stout upstanders say, All's well with us: ruers have nought to rue!
And what the potent say so oft, can it fail to be somewhat true?

Breezily go they, breezily come; their dust smokes around their
    career,
Till I think I am one born out of due time, who has no calling here.

Their dawns bring lusty joys, it seems; their evenings all that is
    sweet;
Our times are blessed times, they cry: Life shapes it as is most
    meet,
And nothing is much the matter; there are many smiles to a tear;
Then what is the matter is I, I say, Why should such a one be
    here?

Let him in whose ears the low-voiced Best is killed by the clash of
    the First.
Who holds that if way to the Better there be, it exacts a full look at
    the Worst.
Who feels that delight is a delicate growth cramped by
    crookedness, custom and fear,
Get him up and be gone as one shaped awry: he disturbs the order
    here.

DATE   Hardy dated this poem 1895–6. The motto, from Psalm 142,
is: 'I looked on my right hand, and beheld, but there was no man
that would know me. No man cared for my soul.'

STYLE   This poem is written in a completely different way from the
first part of 'In Tenebris'. It is not just a matter of very long lines
rather than very short ones: the whole method is different. Instead
of dramatizing his feelings through a series of poetic images, Hardy
tries to argue them out in the form of a dialogue with those who see
a different world from the one that he sees. He also gives us some
idea, in this second poem, of why he is suffering, and it is from a
more complex cause than bereavement.

SUBJECT   There cannot be much doubt about what Hardy is
describing: the reception of *Jude the Obscure* and the way he and his
ideas were abused. This might not have been very painful for
someone who enjoyed controversy and could give back as good as
he got; for Hardy, who was not like that at all, the whole experience
was a nightmare. Having tried to write an honest novel about what
seemed to him to be universal problems, he found himself abused
on all sides as morbid. The ideas which Hardy expresses in this
poem have been discussed at length in Chapter Three. It will be
seen that the poet is not saying that the world is necessarily a bad
place; merely that evils do exist and always have done since the
earliest times (the 'clash of the First' refers to the biblical legend in
which Abel is killed by Cain). 'Delight' again, is by no means

impossible, but it is 'a delicate growth cramped by crookedness, custom, and fear'. This means that people will have to struggle for it if they want to get it, and that, in certain social conditions, they may fail. If one thinks of the prejudices and the outworn conventions which ruin people's lives in *Jude the Obscure* and *Tess of the D'Urbervilles* one begins to understand what he means. Hardy is asking that human beings should be honest about the imperfect state of the world they live in, rather than insisting (as many of the brasher Victorians did) that everything was for the best in the best of all possible worlds. He was always upset when he was accused of being unnecessarily gloomy. In later years he often quoted the line 'if way to the Better there be, it exacts a full look at the Worst', as a truer statement of his feelings, and in the Preface to *Late Lyrics and Earlier*, published in 1922, he said that his philosophy could be called 'evolutionary meliorism'. But in spite of his own clear statements, the myth that Hardy was an incurable pessimist persists.

In Tenebris III

'Heu mihi, quia incolatus meus prolongatus est! Habitavi cum habitantibus Cedar: multum incola fuit anima mea.'

There have been times when I well might have passed and the ending have come –
Points in my path when the dark might have stolen on me, artless, unrueing –
Ere I had learnt that the world was a welter of futile doing:
Such had been times when I well might have passed, and the ending have come!

Say, on the noon when the half-sunny hours told that April was nigh,
And I upgathered and cast forth the snow from the crocus-border.
Fashioned and furbished the soil into a summer-seeming order,
Glowing in gladsome faith that I quickened the year thereby.

Or on that loneliest of eves when afar and benighted we stood,
She who upheld me and I, in the midmost of Egdon together,
Confident I in her watching and ward through the blackening heather,
Deeming her matchless in might and with measureless scope endued.

Or on that winter-wild night when, reclined by the chimney-nook quoin,
Slowly a drowse overgat me, the smallest and feeblest of folk there,

Weak from my baptism of pain; when at times and anon I awoke
there –
Heard of a world wheeling on, with no listing or longing to join.

Even then! while unweeting that vision could vex or that
knowledge could numb,
That sweets to the mouth in the belly are bitter, and dark, and
untoward,
Then, on some dim-coloured scene should my briefly raised curtain
have lowered,
Then might the Voice that is law have said 'Cease!' and the ending
have come.

DATE 1896. The motto is translated in the Authorized Version of
Psalm 120 as 'Woe is me that I sojourn in Mesech, that I dwell in
the tents of Kedar! My soul hath long dwelt with him that hateth
peace.'

STYLE In this third part of the poem Hardy adopts a third kind of
rhythm to express what he wants to say. The very long and slowly
moving lines help to create the mood of the poem, which is
reminiscent, elegiac and sad. It is an impressive piece of work, but
the language has certain faults. Hardy had a weakness for archaic
words like 'overgat' (overcame), and 'unweeting' (unknowing),
which still makes parts of his work, and especially his poetry,
difficult to read. The alliteration is too obvious in places: 'winter-
wild' is a beautiful construction but 'glowing in gladsome faith' and
'matchless in might and with measureless scope endued' sound
artificial and forced. The best lines are the very simple ones where
the words are all short and natural, 'Such had been times when I
well might have passed, and the ending have come!'

SUBJECT This is very different from the first part of 'In Tenebris',
a brief lyrical statement on one man's condition, and from the
second part, which, however sad in its tone, is still *arguing*, still
defending a position. This is a 'dim-coloured' poem, which makes
few direct statements, merely guides the reader back gradually into
the past. Hardy is looking back at the times when he might have
died as a child (as many did). Almost certainly he was thinking of
how he was left for dead as a baby, and also about how for many
years he was a small and very frail boy – 'weak from my baptism of
pain'. It might have been better to have died then because he would
not have discovered the full suffering and complexity which is
involved in being an adult – when he says that 'knowledge could
numb' he is referring to the pain of having to *think*, which seemed to
him and to so many other Victorians to force on him an intolerable
weight of responsibility. Neither in this poem, nor in the *Life*, does

143

he pretend that his childhood was always happy, but at least, he seems to be saying, it offered him security of a kind. It was rather like being able to sit by the fire while the winter winds were raging outside. A small child can derive a real joy from helping to cultivate a garden, because it seems to him that he can control his environment with no real effort, 'glowing in gladsome faith that I quickened the year thereby'. In the same way, he notes that he did not mind being stranded on Egdon Heath after dark, because he was with his mother who 'upheld' him – and, to a child, the mother seems all-powerful. But now he cannot rely on anyone to guide him through the world, which he has come to see as 'a darkling plain', where each man is alone. He is not *wishing* that he had died at that time; he is simply reflecting on the infinite uncertainty of human life and considering how much more complex his own life has become since he was a child.

CONCLUSION The third part of 'In Tenebris' has affinities with some of Hardy's other poems. 'To an Unborn Pauper Child' describes his fears for the future of a child which is going to be born into poverty, his desire to protect it, and his unhappiness in realizing that the child which has no knowledge of the world as yet will eventually have to find out what suffering is. 'The Oxen' is about his childish belief that the animals went on their knees on Christmas Eve, and more importantly how he wishes that he could believe in it still.

As was said above, 'In Tenebris' (whose sections seem to have been written at different times) is not totally unified. The first part belongs with the best of Hardy's short lyrical poems; the second and third parts are very closely related to Hardy's thinking on pessimism and agnoticism. They can usefully be read with the discussion of this subject in Chapter Three.

Hardy wrote one more great poem during his black period:

Wessex Heights

There are some heights in Wessex, shaped as if by a kindly hand
For thinking, dreaming, dying on, and at crises when I stand.
Say, on Ingpen Beacon eastward, or on Wylls-Neck westwardly,
I seem where I was before my birth, and after death may be.

In the lowlands I have no comrade, not even the lone man's
    friend –
Her who suffereth long and is kind; accepts what he is too weak to
    mend:
Down there they are dubious and askance; there nobody thinks as I,

But mind-chains do not clank where one's next neighbour is the
   sky.

In the towns I am tracked by phantoms having weird detective
   ways –
Shadows of beings who fellowed with myself of earlier days:
They hang about at places, and they say harsh heavy things –
Men with a wintry sneer, and women with tart disparagings.

Down there I seem to be false to myself, my simple self that was,
And is not now, and I see him watching, wondering what crass
   cause
Can have merged him into such a strange continuator as this,
Who yet has something in common with himself, my chrysalis.

I cannot go to the great grey Plain; there's a figure against the
   moon,
Nobody sees it but I, and it makes my breast beat out of tune;
I cannot go to the tall-spired town, being barred by the forms now
   passed
For everybody but me, in whose long vision they stand there fast.

There's a ghost at Yell'ham Bottom chiding loud at the fall of the
   night,
There's a ghost in Froom-side Vale, thin-lipped and vague, in a
   shroud of white,
There is one in the railway train whenever I do not want it near,
I see its profile against the pane, saying what I would not hear.

As for one rare fair woman, I am now but a thought of hers,
I enter her mind and another thought succeeds me that she prefers;
Yet my love for her in its fullness she herself even did not know;
Well, time cures hearts of tenderness, and now I can let her go.

So I am found on Ingpen Beacon, or on Wylls-Neck to the west,
Or else on homely Bulbarrow, or little Pilsdon Crest,
Where men have never cared to haunt, nor women have walked
   with me,
And ghosts then keep their distance; and I know some liberty.

DATE   1896. Hardy did not publish it until many years afterwards.

GEOGRAPHY   The heights which Hardy names all stand in different
parts of 'Wessex'. Ingpen Beacon is near Basingstoke, Wylls-Neck
in Somerset, and Bulbarrow and Pildson in Dorset. The 'tall-spired
town' is Salisbury Hardy's Melchester and 'the great grey plain'
may be either Salisbury Plain or Egdon Heath.

REFERENCES J.O. Bailey in *The Poetry of Thomas Hardy* has conjectured that 'the forms now passed' who bar the poet from going to Salisbury may be the long-dead church officials who it is said prevented him from studying theology there. According to Florence Hardy, all the people mentioned in the poem were actual women. They cannot all be identified with any certainty, but one of the ghosts in the sixth verse may be that of Tryphena Sparks. It seems definite that the 'one rare fair woman' who never knew how much Hardy loved her was Florence Henniker, whom he had met and been deeply attracted to three years before.

STYLE Again Hardy uses the long reflective line to create the mood of this poem. Although some parts are difficult to understand immediately, the poem has always had a strong appeal, perhaps because it describes emotions which are almost universal.

SUBJECT 'Wessex Heights' will *always* wring my heart,' Florence Hardy wrote, soon after she married the poet, 'for I know when it was written, a little while after the publication of *Jude*, when he was so cruelly treated.' 1896 was the year when *Jude the Obscure* was being attacked in every newspaper in the country, and when Hardy was literally afraid to go out of doors in case he was stopped and abused for writing an immoral book. We can see how bitter this experience was when we read the third verse of 'Wessex Heights', where he feels that he is being followed about by ghostly detectives:

> They hang about at places, and they say harsh heavy things –
> Men with a wintry sneer, and women with tart disparagings.

'In the towns' he is tormented by the feeling that everybody is watching him, and that he is hopelessly different from other people. 'Nobody thinks as I' – he had discovered this when his novel was published, and it made him feel that his critics (like those in 'In Tenebris II') were wearing 'mind-chains' which made them unable to break with their preconceived ideas. He is desperately lonely. He has no friends at all – not even his wife, it's worth noting – and indeed we know now that Emma had tried to suppress *Jude* and that their marriage had become impossible by the time Hardy wrote 'Wessex Heights'. But he is not only at odds with other people, but also with himself:

> Down there I seem to be false to myself, my simple self that was,
> And is not now, and I see him watching, wondering what crass
>   cause
> Can have merged him into such a strange continuator as this,
> Who yet has something in common with himself, my chrysalis.

Perhaps these are the most interesting lines in the poem, for they reveal that Hardy was very often a prey to inward guilts and tensions, the feeling that he had been 'false to himself'. On the Wessex hills, which had been familiar to him since his earliest childhood, he may indeed have felt that his life had developed in all the wrong ways. He had made the wrong marriage, got into the wrong social set, and spent the greater part of his life doing uncongenial work. His 'simple self' which had known of nothing better than life in Wessex must have seemed very far removed from what he had become.

'I will lift up mine eyes to the hills, from whence cometh my help', says a Psalm which Hardy knew well. It seemed to him, during the crises in his life, that if he could get away on to the hills 'where one's next neighbour is the sky' his real values would come back into perspective. It was not that he disliked other people, as this poem may suggest at a first reading, but he did very often feel the need to escape from a society with which he was deeply out of sympathy. His work shows time and again that, like Wordsworth, and like his own hero, Clym Yeobright, he found that nature could be a soothing and strengthening force.

POSTSCRIPT   It is worth noting that some of the images in this poem are very like the images in *Jude the Obscure*, which of course had only been written a short time before. There are several places, 'in the lowlands', where Hardy literally finds it too painful to go. Jude has the same fear of reviving memories, 'We mustn't go to Alfredston, or to Melchester, or to Shaston, or to Christminster'. Like Jude when he first enters Christminster, Hardy is surrounded by 'phantoms' which appear more real to him than solid flesh-and-blood people. 'I am neither a dweller among men nor ghosts', Jude says, and Hardy in 'Wessex Heights' has the same feeling. In the line, 'I seem where I was before my birth, and after my death may be', he looks forward to becoming a disembodied spirit himself.

Turn of the century poems

There is a whole group of Hardy poems, some of them very fine ones, about the South African war (1899–1902). He was conscious of writing from a minority viewpoint. Most people approved of the sending of British troops to fight the Boers or Dutch settlers; Hardy was much more doubtful about the ultimate wisdom of hanging on to the Empire. Afterwards he wrote to Florence Henniker, 'I am happy to say that not a single one is Jingo or Imperial – a fatal defect according to the judgment of the British majority at present, I dare say'. He refused to glorify the troops, as so many hack writers were doing; instead he wrote out of a deep sense of what a younger poet, Wilfred Owen, would call 'the pity of war':

Drummer Hodge

They throw in Drummer Hodge, to rest
    Uncoffined – just as found:
His landmark is a kopje-crest
    That breaks the veldt around;
And foreign constellations west
    Each night above his mound.

Young Hodge the Drummer never knew –
    Fresh from his Wessex home –
The meaning of the broad Karoo,
    The Bush, the dusty loam,
And why uprose to nightly view
    Strange stars amid the gloam.

Yet portion of that unknown plain
    Will Hodge for ever be;
His homely Northern breast and brain
    Grow to some Southern tree,
And strange-eyed constellations reign
    His stars eternally.

DATE   First published in 1899 with the note, 'One of the drummers killed was a native of a village near Casterbridge (Dorchester)'.

STYLE   This basically simple poem contains a number of exotic words – 'kopje' (small hill), 'veldt' (open uncultivated land), 'karoo' (the wide sandy plain of South Africa). Readers would have been familiar with them from the war reports and from Olive Schreiner's famous novel *Story of an African Farm* (1883), and might have felt they had a good idea of what the South African landscape was like. Nevertheless most of them (including Hardy) had never seen it and would have found it extremely strange; even the stars are in the southern hemisphere and therefore unfamiliar. Juxtaposed against these images is that of an ordinary boy called Hodge, not his real name but the word commonly used for a Dorset agricultural labourer.

SUBJECT   The poem has been compared to Rupert Brooke's 'The Soldier', written in the First World War some fifteen years later:

If I should die, think only this of me,
That there's some corner of a foreign field
That is for ever England.

But in Hardy's poem there is no suggestion that the soldier died for a worthy cause, or that the soil is somehow ennobled by his being in it. It starts with a deliberately brutal image; he is thrown into the earth without a coffin – or other ceremonies, presumably – just as he is found. Not that Hardy attacks the war; that is not his way. He merely suggests, in the second verse, that the boy had no idea what it was about. We are left to ponder the contrast between the southern landscape and the northern invader, and draw our own conclusions.

The war continued to haunt Hardy, as in this poem written three years later:

The Man He Killed

'Had he and I but met
By some old ancient inn,
We should have sat us down to wet
Right many a nipperkin!

'But ranged as infantry,
And staring face to face,
I shot at him as he at me,
And killed him in his place.

'I shot him dead because –
Because he was my foe,
Just so: my foe of course he was;
That's clear enough; although

'He thought he'd 'list, perhaps,
Off-hand like – just as I –
Was out of work – had sold his traps –
No other reason why.

'Yes; quaint and curious war is!
You shoot a fellow down
You'd treat if met where any bar is,
Or help to half-a-crown'.

DATE 1902. A note tells us that the speaker is a Dorset man returned from the Boer War, and that it is set in an inn near Dorchester.

STYLE This is one of Hardy's most Wordsworthian poems; the speaker is an ordinary unsophisticated person and the story is told in what Wordsworth called 'the real language of men'. (Some of it is colloquial; 'traps' means baggage and 'nipperkin' is a Dorset word for a small drink.)

SUBJECT   The moral, like those in many of Wordsworth's ballads, is simple and has universal appeal. I once heard a very aged man, in a film about survivors of the Somme, quote the last verse with great feeling. Like Hardy, the returned soldier is asking *why* – why do things go wrong? 'The eternal question of what Life was/ And why we were there, and by whose strange laws/ That which mattered most could not be' ('After the Visit'). In his mind, this question takes the form of wondering why he should have killed a man very like himself, and the poem is more overtly anti-war than 'Drummer Hodge'. But it is a question which takes other forms in other works by Hardy. The friendly and familiar background of the inn sharpens the contrast with what is being talked about.

In between these two poems, Hardy wrote one that is entirely different:

The Darkling Thrush

I leant upon a coppice gate
  When Frost was spectre-gray,
And Winter's dregs made desolate
  The weakening eye of day.
The tangled bine-stems scored the sky
  Like strings of broken lyres,
And all mankind that haunted nigh
  Had sought their household fires.

The land's sharp features seemed to be
  The Century's corpse outleant,
His crypt the cloudy canopy,
  The wind his death-lament.
The ancient pulse of germ and birth
  Was shrunken hard and dry,
And every spirit upon earth
  Seemed fervourless as I.

At once a voice arose among
  The bleak twigs overhead
In a full-hearted evensong
  Of joy unlimited;
An aged thrush, frail, gaunt, and small
  In blast-beruffled plume,
Had chosen thus to fling his soul
  Upon the growing gloom.

So little cause for carolings
  Of such ecstatic sound

Was written on terrestrial things,
　　Afar or nigh around,
That I could think there trembled through
　　His happy good-night air
Some blessed Hope, whereof he knew
　　And I was unaware.

DATE　　This poem was first published in the last days of 1900, under the title 'By the Century's Deathbed'.

STYLE AND LITERARY BACKGROUND　　Nobody else could conceivably have written this poem, yet it owes a good deal to two masterpieces by the younger Romantics, Keats's 'Ode to a Nightingale' and Shelley's 'To a Skylark'. Hardy knew both these poems well, and 'The Darkling Thrush' is written from the same point of view. In all three poems, the bird's song reveals a new, mysterious and joyful world to the poet, who is deeply unhappy and dissatisfied with the world as it is. Keats, listening to the nightingale, wishes to 'leave the world unseen/And with thee fade away into the forest dim',

Fade far away, dissolve, and quite forget
　　What thou among the leaves has never known,
The weariness, the fever, and the fret,
　　Here, where men sit and hear each other groan;
Where palsy shakes a few, sad, last gray hairs,
　　Where youth grows pale, and spectre-thin, and dies;
　　　　Where but to think is to be full of sorrow
　　　　And leaden-eyed despairs;
Where Beauty cannot keep her lustrous eyes,
　　Or new Love pine at them beyond tomorrow.

Shelley also feels that the skylark is living in a much happier state than human beings can ever reach:

Yet if we could scorn
Hate, and pride, and fear;
If we were things born
Not to shed a tear,
I know not how thy joy we ever should come near.

Unhappiness, a feeling of deadness and desolation, is the point from which Hardy begins 'The Darkling Thrush'. The first two verses show a landscape on a winter evening, which mirrors the 'fervourless' state of the poet's mind. In the third verse, and quite unexpectedly, he suddenly hears the thrush 'fling his soul/Upon the growing gloom'. The language is similar to that of Keats, who imagines the nightingale 'pouring forth thy soul abroad/In such an ecstasy' (the thrush is 'ecstatic' too). Yet the overall impression of this poem is quite different from that of Keats's, or Shelley's. Shelley imagines the singing bird as a 'blithe spirit', 'an unbodied joy', or 'a star of heaven in the broad daylight' (it is significant that he cannot actually *see* it). The nightingale in the Keats ode is also invisible, an ethereal being which was 'not born for death'. Both of them seem unaware that this marvellous music actually comes from a little, ordinary bird. Hardy, on the other hand, can see the bird clearly:

> An aged thrush, frail, gaunt, and small,
> In blast-beruffled plume.

This bird obviously *is* born for death. It is old, frail, and knocked about by the winter winds, yet this does not destroy the core of happiness which makes it sing.

Although, as we noted, some expressions in this poem (including the word 'darkling') were suggested by the Keats ode, this is a deliberately plain and simple piece of work which keeps well clear of the 'poetic' imagery used by the two earlier writers. 'I leant upon a coppice-gate' is very different, as an opening line, from 'Hail to thee, blithe spirit!', and this is characteristic of Hardy's writing.

SUBJECT We know that the 1890s were a bad time for Hardy, with the attacks on his last two novels and troubled marriage (and if we didn't know, we could guess it from 'In Tenebris' and 'Wessex Heights'). He must also have felt that the nineteenth century had been a time of terrible human suffering, bearing in mind that the South African war was being fought as he wrote. This tended to make him feel that the only way to live without being hurt was in a state of 'unhope'. In this frame of mind he becomes aware of the thrush, which is singing joyfully as the landscape grows darker, although for no apparent reason:

> So little cause for carolings
> Of such ecstatic sound
> Was written on terrestrial things
> Afar or nigh around.

The thrush, then, seems to know about 'some blessed Hope' of which the poet is 'unaware'. Some critics have thought that this 'blessed Hope' must be God. Perhaps, but then Hardy had always believed that human life contained hopeful elements (this poem is never cited by those who call him a pessimist). He had shown how the same thing happened to Tess Durbeyfield, after her 'fall': 'Some spirit within her rose automatically as the sap in the twigs. It was unexpended youth, surging up anew after its temporary check, and bringing with it hope, and the invincible instinct towards self-delight'. It is this 'invincible instinct towards self-delight' which makes the thrush sing, just as it makes the sap rise (Hardy describes how 'the ancient pulse of germ and birth/Was shrunken hard and dry', but we can scarcely doubt that, in spring, it will begin all over again). Hardy's point seems to be that the bleakest of lives can still offer sources of happiness, even if this is only the song of an elderly thrush.

Less optimistic is another poem about a wintry landscape:

New Year's Eve

'I have finished another year,' said God,
     'In grey, green, white, and brown;
I have strewn the leaf upon the sod,
Sealed up the worm within the clod,
     And let the last sun down.'

'And what's the good of it?' I said;
     'What reasons made you call
From formless void this earth we tread,
When nine-and-ninety can be read
     Why nought should be at all?

'Yea, Sire; why shaped you us, "who in
     This tabernacle groan" –
If ever a joy be found herein,
Such joy no man had wished to win
     If he had never known!'

Then he: 'My labours – logicless –
     You may explain; not I:
Sense-sealed I have wrought, without a
     guess
That I evolved a Consciousness
     To ask for reasons why.

'Strange that ephemeral creatures who
     By my own ordering are,
Should see the shortness of my view,
Use ethic tests I never knew,
     Or made provision for!'

He sank to raptness as of yore,
     And opening New Year's Day
Wove it by rote as heretofore,
And went on working evermore
     In his unweeting way.

153

DATE   First published in January 1907, probably written late in 1906.

STYLE   The first verse is the best in this poem, with its startling opening line and its lovely evocation of early winter, painted in the colours of the English countryside – 'grey, green, white and brown'. It has an easy conversational movement and a simplicity of language which is lost as the poem goes on. '"I have finished another year," said God', is ordinary English (however surprising it may sound!); so is, '"And what's the good of it?" I said.' But the third verse is written in Hardy's most convoluted style ('Yea, Sire, why shaped you us'), and much of the rest of the poem sounds forced. Words like 'herein', 'yore', 'heretofore', 'evermore', and 'unweeting' are examples of the unnatural language which he too often used.

SUBJECT   This is one of several poems in which Hardy deeply shocked the conventional Christians of his time. The speaker is called 'God', and it was a daring idea to write a dialogue between God and the poet in which the poet distinctly comes off better. But this is not a God of love, or one who is closely involved with his creation. His job is to keep the universe ticking over:

> I have strewn the leaf upon the sod,
> Sealed up the worm within the clod,
> And let the last sun down.

He has, apparently, no other interests.

The poet asks God to explain the problem of pain – why human beings are forced to suffer in what the Bible calls 'this tabernacle of flesh'. But God has no answer. He is 'sense-sealed', that is, he only cares about the processes of nature, not the spiritual struggles of human beings, (an extraordinary thing, incidentally, to say about God). Perhaps it would be easier to understand this poem if Hardy had called this God *Nature*. He is obviously thinking in terms of a force which keeps the universe going, but which is not conscious or moral, and which, of course, would not be capable of holding a conversation with an individual man!

Hardy often said that he thought the cause of things was 'neither moral nor immoral, but *unmoral*'; at times he went further and imagined a God who resembled a sleepwalker. Sue in *Jude the Obscure* speculates that 'the First Cause worked automatically like a somnambulist, and not reflectively like a sage'.

POSTSCRIPT   Many years later the Catholic poet Alfred Noyes accused Hardy of visualizing a God who enjoyed tormenting human beings, and cited this poem among others to prove his point. Hardy said that he had never believed any such thing, and that 'New Year's Eve' and other poems like it were merely 'fanciful impressions of the moment' (*Life*, 409).

We may close this section with Hardy's famous poem about the *Titanic*, written a few months before Emma died and his poetry changed course. It is the best of his 'public' poems, and raises questions about what kind of Poet Laureate he might have been, in the unlikely event of him having been offered and accepted the post:

The Convergence of the Twain
(*Lines on the loss of the 'Titanic'*)

In a solitude of the sea
Deep from human vanity,
And the Pride of Life that planned her, stilly couches she.

Steel chambers, late the pyres
Of her salamandrine fires,
Cold currents thrid, and turn to rhythmic tidal lyres.

Over the mirrors meant
To glass the opulent
The sea-worm crawls – grotesque, slimed, dumb, indifferent.

Jewels in joy designed
To ravish the sensuous mind
Lie lightless, all their sparkles bleared and black and blind.

Dim moon-eyed fishes near
Gaze at the gilded gear
And query: 'What does this vaingloriousness down here?' . . .

Well: while was fashioning
This creature of cleaving wing,
The Immanent Will that stirs and urges everything

Prepared a sinister mate
For her – so gaily great –
A Shape of Ice, for the time far and dissociate.

And as the smart ship grew
In stature, grace and hue,
In shadowy silent distance grew the Iceberg too.

Alien they seemed to be:
No mortal eye could see
The intimate welding of their later history,

> Or sign that they were bent
> By paths coincident
> On being anon twin halves of one august event,
>
> Till the Spinner of the Years
> Said 'Now!' And each one hears,
> And consummation comes, and jars two hemispheres.

DATE April 24th 1912 – the *Titanic* had gone down on April 15th and the poem was commissioned in aid of the diaster fund.

STYLE The three-line verses – one of many forms which Hardy experimented with – are very effective, the long last lines slowing the pace and giving the effect of a meditation on human vanity. The first five give us a series of pictures, imaginatively reconstructing what the great ship would look like on the bed of the sea. Jewels, mirrors and the rest are contrasted with dirt and darkness. Hardy's interest in non-human life (as in the lyric about the animals at Waterloo) adds another dimension; to think of the fishes' moon-eyes surveying the grand ruin is to ask ourselves what is the real value of all that 'gilded gear'. It goes on to describe the 'convergence' between the iceberg and the ship.

SUBJECT Over two-thirds of the passengers and crew on the *Titanic* were drowned. Two of them had been personally known to Hardy, including the great reforming newspaper editor W.T. Stead. Others who wrote about the tragedy highlighted other aspects, such as its unnecessariness, or the heroism of many people involved. Hardy's poem has been criticized because it says nothing about the steerage passengers, for instance, and because it seems to assume that the disaster was inevitable. What it does is to concentrate on one particular aspect, the 'pride of life' and its destruction.

The *Titanic* had on board several millionaires and every conceivable luxury. Some passengers used the wireless to send messages to their stockbrokers, perhaps one reason why the overworked radio men ignored warnings of ice. The ship was the biggest and most modern in the world, widely believed to be unsinkable, and her maiden voyage was something of a celebration. Hardy's poem is like one of those medieval stained-glass windows which shows three kings, splendidly dressed, riding out to meet Death. 'Human vanity', 'vaingloriousness', the cheapness of the sparkling jewellery is the most powerful impression conveyed.

The Spinner of the Years, or Immanent Will, appears to be a godlike being who has caused the crash. Hardy would probably not have defended this position, since he often said that his work merely explored ideas and should not be taken literally. His later novels show an interest in the idea that there are 'twin halves' wandering about the world, such as a man and woman who do not meet until it is too late. But these 'halves' need not be persons; other examples are Halley and his comet, or the *Titanic* and the iceberg. The poem does not state dogmatically that they had to collide, only notes the obvious fact that they did. The 'two hemispheres' in the last line are Europe and America.

The *Titanic* has continued to fascinate those who read about it, more so than later, and even bigger disasters. Some who looked back on it after the war saw it as a symbol of a society careering towards doom. Perhaps it is the contrast between the doom and the 'vaingloriousness' (not just the luxury but the faith in technology) which is so striking. Hardy's poem, written just after the event, surpasses all the many others.

Poems to Emma

Hardy wrote few poems about his first wife until after her sudden death. The shock made his mind go back years into the past, releasing a whole group of superb elegies, and, in a sense, he fell in love with her all over again. The three poems here were written during or soon after his visit to Cornwall in March 1913, when he revisited Emma's 'olden haunts' on the forty-third anniversary of their meeting:

After a Journey

Hereto I come to view a voiceless ghost;
    Whither, O whither will its whim now draw me?
Up the cliff, down, till I'm lonely, lost,
    And the unseen waters' ejaculations awe me.
Where you will next be there's no knowing,
    Facing round about me everywhere,
        With your nut-coloured hair,
And gray eyes, and rose-flush coming and going.

Yes: I have re-entered your olden haunts at last;
    Through the years, through the dead scenes I have tracked you;
What have you now found to say of our past –
    Scanned across the dark space wherein I have lacked you?
Summer gave us sweets, but autumn wrought division?
    Things were not lastly as firstly well
        With us twain, you tell?
But all's closed now, despite Time's derision.

I see what you are doing: you are leading me on
    To the spots we knew when we haunted together,
The waterfall, above which the mist-bow shone

At the then fair hour in the then fair weather,
And the cave just under, with a voice still so hollow
   That it seems to call out to me from forty years ago,
      When you were all aglow,
And not the thin ghost that I now fraily follow!

Ignorant of what there is flitting here to see,
   The waked birds preen and the seals flop lazily;
Soon you will have, Dear, to vanish from me,
   For the stars close their shutters and the dawn whitens hazily.
Trust me, I mind not, though Life lours,
   The bringing me here; nay, bring me here again!
      I am just the same as when
Our days were a joy, and our paths through flowers.

DATE   1913. A note tells us that the setting is Pentargan Bay.

STYLE   This poem follows on naturally from 'The Voice' (page 36), written a few months earlier in Dorset. As in that poem, Hardy takes stylistic risks, using double and even triple rhymes ('lazily/hazily') which a lesser poet would not have got away with. He also uses the same kind of imagery; a young and beautiful Emma, with rose-flush and nut-coloured hair, hovers tantalizingly just ahead of him, yet the elderly bereaved husband knows he will not reach her. However, something which cannot be seen or touched may still be real. 'The Voice' is dominated by the image of wind, and says that Emma's physical reality has been 'dissolved'. In this poem, the water is 'unseen', but awesome. The 'mist-bow', like wind and voices, has no substance. Nor has Emma; the birds and seals, like the fish surveying the wreck of the *Titanic*, are not interested.

SUBJECT   More directly than in some other poems from this sequence, Hardy refers to the estrangement between himself and his wife. Between their early courtship and the present is a 'dark space' where unmentionable things happened, but – he maintains at the end of the second verse – the circle has now been closed. Forty years on, he is back on a private pilgrimage to the places where he fell in love with Emma. What he is doing – following a ghost – would seem meaningless to outsiders but for him it is necessary, in order to come to terms with his past and her death. In the last verse he has accepted that she will vanish but his mood is calm and even cheerful. Perhaps, like stars fading and dawn breaking, death is a natural process.

Beeny Cliff (Aug. 22. '70)

The Figure in the Scene.

....."I stood back that I might pencil it
With her amid the scene ;
  Till it gloomed & rained."

(Moments of Vision.)

Hardy's drawing of Beeny Cliff

Beeny Cliff

I

O the opal and the sapphire of that wandering western sea,
And the woman riding high above with bright hair flapping free –
The woman whom I loved so, and who loyally loved me.

II

The pale mews plained below us, and the waves seemed far
  away
In a nether sky, engrossed in saying their ceaseless babbling say,
As we laughed light-heartedly aloft on that clear-sunned March
  day.

III

A little cloud then cloaked us, and there flew an irised rain,
And the Atlantic dyed its levels with a dull misfeatured stain,
And then the sun burst out again, and purples prinked the main.

IV

– Still in all its chasmal beauty bulks old Beeny to the sky,
And shall she and I not go there once again now March is nigh,
And the sweet things said in that March say anew there by and by?

V

What if still in chasmal beauty looms that wild weird western
  shore,
The woman now is – elsewhere – whom the ambling pony bore,
And nor knows nor cares for Beeny, and will laugh there
  nevermore.

DATE The poem is subtitled 'March 1870–March 1913'. The
subject is two March days, the first in 1870 when Hardy and Emma
went to the cliff together, and the second, forty-three years later,
when he returned alone.

PLACE Beeny Cliff, also known as the Cliff Without a Name, is a
few miles from the village of St Juliot. Hardy walked there with
Emma while she rode her pony. In his notebook he described the
scene:

> Beeny Cliff . . . green towards the land, blue-black towards the
> sea. Every ledge has a little, starved, green grass upon it: all
> vertical parts bare. Seaward, a dark-grey ocean beneath a pale
> green sky, upon which lie branches of red cloud. A lather of foam
> around the base of each rock. The sea is full of motion internally,
> but still as a whole. Quiet and silent in the distance, noisy and
> restless close at hand.

Emma has left her own description of their courtship:

> Scarcely any author and his wife could have had a much more
> romantic meeting, with its unusual circumstances in bringing
> them together from two different, though neighbouring counties
> to this one at this very remote spot, with a beautiful sea-coast,
> and the wild Atlantic Ocean rolling in with its magnificent waves
> and spray, its white gulls, and black choughs and grey puffins,
> its cliffs and rocks and gorgeous sunsettings, sparkling redness in
> a track widening from the horizon to the shore. All this should
> be seen in the winter to be truly appreciated. No summer visitors
> can have a true idea of its power to awaken heart and soul. It
> was an unforgettable experience to me, scampering up and down
> the hills on my beloved mare alone, wanting no protection, the
> rain going down my back often, and my hair floating on the
> wind.

(Life, p. 69)

STYLE   This is one of the most lyrical of Hardy's poems. Here he
does not 'avoid the jewelled line', as was his normal practice (he
even uses the names of jewels to evoke the mood of the first line),
and the alliteration, and the very simple verse form, make it a more
traditional, even a more 'Victorian' poem than he usually wrote.

SUBJECT   The subject also is very simple; the contrast between
'then' and 'now'. The first three verses are all set in the past. The
brilliant word pictures here make us *see* the cliff, the spring sunshine
and the fair-haired girl on her pony, pictures which have shone in
the poet's memory for over forty years. They give a clear impression
of how happy and easy everything seems for the young lovers. Even
the rain only lasts for a few minutes. Emma is riding 'high above'
the cliff and the sea; they are both 'aloft' and laughing light-
heartedly: the waves seem a long way away. The 'mews' – seagulls
– are in the mid-air, lower down. We get the feeling that we are
looking up at them from a great distance, and that they cannot see
the abyss and the vast Atlantic under their feet. They have no idea,
on that first spring day, that youth and happiness do not last for
ever. Hardy knows it now, and in the last verse he faces the fact
that the 'chasmal beauty' of the coastline means nothing to him
now that Emma is gone.

Hardy deliberately simplified this poem by leaving out every hint
of his long estrangement from Emma. She is quite straightforwardly
'the woman whom I loved so, and who loyally loved me'. Nothing,
in 'Beeny Cliff', is allowed to darken the picture of the two lovers.
Time and death are the sole forces they have to fear.

At Castle Boterel

As I drive to the junction of lane and highway,
  And the drizzle bedrenches the waggonette,
I look behind at the fading byway,
  And see on its slope, now glistening wet,
    Distinctly yet

Myself and a girlish form benighted
  In dry March weather. We climb the road
Beside a chaise. We had just alighted
  To ease the sturdy pony's load
    When he sighed and slowed.

What we did as we climbed, and what we talked of
  Matters not much, nor to what it led, –
Something that life will not be balked of
  Without rude reason till hope is dead,
    And feeling fled.

It filled but a minute. But was there ever
  A time of such quality, since or before,
In that hill's story? To one mind never,
  Though it has been climbed, foot-swift, foot-sore,
    By thousands more.

Primaeval rocks form the road's steep border,
  And much have they faced there, first and last,
Of the transitory in Earth's long order;
  But what they record in colour and cast
    Is – that we two passed.

And to me, though Time's unflinching rigour,
  In mindless rote, has ruled from sight
The substance now, one phantom figure
  Remains on the slope, as when that night
    Saw us alight.

I look and see it there, shrinking, shrinking,
  I look back at it amid the rain
For the very last time; for my sand is sinking
  And I shall traverse old love's domain
    Never again.

DATE   March 1913. Castle Boterel is Boscastle; the steep lane above the town, overlooking the sea, is bordered by rocks which are rich in fossils.

STYLE   Once again, the poet juxtaposes past and present, the 'substance' and the 'phantom' of Emma, but this poem is written in a lower key than some others. Until the end, he avoids using the word 'love' to describe their relationship, merely calling it 'something that life will not be balked of'. The images are of a gloomy, rainy day and the 'primaeval rocks' beside the road. He had used the same image of Cornish rocks in the famous passage from *A Pair of Blue Eyes*, which contrasts their great age with the brief lifespan of man. Thousands have climbed this hill; to most of them, probably, it had no emotional significance, but for Hardy the scene which took place there was so important that it colours the landscape permanently so long as he is there to see it. At the same time he recognizes that, in a sense, the experience 'matters not much'; for others, the crucial encounters of their lives will have different settings, or the road itself may mean something different.

SUBJECT It sounds as if Hardy is in a cab, being driven away from the town, and this time Emma is not leading him on but remaining behind. Although her body was buried in Stinsford churchyard, the young woman whom Hardy had fallen in love with seems to belong permanently to her native place. In the last verse, which is all the more powerful for being written in extremely simple language, the poet acknowledges that he is old, perhaps soon to die, and is not coming back. Her image is 'shrinking, shrinking' because he is moving away from it – physically in the cab, emotionally in time as sand runs through an hourglass – and perhaps will disappear altogether once he is dead. For all its starkness, this last verse suggests that he had made his peace with Emma's ghost.

Late Poems

We have seen that Hardy went on writing poetry until about a month before he died. Remarkably, he wrote some of his best lyrics when he was in his seventies; 'In Time of "The Breaking of Nations"' is among the most celebrated. It was composed at the time of the Great War, when he was also writing several minor patriotic pieces, but it is probably his ultimate comment on that, or any, war:

In Time of 'The Breaking of Nations'

I

Only a man harrowing clods
   In a slow silent walk
With an old horse that stumbles and nods
   Half asleep as they stalk.

II

Only thin smoke without flame
From the heaps of couch-grass;
Yet this will go onward the same
Though Dynasties pass.

III

Yonder a maid and her wight
Come whispering by:
War's annals will cloud into night
Ere their story die.

DATE   1915.

TITLE   The title is taken from a verse in the Old Testament, 'With thee will I break in pieces the nations, and with thee will I destroy kingdoms' (Jeremiah, 51:20).

STYLE   This is a deceptively simple poem; the short lines and apparently ordinary observations hiding the real depth of the thought. Hardy gives each verse a separate number, and at first there seems to be no connection between them. It is only at the end of the poem that we see how these apparently arbitrary and disconnected images fix together.

SUBJECT   Hardy was, of course, thinking about the Great War, but strangely enough it had been suggested forty-five years earlier, when the Franco-Prussian War of 1870 was being fought and he was in Cornwall with Emma.

> On the day that the bloody battle of Gravelotte was fought they were reading Tennyson in the grounds of the rectory. It was at this time and spot that Hardy was struck by the incident of the old horse harrowing the arable field in the valley below, which, when in far later years it was recalled to him by a still bloodier war, he made into the little poem of three verses entitled 'In Time of "The Breaking of Nations"'.
>
> (*Life*, pp. 78–9)

It is not, perhaps, surprising that the idea (like the image of Emma on Beeny Cliff) had lain dormant in his mind for nearly half a century. Throughout his life Hardy had always believed that *written* history, the stories of kings and queens and battles, had at most only a very tenuous connection with the history that really mattered. In *Jude the Obscure* he suggested that the Crossway in Christminster 'had more history than the oldest college in the city' because it had long been a focus and gathering-point for ordinary people 'whom nobody ever thought of now'. The man and the old horse ploughing a field, the 'thin smoke without flame' and the two lovers will never get in any history book. Yet they seem to him to have more reality than the battle which is being fought elsewhere on the same day. *The Dynasts* had also studied the relationship between everyday life and high politics, and its title is taken up in the word 'dynasties'. The Franco-Prussian war had wiped out one dynasty; the Great War would wipe out three, and change the whole course of European history. But the 'maid and her wight' will presumably marry and have children, and this, Hardy suggests, is more important.

Heredity

I am the family face;
Flesh perishes, I live on,
Projecting trait and trace
Through time to times anon,
And leaping from place to place
Over oblivion.

The years-heired feature that can
In curve and voice and eye
Despise the human span
Of durance – that is I;
The eternal thing in man,
That heeds no call to die.

DATE First published in 1917, but Hardy may have nursed the idea since 1889 when he made a note in his journal: 'The story of a face which goes through three generations or more, would make a fine novel or poem of the passage of Time. The differences in personality to be ignored.' He had followed this through in his novel about three generations, *The Well-Beloved*.

STYLE This is a short, bare, striking poem in which the 'I' is not an individual but a face that 'leaps' across the years. The forceful verb suggests that we are talking about something very powerful, which 'despises' and can afford to break ordinary rules. Perhaps the three strong rhymes in each verse echo Hardy's idea about three generations.

SUBJECT 'The eternal thing in man' traditionally meant the soul. Flesh perishes – so the Church teaches – but the individual human spirit lives on. Hardy did not believe this and in fact seems to take a materialist position, that the family face survives although the individuals who bear it may have completely different personalities.

However, there is a suggestion that 'trait' (characteristics) may be inherited along with the family features. Hardy's writings about his own family, and the doomed and feckless families in *Tess of the D'Urbervilles* and *Jude the Obscure*, show that he did believe this. Tess distinctly resembles the vicious-looking D'Urberville women in the ancestral pictures, and we are also told that she has inherited some of their characteristics, such as recklessness. Jude and Sue are cousins, their family history is unfortunate and their children do not survive because of their bad heredity.

It is worth noting that Hardy had certainly brooded on his failure to continue the family line and that the art of photography, invented in his childhood, made it possible for everyone to study the variations of 'the family face'.

Old Furniture

I know not how it may be with others
   Who sit amid relics of householdry
That date from the days of their mothers' mothers,
    But well I know how it is with me
      Continually.

I see the hands of the generations
   That owned each shiny familiar thing
In play on its knobs and indentations,
    And with its ancient fashioning
      Still dallying:

Hands behind hands, growing paler and paler,
   As in a mirror a candle-flame
Shows images of itself, each frailer
    As it recedes, though the eye may frame
      Its shape the same.

On the clock's dull dial a foggy finger,
   Moving to set the minutes right
With tentative touches that lift and linger
    In the wont of a moth on a summer night
      Creeps to my sight.

On this old viol, too, fingers are dancing –
   As whilom – just over the strings by the nut,
The tip of a bow receding, advancing
    In airy quivers, as if it would cut
      The plaintive gut.

And I see a face by that box for tinder,
   Glowing forth in fits from the dark,
And fading again, as the linten cinder

Kindles to red at the flinty spark,
  Or goes out stark.

Well, well. It is best to be up and doing,
  The world has no use for one today
Who eyes things thus – no aim pursuing!
  He should not continue in this stay,
    But sink away.

DATE   First published 1917.

STYLE   Hardy uses all his stylistic resources – an artful sense of rhyme, alliteration, a quiet conversational tone – to give universal significance to what is apparently a commonplace subject. The pictures come to us as if lit up by sudden flares of a match – shiny knobs, hands in a mirror, the clock, a moth (a traditional symbol of death).

SUBJECT   Hardy's parents had both died (his mother about ten years before at the age of ninety-one) when he wrote this poem. He imagines himself surrounded with the old-fashioned cottage furniture which had been used by them and probably by generations before them. This was not a throwaway age; he had referred in 'The Three Strangers' to 'the family mug – a huge vessel of brown ware, having its upper edge worn away like a threshold by the rub of whole generations of thirsty lips that had gone the way of all flesh', and he was fascinated by the way in which objects survive people. The most prominent piece of 'furniture' in this poem is his father's violin, so often played in church and at dances. Musical instruments have been cited many times in discussions of death and immortality; even after the instrument is broken, the music survives. Hands and faces appear to him, going further and further back (he can remember his ancestors, even those he has not seen, but cannot look forward, having no descendants). The overwhelming impression is of a light growing ever frailler, and at last going out. Possibly, he suggests, the furniture and the memories will have no value once he is gone, and the last verse recalls the poems of Hardy's black period, saying that dreamers like himself, now very old and continually brooding on the past, are of no use.

Afterwards

When the Present has latched its postern behind my tremulous
    stay,
  And the May month flaps its glad green leaves like wings,
Delicate-filmed as new-spun silk, will the neighbours say,
  'He was a man who used to notice such things'?

If it be in the dusk when, like an eyelid's soundless blink,
  The dewfall-hawk comes crossing the shades to alight
Upon the wind-warped upland thorn, a gazer may think,
  'To him this must have been a familiar sight.'

If I pass during some nocturnal blackness, mothy and warm,
  When the hedgehog travels furtively over the lawn,
One may say, 'He strove that such innocent creatures should come
  to no harm,
  But he could do little for them; and now he is gone.'

If, when hearing that I have been stilled at last, they stand at the
  door,
  Watching the full-starred heavens that winter sees,
Will this thought rise on those who will meet my face no more,
  'He was one who had an eye for such mysteries?'

And will any say when my bell of quittance is heard in the gloom,
  And a crossing breeze cuts a pause in its outrollings,
Till they rise again, as they were a new bell's boom,
  'He hears it not now, but used to notice such things'?

DATE First published in 1917. Hardy was in his mid-seventies
when he wrote 'Afterwards' and in some ways it is a deliberate
valediction. In the nature of things, he felt, it was not very likely
that he had much more time ahead (though he did, in fact, live for
another ten years).

STYLE The movement of this poem is slow, gentle, and rather
hesitating (perhaps Hardy's own word, 'tremulous', is the best one
to use). The images in each verse are the most memorable part of it,
and these build up an impression that Hardy is, not exactly confident,
but at least hopeful that he will be remembered by a few people,
not as a poet or novelist but simply as a loving observer of nature.

SUBJECT In its quiet way, this is a curiously optimistic poem, and
one which is concerned not so much with death as with the
possibilities of life. Each verse gives a different picture of the world
he will be leaving, and these pictures are very moving and convincing. The real focus of interest is not himself, but the animals, birds,
leaves and stars.

There is a distinct feeling of gaiety in the first verse, that we
might not expect in a poem which is 'about' death. 'The May
month flaps its glad green leaves like wings,' – Hardy sees this
happening after he is gone, just as the bells of Christminster rang
'joyously' when Jude was in his coffin, and does not resent it at all.
He only hopes that it may bring him to mind momentarily, because
he was 'a man who use to notice such things'. In the rest of the

poem there is more evidence that he was, in fact, a keen observer of the world around him. For example, how many of us would think of comparing the flight of a hawk to an *eyelid*? But this image very skilfully evokes the ideas of speed and soundlessness.

Hardy was fond of hedgehogs, and throughout his life campaigned vigorously against cruelty to animals and birds. Many people were amused when, asked for his comments on modern warfare, he suggested that armies should at least stop using horses on the battlefield. In the third verse of 'Afterwards', he recognizes that he could do little for dumb animals, but, at the same time, holds on to his belief that even a hedgehog has a right to live, and a value and worth of its own.

The fourth verse moves out from the homely image of hedgehogs and moths on the lawn of Hardy's house to the 'mystery' of the starry sky, and the questions it raises in our minds about man's place in the universe, which he had described, long before, in *Far from the Madding Crowd* (though it is characteristic that, in the last verse of all, he should move back from this to the familiar sound of bells from a country church). It is not a religious image; after all those years of searching, Hardy felt that he was still no nearer an answer to 'the eternal question of what Life was, and why we were there'. He can only comment on the everyday things which he does understand, and keep his sense of wonder in the face of the unknown. The poem makes no dogmatic statements. It merely suggests, rather tentatively, that an individual man can make only the faintest of marks on the universe, and that the most he can hope for is to be remembered with kindness by a few people after he dies. It also suggests that there is nothing tragic about this; if anything, it is a happy thing, when the time comes, to be absorbed back into the natural world.

This is what happens to most of us, of course, but it has not in fact happened to Hardy. One of the most modest of men, he would not have thought of claiming, like Shakespeare, 'Not marble nor the gilded monuments/Of princes shall outlive this powerful rhyme', even though in his case it was true. 'Afterwards' is among the small group of Hardy poems which make his place in literature secure.

At Lulworth Cove a Century Back

Had I but lived a hundred years ago
I might have gone, as I have gone this year,
By Warmwell Cross on to a Cove I know,
And Time have placed his finger on me there:

'You see that man?' – I might have looked, and said,
'O yes: I see him. One that boat has brought

> Which dropped down Channel round Saint Alban's Head.
> So commonplace a youth calls not my thought'.
>
> *'You see that man?'* – 'Why, yes, I told you; yes:
> Of an idling town-sort; thin; hair brown in hue;
> And as the evening light scants less and less
> He looks up at a star, as many do.'
>
> *'You see that man?'* – 'Nay, leave me!' then I plead,
> 'I have fifteen miles to vamp across the lea,
> And it grows dark, and I am weary-kneed:
> I have said the third time; yes, that man I see!'
>
> 'Good. That man goes to Rome – to death, despair;
> And no one notes him now but you and I:
> A hundred years, and the world will follow him there,
> And bend with reverence where his ashes lie.'

DATE   September 1920. A note tells us that 'in September 1820 Keats, on his way to Rome, landed one day on the Dorset coast, and composed the sonnet, "Bright Star! would I were steadfast as thou art". The spot of his landing is judged to have been Lulworth Cove'.

STYLE   The first and last verses are a frame for the three middle ones, with their repeated question, *'You see that man?'*. Unlike the majestic sonnet which inspired it, the tone is relaxed and conversational. Hardy presents himself as an ordinary man, preoccupied by his long walk home (it is fifteen miles from Lulworth to Dorchester) and unable to see what is in front of him, even when he is being nudged by Time itself.

SUBJECT   Hardy was naturally interested in the story that Keats had cousins in Dorset, and already knew the 'splendid caverns and grottoes' at Lulworth when he landed there on his way to Rome. He was very ill with consumption (a fact the spectator doesn't notice) and would die in Rome a few months later. Along with Shelley he had become a cult-figure for the Victorians, and there was a legend that he had been killed by unkind reviews. Certainly during his short lifetime (he was twenty-five when he died) his work was under-appreciated. Hardy had visited the Protestant cemetery in Rome where he lies with Shelley and had written a poem about it, 'At the Pyramid of Cestius near the Graves of Shelley and Keats'.

As in so many of his poems, Hardy is pleading with his readers to appreciate the full value of the apparently ordinary. The figure of Keats, like the bird in 'The Darkling Thrush', seems an unlikely vehicle for great art. He looks 'commonplace' and 'an idling town-sort'. Only in the final verse is this ordinary young man transformed by the great words 'death, despair'. We are then told that he is, in fact, a genius, and that the people who ignore him now would one day be glad to have taken notice of him. But Hardy is quite aware that this encounter did not happen and that if he had really met Keats he would probably not have paid him much attention. His feeling is that we constantly fail to appreciate the things that matter, a point made forcibly in the earlier poem, 'The Self-Unseeing':

> Childlike, I danced in a dream;
> Blessings emblazoned that day;
> Everything glowed with a gleam;
> Yet we were looking away!

Part Three
Reference Section

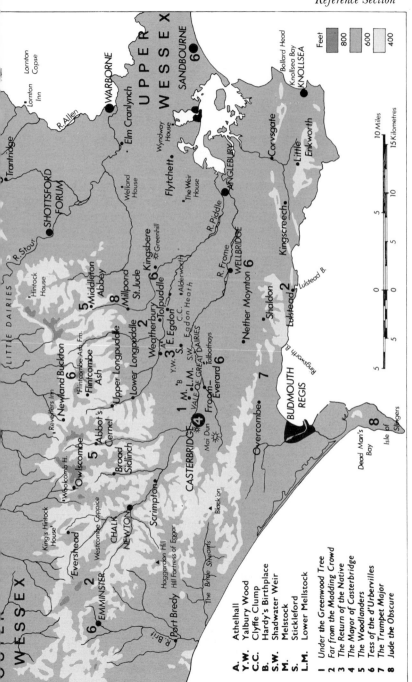

Feet
800
600
400

10 Miles
15 Kilometres

A.   Athelhall
Y.W.   Yalbury Wood
C.C.   Clyffe Clump
B.   Hardy's Birthplace
S.W.   Shadwater Weir
M.   Melstock
S.   Stickleford
L.M.   Lower Mellstock

1   Under the Greenwood Tree
2   Far from the Madding Crowd
3   The Return of the Native
4   The Mayor of Casterbridge
5   The Woodlanders
6   Tess of the d'Urbervilles
7   The Trumpet Major
8   Jude the Obscure

Map of Hardy's Wessex

Short biographies

ARCH, JOSEPH, 1826–1919. The son of a shepherd in Warwickshire, Arch worked in the fields scaring rooks as a child. He bought as many books as he could and became a skilled worker and a Methodist lay preacher. The terrible conditions among agricultural labourers made him a radical, and in 1872 he agreed to organize the Warwickshire labourers into a union which soon spread over much of the countryside. It was a miracle to many people that this class had any spirit, and Arch was held responsible for it. He became a kind of bogeyman to the farmers. Although the Union collapsed in the end, it managed to do a great deal for the labourers. In later life, Arch went into parliament as a Liberal. His autobiography, *The Life of Joseph Arch* (1898, reprinted 1971) is essential reading for anyone interested in English rural history. Hardy publicly paid tribute to him in his article, 'The Dorsetshire Labourer', for his reasonableness and moderation.

ARNOLD, MATTHEW, 1822–88. Son of Thomas Arnold, the famous headmaster of Rugby. Although he earned his living as an inspector of schools, Arnold was one of the foremost Victorian poets and critics; he also did a great deal for popular education. For a time he was Professor of Poetry at Oxford. He was concerned with the survival of culture, the humanization of English society, and, above all, with the problem of how religion could be adapted to the modern mind. He had been deeply influenced by the Oxford Movement, but felt that a more enlightened form of Christianity must be evolved if it was to survive at all. Hardy (who met him socially in London and who shows him apostrophizing Oxford University in *Jude the Obscure*) disapproved of his efforts. He thought that if religion had to be propped up by 'hair-splitting' like Arnold's it must be in a desperate state.

BARNES, WILLIAM, 1801–86. A Dorset farmer's son, Barnes became first a lawyer's clerk, then a schoolmaster, and finally a clergyman, after he had taken an external degree at Oxford over a period of ten years. He was and is best known for his dialect poetry, although he also wrote poems in ordinary English. A great, though entirely self-educated linguist, he was devoted to old-fashioned forms of speech and according to Hardy thought that a bicycle should have been called a 'wheelsaddle'. A collected edition of his poems was published in 1879 and Hardy edited a selection in 1908, his one venture into literary criticism. He thought that Barnes's pictures of the

Dorset labourers were generally too happy to be realistic: this is mostly, but not always, true. Apart from Burns, he was probably the greatest of all our dialect poets.

DARWIN, CHARLES, 1809–82. Generally considered to be rather stupid at school and university, Darwin as a young man accompanied the ship *Beagle* on a voyage round the world as a naturalist. It was in the Galapagos islands off the coast of Ecuador that he made the observations about animal development which led him to work out the theory of evolution. He did not publish his findings as *Origin of Species* until 1859, when he heard that another scientist, Alfred Russel Wallace, had independently reached the same conclusions. A semi-invalid, Darwin kept out of the resulting furore as much as he could. Like Hardy, he was a modest man and hated the notoriety which his work brought him.

ELIOT, GEORGE (Mary Ann Evans), 1819–81. This great novelist is remembered by her pseudonym, used because she feared that a woman's novels would not be taken seriously. By the time Hardy was beginning to be published the secret was out, but she was respected almost universally for her tremendous intellect. She was a member of the small group of advanced intellectuals who wrote for the *Westminster Review*. Hardy considered her to be one of the greatest living thinkers, although he was doubtful whether her novels had anything of value to say about country life.

HARDY, EMMA (née Gifford), 1840–1912. Emma Gifford was born a solicitor's daughter in Plymouth and when Hardy met her she was living with her elder sister, the wife of the rector of St Juliot. Having no money of her own, she encouraged Hardy to keep on with his writing, although this meant that they could not afford to get married for four years. In later life her behaviour became increasingly odd, and Hardy's poem 'The Interloper' expresses the fear that she might be insane. Emma has had a bad press from the critics, but Hardy himself was much more charitable about her memory. Her writings show that she was capable of thinking for herself and had many original ideas.

HARDY, FLORENCE EMILY (née Dugdale), 1879–1937. Hardy had known Miss Dugdale for several years when he married her in 1914. She was a much more competent and self-effacing person than Emma, and in spite of the great difference in age it was a happy marriage. His poems 'After the Visit' and 'I Sometimes Think' give us an idea of how much she helped him. After his death she arranged and published the *Life*, which was very largely written by Hardy himself, although it appeared under Florence's name.

HARDY, JEMIMA (née Hand), 1813–1904. The novelist's mother. Hardy described her as 'a girl of unusual ability and judgment, and an energy that might have carried her to incalculable issues'. Her own mother was a widow with a large family and she had a very hard life before she was married. She liked reading, and taught her son to do the same, and she had an impressive knowledge of local traditions. She is thought to have inspired the character of Mrs Yeobright in *The Return of the Native*.

HARDY, THOMAS (the First), 1778–1837. Hardy heard a good deal of family reminiscences about his grandfather, who died three years before he was born. He was said to have been a smuggler, and he and his two sons had practically created the choir at Stinsford Church. His wife, Mary Head, who lived with the family when Hardy was a child, had grown up as an orphan at Great Fawley in Berkshire, the 'Marygreen' of *Jude the Obscure*. Some of her childhood experiences may have been incorporated in the novel.

HARDY, THOMAS (the Second), 1811–92. Hardy's father was a master-mason and a very good violinist. He was a sociable man with no great ambition for himself or his children, and he spent his entire life in the cottage at Higher Bockhampton where he was born. He is buried in Stinsford churchyard with the other members of the Hardy family. Hardy, who was very attached to him, records that almost the last thing his father had asked for was water fresh drawn from the well – which was brought and given him; he tasted it and said, 'Yes – that's our well-water. Now I know I am at home' (*Life*, p. 248).

HENNIKER, HON. FLORENCE, 1855–1923. A society hostess and occasional novelist, married to a Major-General. Hardy met her in Dublin in 1893, when his marriage was in difficulties. She was a charming woman and he was soon very attracted to her, although he realized that there was not much hope for him. They had a good deal in common emotionally, particularly a love of literature and a hatred of cruelty to animals, though Hardy was annoyed with her for remaining an orthodox Christian. They worked together on a short story, 'The Spectre of the Real'. In later years their friendship became less emotionally charged. Hardy's letters to her have been collected by F.B. Pinion and Evelyn Hardy in *One Rare Fair Woman* (1972).

HUXLEY, THOMAS HENRY, 1825–95. Scientist who became the foremost defender of Darwin's theory of evolution. He used to say that he had been named after the Apostle with whom he had the most sympathy, 'Doubting Thomas'. His place in the history of intellectual progress is assured by his thoughtful essays on science and agnosticism. He was a member of the London School Board during the brief time that Hardy was designing buildings for it, and was a distinguished educator. *Man's Place in Nature* (1863) is his chief non-technical book.

MILL, JOHN STUART, 1806–73.   One of the most remarkable thinkers of his age, almost worshipped by Hardy as a young man. He was ahead of his time in many ways; during his short career in Parliament he proposed a Bill giving the vote to women which nobody else would vote for, and he became unpopular when he tried to prosecute Governor Eyre of Jamaica for summarily hanging some of the 'natives'. The full extent of his influence on Hardy has probably not yet been traced. His most influential works are *On Liberty* (1859) and *Utilitarianism* (1863).

MOULE, HORACE, 1832–73.   The son of a much-loved Dorchester clergyman, Horace Moule was one of the strongest influences on the young Hardy. He helped him to widen his reading, and wrote encouraging reviews of his earliest books. Though a brilliant scholar, it took him many years of intermittent study at Oxford and Cambridge to get his degree. Hardy was shocked when he committed suicide, although his family had known for years that there was a danger of this. The poem, 'Standing by the Mantelpiece', is based on his death. Hardy may well have had this tragedy in mind when he began planning *Jude the Obscure*; it has also been suggested that Moule was a model for the intellectual hero Knight in *A Pair of Blue Eyes*.

NEWMAN, JOHN HENRY, 1801–90   Beginning his career as an Anglican clergyman and a Fellow of Oriel College, Newman was one of the leading spirits in the Oxford Movement, which strove to make the Church of England more 'Catholic'. He wrote several of the *Tracts for the Times* which led to the movement being called Tractarian, and his sermons in the University Church had a deep influence on many undergraduates. One of his disciples was the Jesuit poet Gerard Manley Hopkins. When he joined the Catholic Church in 1845 the movement effectively broke up. In 1864, after an attack by Charles Kingsley, he published *Apologia Pro Vita Sua* which won him many admirers outside his own church. Horace Moule recommended it to Hardy, who, however, was not convinced. Another distinguished work of Newman's was the *Grammar of Assent* (1870). His chief argument, which Hardy quotes in *Jude the Obscure*, was that 'probabilities which did not reach to logical certainty might create a mental certitude'. Newman was made a cardinal in 1879.

SPARKS, TRYPHENA, 1851–90.   Hardy's cousin, a pupil-teacher in Puddletown, with whom he fell in love after he came back from

London in 1867. Nothing was known of her until Lois Deacon and Terry Coleman published *Providence and Mr Hardy* in 1966. After such a long space of time, very few facts about her are ascertainable. There are many theories about the relationship, but although we can be almost certain that she meant a good deal to Hardy at one time, and that she had some influence on *Jude the Obscure*, we are unlikely ever to know the full truth.

STEPHEN, LESLIE, 1832–1904. Critic and editor of the *Cornhill Magazine*, which published two of Hardy's novels. He was the first editor of the *Dictionary of National Biography*; he also wrote several books, including one on George Eliot which is still widely read. Hardy was deeply influenced by Stephen's agnostic philosophy, and witnessed his formal (and belated) renunciation of the holy orders he had taken at Cambridge as a young man. Stephen is best remembered as the father of Virginia Woolf, who drew a cruel portrait of him as Mr Ramsay in *To the Lighthouse*.

SWINBURNE, ALGERNON CHARLES, 1837–1909. Although he was only a little older than Hardy, Swinburne became established as a writer at a very much earlier date. *Poems and Ballads* caused a sensation when it came out in 1866; it was followed by the equally daring *Songs before Sunrise*. Swinburne's early poems were very popular with Hardy's generation – perhaps more popular than they deserved. Hardy often quoted them in his novels. Swinburne was passionately devoted to the idea of liberty, particularly to the crusade for a united Italy which attracted a great deal of sympathy in England. But his radicalism was romantic, not systematic. In his old age he became a Jingo and wrote some bellicose poems about the Boer War, to Hardy's distress. By this time he had written nothing significant for a great many years.

TENNYSON, ALFRED, 1809–92. Poet Laureate after the death of Wordsworth, and raised to the peerage in 1884, Tennyson was very much the Victorians' favourite poet. Hardy had little in common with him as a writer, but found him unexpectedly endearing when he visited him in London. His reputation has shrunk in the twentieth century, but he is likely to survive as a poet. *In Memoriam*, which goes considerably deeper than his later work, is generally accepted as his greatest achievement.

Gazetteer

Everybody has heard of Wessex; few know that it was Hardy who revived the old name for the south-west of England. His decision to be a local or regional novelist compelled him to limit his scene of action to Dorset and the neighbouring counties (though it is exclusively in Dorset that most of the Wessex novels are set). He said of this decision:

> The geographical limits of the stage here trodden were not absolutely forced on the writer by circumstances; he forced them upon himself from judgment. I considered that our magnificent heritage from the Greeks in dramatic literature found sufficient room for a large proportion of its action in an extent of their country not much larger than the half-dozen counties here reunited under the old name of Wessex, that the domestic emotions have throbbed in Wessex nooks with as much intensity as in the palaces of Europe, and that, anyhow, there was quite enough human nature in Wessex for one man's literary purpose. So far was I possessed by this idea that I kept within the frontiers when it would have been easier to overleap them and give more cosmopolitan features to the narrative.
>
> (General Preface to the Novels and Poems)

The map which can be found in almost all editions of Hardy's novels ('Fictitious names as Exonbury; real names as Portsmouth') shows the track of country which Hardy wrote about almost exclusively. If it is checked against the real map it will be found to comprise the whole of Dorset, with parts of Hampshire, Wiltshire, Berkshire, Devon and Somerset (and Cornwall on a sketch-map in the corner). More detailed notes on places which were important in Hardy's life and writings follow.

Berkshire

GREAT FAWLEY   This is a small village, nestling among the Berkshire downs, where Hardy's grandmother, Mary Head, grew up. He depicted it as 'Marygreen', the childhood home of Jude Fawley. The ugly Gothic church which he describes in the novel can still be seen.

READING   Known in *Jude* as 'Aldbrickham'. This was the kind of bustling industrial town which held little interest for Hardy.

WANTAGE   Appears in *Jude* as 'Alfredston', the place where Jude was apprenticed. There is a statue of King Alfred in the market place. (Hardy's last novel is the only one which has a setting some way to the north of Dorset.)

Cornwall

BEENY CLIFF   This is also known as 'the Cliff without a Name'. Hardy visited it in his youth with Emma, and wrote one of his famous love poems about it. In *A Pair of Blue Eyes*, his only novel with a Cornish setting, it is almost a major actor; there is a most dramatic scene where the hero is trapped and nearly killed on this cliff.

ST JULIOT   The old church which Hardy restored is still standing. There is a memorial to Emma, designed by her husband.

Devon

BARNSTAPLE (Downstaple) and EXETER (Exonbury).   Both mentioned in Hardy's fiction.

PLYMOUTH   Was the childhood home of Emma Gifford. Tryphena Sparks was headmistress of the Plymouth Public Free School.

Dorset

The majority of the Wessex Novels are set here.

BEAMINISTER   The home of Angel Clare's parents.

BERE REGIS   This was one of the traditional seats of the aristocratic Turberville family, as described in *Tess*. There is a fine church with a Turberville window, showing the family crests.

BULBARROW   Mentioned in 'Wessex Heights', this is a hill south of Sturminster Newton which gives some magnificent views over the Vale of Blackmore. Hardy thought these views were among the finest in the country.

CERNE ABBAS   Stands at one end of the road which runs through the *Woodlanders* country to Sherborne. It is particularly famous for the chalk giant on the nearby hill, which is of uncertain age. There is also a beautiful gatehouse, all that is left of the medieval abbey.

CRANBORNE   'Chaseborough', the town where Alec D'Urberville's employees went on Saturday nights to get drunk.

DORCHESTER   The county capital is particularly rich in associations for the student of Hardy. His house, Max Gate (now privately owned), stands on the edge of the town. The County Museum (which has a statue of William Barnes outside the door) contains a reconstruction of Hardy's study, the manuscript of *The Mayor of Casterbridge*, and several other documents concerning Hardy, mainly of interest to scholars. Readers of *The Mayor of Casterbridge* will find several parts of the town familiar. There are 'walks' or avenues of trees, which have hardly changed since he wrote. The amphitheatre on the Weymouth Road, Maumbury Rings, is unchanged too. Following the London Road out of town one crosses Hardy's two bridges, the first covers a small stream flowing along the Mill Lane area; the second is Grey's Bridge, where Henchard often stood. It is a fine stone construction and carries a small plaque (the original can be seen in the County Museum) threatening that anyone who damages the bridge will be transported! Ten Hatches Weir is only a little way from this bridge, and across the meadows is the old hangman's cottage. From this end of the town, which merges rapidly into the countryside, there is a good view of the tower of Fordington church. The Reverend Henry Moule preached here for many years, and was active in the cholera epidemic which broke out in the slum quarter of Mill Lane when Hardy was a boy. This church is full of interest, and so is St Peter's (near the museum), which has some interesting monuments and two architectural drawings by Hardy. The monument to the writer stands on the Bridport Road at Top o' Town.

Two prehistoric camps, Poundbury and Mai-Dun, stand at a short distance from Dorchester.

EGDON HEATH   When Hardy wrote *The Return of the Native* there were 'at least a dozen' scattered stretches of heathland in Dorset, although for the purposes of his novel he united them under one name. Today the heath is not easy to find, as some of it has been planted with rhododendrons and other parts are used by the army. There are still several miles of heath around Puddletown, Wareham and Bere.

HIGH-STOY   Another of the 'Wessex heights' which Hardy loved. It stands near the Sherborne-Cerne Abbas road, giving a fine view over the countryside.

KINGSTON MAURWARD   The local 'great house' when Hardy was a boy. It stands near the road from Dorchester to Stinsford. The lady of the manor, Mrs Martin, made a great favourite of the child Hardy and gave him lessons. It is now an agricultural college.

HIGHER BOCKHAMPTON   The cottage where Hardy was born and grew up now belongs to the National Trust. It has not changed a great deal and it is a picturesque place. It is open to visitors by arrangement.

MARNHULL   Tess Durbeyfield's village. There is an interesting church.

PUDDLETOWN   Hardy knew this small village very well, and described it as 'Weatherbury' in *Far from the Madding Crowd*. Tryphena Sparks grew up there.

SHAFTESBURY   'One of the queerest and quaintest spots in England', Hardy said when he described this little Dorset town under its old name of Shaston in *Jude the Obscure*. He found it strange that this interesting place was so little known. Standing on a hill, it gives some extensive views which Hardy mentioned as being among the finest he knew. There is one lovely street, Gold Hill, which is full of old-fashioned houses and must be one of the steepest climbs in any English town.

SHERBORNE   'Sherton Abbas' in *The Woodlanders*. There is a magnificent Norman abbey which Hardy knew well.

STINSFORD   The village between Dorchester and Bockhampton whose church contains graves of the Hardy family, to which has now been added that of Cecil Day Lewis. The church boasts several unusual 'gurgoyles'.

STURMINSTER NEWTON   Hardy and his wife lived at Riverside Villa here while he was writing *The Return of the Native*.

TOLPUDDLE   One of a number of small villages near the Trent or Puddle River whose names are based upon it. It is famous for its contribution to trade union history. The Martyrs' Oak where the six labourers met is still standing, and there is an excellent museum in one of the six cottages which have been built in their honour.

WEYMOUTH   Appears in several of Hardy's writings as Budmouth. It was a fashionable watering-place in the time of George III, of whom there is a great chalk figure on a hill outside the town. Hardy worked as an architect here from 1869 to 1870.

WIMBORNE MINSTER   Hardy lived here while he was writing *Two on a Tower*. It is an ancient town with an interesting church.

WINTERBOURNE ABBAS   Interesting because the church has an old minstrels' gallery which is one of the few that have not been pulled down. The choir survived longer here than in most villages, and there is a memorial to the last surviving member of it, a shepherd, who did not die until the Second World War.

WOOL   Described in *Tess* under the name of 'Wellbridge'. There is an old manor house here which belonged to the Turberville family; nearby are the ruins of Bindon Abbey, and a flour-mill, which are both described in the novel.

Hampshire

BASINGSTOKE   Described in *Jude* as Stoke-Barehills, the site of the big agricultural show.

WEYHILL   'Weydon-Priors', where Henchard sold his wife to the sailor. A great sheep-selling fair was traditionally held here every year.

WINCHESTER   Hardy knew this ancient cathedral town well. He gives a long description of it in the last chapter of *Tess*, where he indirectly relates how she is hanged at the County Gaol for Alec's murder.

London

Greatly changed since Hardy knew it. His grave can be seen in the Poets' Corner at Westminster Abbey.

Oxford

As 'Christminster', the ancient university town is the emotional centre of *Jude the Obscure*. The landmarks of the novel are still there – the Cathedral, the High Street which he described as the loveliest in Europe, Christ Church Meadow, and the 'Church of Ceremonies' – St Barnabas, in the working-class part of the town which he called 'Beersheba'. Although he never lived in Oxford, Hardy seems to have known it well. Real colleges are satirized under the names of 'Rubric' and 'Biblioll'. The University was not flattered by his last novel, and did not honour him until he was a very old man.

Somerset

BATH   Mentioned several times under its own name in the Wessex novels. Bathsheba went there to get married, as did Viviette in *Two on a Tower*.

WELLS   Hardy probably knew this small cathedral town closely, but did not write about it much. It appears on his map as 'Fountall'.

Wiltshire

SALISBURY   Hardy wrote enthusiastically about the cathedral which dominates the city – 'the most graceful architectural pile in England'. An important section of *Jude the Obscure* is set here ('At Melchester'). His sisters went to the training college here, which he described as the temporary home of Sue Bridehead.

STONEHENGE   This is where Tess and Angel take refuge just before the police catch up with them – Tess lying on the stone altar in the centre.

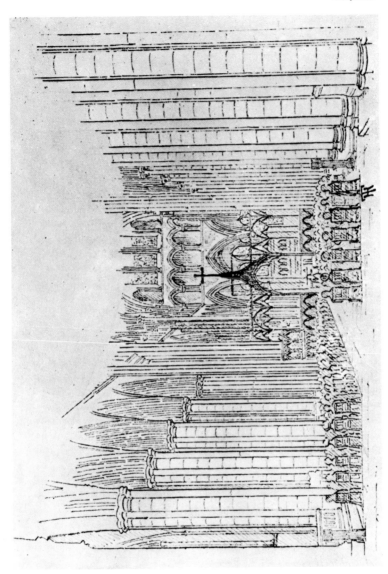

Sketch of Salisbury Cathedral by Hardy.
Melchester, 'the most homogenous pile of medieval architecture in England' (*Jude*).

Further Reading

Hardy's novels and most of his short stories are widely available in the New Wessex edition (Macmillan), as are his *Complete Poems* edited by James Gibson (1976). A good shorter selection is *Selected Poems* (Everyman, 1982, edited by Walford Davies). The most recent collection is *Thomas Hardy: Selected Poems* (Longman Annotated Texts, 1993, edited by Tim Armstrong).

Biography

F.E. HARDY, *The Early Life of Thomas Hardy* (1928) and *The Later Years of Thomas Hardy* (1930), reprinted in one volume, *The Life of Thomas Hardy* (1962). This was mainly written by Hardy himself.

ROBERT GITTINGS, *Young Thomas Hardy* (1975) and *The Older Hardy* (1978).

MICHAEL MILLGATE, *Thomas Hardy: A Biography* (1982).

Bibliography

RICHARD LITTLE PURDY, *Thomas Hardy: A Bibliographical Study* (1954).

RICHARD LITTLE PURDY and MICHAEL MILLGATE (eds), *The Collected Letters of Thomas Hardy* (seven volumes, 1978–88).

HAROLD OREL (ed.), *Thomas Hardy's Personal Writings* (1966).

RICHARD H. TAYLOR (ed.), *The Personal Notebooks of Thomas Hardy* (1978).

LENNART BJORK (ed.), *The Literary Notebooks of Thomas Hardy* (1985).

General background

F.B. PINION, *A Hardy Companion* (1968).

R.G. COX (ed.), *Thomas Hardy: The Critical Heritage* (1970).

Selected criticism

J.O. BAILEY, *The Poetry of Thomas Hardy: A Handbook and Commentary* (1970).

KRISTIN BRADY, *The Short Stories of Thomas Hardy* (1982).

DOUGLAS BROWN, *Thomas Hardy* (1954).

PETER CASAGRANDE, *Unity in Hardy's Novels* (1982).

DONALD DAVIE, *Thomas Hardy and British Poetry* (1973).

DALE KRAMER (ed.), *Critical Approaches to the Fiction of Thomas Hardy* (1979).

D.H. LAWRENCE, *Study of Thomas Hardy*, in *Phoenix* (1936).

MICHAEL MILLGATE, *Thomas Hardy: His Career as a Novelist* (1971).

ROY MORRELL, *Thomas Hardy: The Will and the Way* (1978).

NORMAN PAGE, *Thomas Hardy* (1977).

NORMAN PAGE (ed.), *The Thomas Hardy Annual* (1982–).

RICHARD H. TAYLOR, *The Neglected Hardy: Thomas Hardy's Lesser Novels* (1982).

HARVEY C. WEBSTER, *On a Darkling Plain* (1947).

PETER WIDDOWSON, *Hardy in History: A Study in Literary Sociology* (1989).

MERRYN WILLIAMS, *Thomas Hardy and Rural England* (1972).

Appendix: serialization and Hardy's texts

Hardy's novels have reached us in their familiar form after surviving a process of censorship, dismemberment and reconstitution that is at times painful to contemplate but so essential as evidence of Victorian literary taste that no serious student can afford to ignore it. It was serial publication that caused so much irritation to writers and left indelible marks upon their books even when restored to the safety of the hardback version. To different degrees a forgotten hack writer and a serious artist alike had to accommodate original ideas to the demands of the serial editor if they were to reach the widest public instead of a more discerning body alone.

Leslie Stephen, Hardy's most distinguished periodical editor, stated as a general principle in one of his letters to the novelist: 'Though I do not want a murder in every number it is necessary to catch the attention of the reader by some distinct and well-arranged plot.' Some kind of strategy was then required to meet these demands. Ways of involving the minds of regular readers and retaining them as subscribers were various. A writer might simply favour the more melodramatic cliff-hanging incident for the end of the instalment, or embark upon a series of complex legal and financial problems hinging upon the favourite laws of inheritance and property, or create mysterious characters whose identities are slow to be revealed. In the end, when the novel emerged in the customary two or three volume form, no matter how much detail of dialogue, incident or description might be revised, these character-istics would remain. What follows here is by way of tracing the composition, erasures and revisions required by a magazine editor on two occasions.

To simplify a situation in which there are many variations let us consider three stages:

1 A manuscript as it was written and intended for the press.
2 A revised version prepared for a magazine with passages removed for reasons of length and cuts insisted upon in the interests of morality.
3 A return to a version of (1) usually abandoning all the cuts and revisions of the serial text and intended for the publisher of the hardback edition. While this often provides the modern text, it may be noticed that Hardy revised his texts voluntarily in various ways for collected editions of his novels in 1895 and 1912. This final

establishment of a text is the sum total of years of alterations but is in itself rarely of great moment.

The Mayor of Casterbridge, first published in *The Graphic* from January to June 1886, documents most of the problems of serial authorship and is drawn upon for a number of revealing incidents. There seems to have been no objection to the initial act of wife-selling since it created a sensational impact: it was the later marital tangles of Michael Henchard that called for reserves of patience in the novelist.

Lucetta, crossing the paths of the two principal male characters as she does, has been criticized even in the completed version. Her arrival at Casterbridge from earlier days in Jersey created many of the textual confusions. It is in Chapter 12 that the problems of her past present themselves in flashback. As it was originally defined, the incident was inconsistent with Victorian family reading, though it is, one would think, hardly substantial enough to raise objections. The original version is the one we know today:

> . . . one autumn when stopping there I fell quite ill, and in my illness I sank into one of those gloomy fits I sometimes suffer from, on account o' the loneliness of my domestic life . . . While in this state I was taken pity on by a woman – a young lady I should call her, for she was of good family, well bred, and well educated – the daughter of some harum-scarum military officer who had got into difficulties, and had his pay sequestrated . . . This young creature was staying at the boarding-house where I happened to have my lodgings: and when I was pulled down she took upon herself to nurse me. From that she got to have a foolish liking for me. Heaven knows why, for I wasn't worth it. But being together in the same house, and her feelings warm, we got naturally intimate. I won't go into particulars of what our relations were. It is enough to say that we honestly meant to marry. There arose a scandal, which did me no harm, but was of course ruin to her . . . At last I was well and came away. When I was gone, she suffered much on my account, and didn't forget to tell me so in letters one after another; till, latterly, I felt I owed her something, and thought that, as I had not heard of Susan for so long, I would make this other one the only return I could make, and ask her if she would run the risk of Susan being alive (very slight as I believed) and marry me, such as I was. She jumped for joy, and we should no doubt soon have been married – but, behold, Susan appears!

Here it is as Hardy altered it. It will be seen that a highly sensational boating accident is added and that, from here onwards, the book is overburdened with marriages and remarriages; in themselves the entanglements which readers of popular serials were known to appreciate.

'Well, this summer I was there, and met with an accident. I fell out of a boat in the harbour, and struck my head in falling. If somebody had not helped me instantly, I should have been drowned. An account of it was in our local newspapers at the time.'

'Indeed. And it's all haphazard in this life!'

'But the account was not complete. The person who saved me was a woman – a merchant's daughter – a woman who – God knows why, for I never gave her encouragement! – who has had a foolish liking for me more than five years since I first knew her from going over there to deal with her father. So when I found I owed my life to her, in a moment of gratitude and excitement I offered to marry her. I did marry her – I married her at St Heliers a fortnight ago. Three days after I came home here to get the house ready for her, and await her coming. But from the moment I landed, I felt I had acted rashly. It was not that I dreamed of Susan living: but I felt I did not care for this young woman, much as she might like me. Odd as it may seem to you, I've always liked Susan in my heart, and like her best now. Well, now Susan has returned to life, and you begin to see the colour o't; for the other is coming by the packet tomorrow night.' Henchard's voice grew brokenly indicative of passionate revolt against eighteen years of caution. 'I've compromised myself by acting a fortnight too soon!'

Explanations are unnecessary, but the return of Lucetta to the forefront of the action, alternately claimed by Henchard and Farfrae, occasioned an amount of accommodating minor revision. For example, take an incident in Chapter 27 as it stands today:

'But you ought to hear it,' said he [Henchard].

'It came to nothing; and through you. Then why not leave me the freedom that I gained with such sorrow! Had I found that you proposed to marry me for pure love I might have felt bound now. But I soon learnt that you had planned it out of mere charity – almost as an unpleasant duty – because I had nursed you, and compromised myself, and you thought you must repay me. After that I did not care for you so deeply as before.'

'Why did you come here to find me, then?'

'I thought I ought to marry you for conscience's sake, since you were free, even though I – did not like you so well.' . . .

This unluckily aroused Henchard. 'You cannot in honour refuse me,' he said. 'And unless you give me your promise this

very night to be my wife, before a witness, I'll reveal our intimacy
– in common fairness to other men!'

With this passage compare the following, the result of an editor's
blue pencil and an obedient rewriting. (Only the important phrases
are given):

'Had I found that you married me for pure love I might have
felt the vow binding, though it was not legal. But I soon learnt
that you had done it out of mere charity – almost as an
unpleasant duty – because I had helped save your life and you
thought you must repay me in some way . . .'
'I thought I ought to remarry you for conscience' sake.' . . .
'You belong to me and you cannot in honour refuse me . . .
And unless you give me your promise this very night to be my
legal wife, before a witness, I'll disclose all – in common fairness
to other men.'

Comparative study of different versions reveals Hardy's problems
with the return of Richard Newson, the true father of Elizabeth-
Jane. On his first visit to Casterbridge he is told that his daughter
is dead and he departs; but there is a picturesque incident (Ch. 43)
in which Henchard spots him through his telescope and which is
his cue to depart. The serial version made for difficulties in
consistency and motivation of character by making Elizabeth-Jane
already aware of her father's identity and known to him. Having
met him many times during her walks along the Budmouth road
she is still obliged to return to her stepfather's home without any
revelations or recriminations. The original and final text is over-
whelmingly superior in this respect since her continued silence is
completely improbable, threatening to pull the book's credibility
apart, even though Hardy consented to produce this inartistic effect.
   There were minor revisions to the text made between 1886 and
1912, some of them explained in an author's Preface. They concern
passages in Chapters 12, 18, 34, 43 and 44, and the ones with which
many people are familiar concern the author's later thoughts on the
Scots dialect attributed to Donald Farfrae. Without any external
pressure Hardy, who it will be remembered was a devotee of
William Barnes, would attempt to rectify linguistic matters. At the
same time his conception of Wessex as an entity was growing more
specific, rechristening places with new names and rendering the
speech more correct on the principle that a spoken language is an
index to the society that produced it. Thus he wrote 'zilver
zaxpence' and "oman' where standard spellings had originally
prevailed. In the end Wessex had grown into an autonomous world

of his own imagination that he was at times loath to identify with the map of Dorset and its neighbouring counties.

Chapter 4 of *The Mayor of Casterbridge* follows two women into the town and the eye travels to collect a bird's eye view of the whole scene. In the shop windows is arrayed a great profusion of scythes, reap-hooks, or in the words of Gerard Manley Hopkins, 'all trades, their gear and tackle and trim'. Even so, in the serial edition of the opening chapter Henchard is shown with what is called merely an 'implement'. In the novel it was to be identified; although all Hardy's novels have their quota of literary references, biblical allusions and the like, the implement is given as a 'hoe': when he wished Hardy could call a spade a spade.

The second part of this Appendix is devoted to *Tess of the D'Urbervilles* or *Too Late Beloved* as it was originally known. In this case Hardy had begun writing in 1888, designing the text for a rather different means of dissemination: a newspaper fiction syndicate which would buy a novel and lease it to a chain of local newspapers up and down the country for simultaneous publication. The manuscript was under contract, and was in the printer's hands in 1889 without any alterations, the seduction scene and the illegitimate child notwithstanding. However, as the narrative came fully to the attention of the editor he cancelled the contract and returned portions already standing in print. To the author's mortification it was the prelude to a period of frustration and evasion: not until 1891, when he prepared a revised text for *The Graphic* once more, was he able to place the novel with an editor and one of the greatest of his works was cynically submitted to a process he called 'dismemberment'.

We shall document the late-night seduction scene: Chapters 10 and 11. Hardy's original conception is one that would seem to the modern reader to have come under a mild censorship already, for there is a restraint and ambiguity in the presentation of Alec's approach to the sleeping girl:

> D'Urberville stooped; and heard a gentle regular breathing. He knelt and bent lower, till her breath warmed his face, and in a moment his cheek was in contact with hers. She was sleeping soundly, and upon her eyelashes there lingered tears.

At this point the author's viewpoint changes and he turns to a historical meditation. The bowdlerized text jettisons the whole of the village dance that leads to the seduction and treats the incident in flashback (as if it were no more urgent than Henchard's behaviour in Jersey) when Tess returns to her mother. The differences are startling:

'Well! – my dear Tess!' exclaimed her surprised mother, jumping up and kissing the girl. 'How be ye? I didn't see you till you was in upon me! Have you come home to be married?'

'No, I have not come for that, mother.'

'Then for a holiday?'

'Yes – for a holiday; for a long holiday,' said Tess.

Her mother eyed her narrowly. 'Come, you have not told me all,' she said.

Then Tess told.

'He made love to me, as you said he would do, and he asked me to marry him, also just as you declared he would. I never have liked him, but at last I agreed, knowing you'd be angry if I didn't. He said it must be private, even from you, on account of his mother; and by special licence, and foolish I agreed to that likewise, to get rid of his pestering. I drove with him to Melchester, and there in a private room I went through the form of marriage with him as before a registrar. A few weeks after, I found out that it was not the registrar's house we had gone to, as I had supposed, but the house of a friend of his, who had played the part of the registrar. I then came away from Trantridge instantly though he wished me to stay: and here I am.'

'But he can be prosecuted for this,' said Joan.

Even without the disclosure of the fraudulence of the ceremony, a marriage by special licence strikes against the credibility of characterization. There is no illegitimate child in the serial so that neither its baptism nor burial need to be recorded, but less probable still is the behaviour of Angel Clare. Because Tess is perfectly justified in living with Alec, to whom she believes herself married, Angel is made monstrously unfeeling to reject her on that score. These are the dismantlings of a work of art caused by the susceptibilities of an editor but tolerated by its creator in a way that shocks us today.

Hardy, aware that this novel represented his art extended to the full ('I have put in it the best of me') was reluctant to see it sink in periodical form without a fight. In May 1891, before the serial began to appear there was published in the *Fortnightly Review* a piece entitled 'Midnight Baptism, a Study in Christianity'. This is the incident that was not to be allowed to stand in its due place in the serial. Then, in November of that year while the serial was in progress, he published the night seduction scene separately in the *National Observer* under the title 'Saturday Night in Arcady'. Even with all the instalments and the two fugitive pieces together the reader was still puzzled because the fragments bore none of the names that identified them with the new novel: in the end, with all the cancelled passages visible in the three-volume copy, the novelist's method of self-defence should have been obvious, and not, in the long run, unheeded.

Still consistent with Victorian magazine ethics words like God, Hell and Damnation disappeared from the serial copy of *Tess* and when Angel Clare finds Tess with Alec in the hotel at Sandbourne he is made to imagine perfect discretion and separate rooms occupied by Mr D'Urberville and Miss D'Urberville for reasons simple to understand. Finally, however, an instance that amused Hardy in later years, Angel Clare carries the milkmaids one by one across a flooded road but not in the pages of *The Graphic*. It is a happy incident, but at a late date in the preparation of copy for the paper Hardy was made to give Angel a wheelbarrow to transport the girls. Agricultural implements are always in evidence in the Wessex novels.

Mary Ellen Chase's study, *Thomas Hardy, from Serial to Novel*, has a wealth of further documentation and also takes *Jude the Obscure* into detailed account. It has been pointed out that without recourse to the manuscripts where the changes are evident Miss Chase is not entirely correct in some of her judgements, but she shows us without the slightest doubt the extent of the tyranny of editorial taste over the creative writer. Indeed, it exposes a piece of cultural history and provides texts for the history of censorship and a discussion that is still in progress.

Regarding the process we have been tracing, the American Hardy scholar, Joseph Warren Beach, writing in 1927, remarked that English fiction in the latter half of the nineteenth century was lacking in profundity, seriousness and depth. It is a verdict that may well spring from the same casual and patronising habit as Henry James's. His verdict on 'the good little Thomas Hardy' was that *Tess*, though much impaired was a surprising success. Hardy with a more peasantlike isolated and rocky quality about himself and his work accorded very little with a man of James's refinement and those mannered novels which at times appear to be endlessly undulating and circling in their moral refinements, turning in upon themselves and sometimes disappearing altogether. Possibly as a result of technical expectations that Hardy did not acknowledge in the first place and his consequent failure to observe them in his novels Hardy's standing has been depressed for too much of the present century.

Finally, it is tempting to compare him with another figure that now emerges so clearly out of the Victorian and Edwardian eras, Sir Edward Elgar. This most distinguished composer had to establish himself in spite of the tyranny of Victorian oratorio which had almost contrived to set the entire Bible to music. What Elgar recognized (like Hardy with *Tess*) in *Dream of Gerontius*, his setting of Cardinal Newman's poem, as 'the best of me' was first performed much against the grain of the nonconformist conscience of the English provinces. But both Hardy and Elgar displayed the courage to work and to grow, overcoming contemporary prejudices and now stand firm as masters of their arts.

MAURICE HUSSEY

Index

General Index

Index to Hardy's Poetry and Prose

Index